PATHWAYS TO SELF-DISCOVERY AND CHANGE

PATHWAYS TO SELF-DISCOVERY AND CHANGE:
Criminal Conduct and Substance Abuse Treatment for Adolescents

The Participant's Workbook

Harvey B. Milkman
Metropolitan State College of Denver

Kenneth W. Wanberg
Center for Addictions Research and Evaluation, Denver, Colorado

SAGE Publications
Thousand Oaks ▪ London ▪ New Delhi

This document was prepared under contract number OE IHM NC030000031 with the Colorado Department of Human Services, Alcohol & Drug Abuse Division. Funding for this project was $37,000.00 through the Colorado Department of Public Safety, Division of Criminal Justice, Office of Juvenile Justice.

For information:

Sage Publications, Inc.
2455 Teller Road
Thousand Oaks, California 91320
E-mail: order@sagepub.com

Sage Publications Ltd.
1 Oliver's Yard
55 City Road
London EC1Y 1SP
United Kingdom

Sage Publications India Pvt. Ltd.
B-42 Panchsheel Enclave
Post Box 4109
New Delhi 110017
India

Printed in the United States of America
Pathways to Self-Discovery and Change:
Criminal Conduct and Substance Abuse Treatment for Adolescents
The Participant's Workbook

ISBN # 1-4129-0614-8

Correspondence should be sent to:
The Center for Interdisciplinary Studies
899 Logan Street, Suite 207
Denver, Colorado 80203
e-mail: cisdenver@msn.com

04   05   06   07   10   9   8   7   6   5   4   3   2   1

Harvey B. Milkman, Ph.D. is Professor of Psychology at Metropolitan State College of Denver and Director of the Center for Interdisciplinary Studies, Denver, Colorado. Kenneth W. Wanberg, Th.D., Ph.D. is a private practice psychologist and Director of the Center for Addictions Research and Evaluation (CARE), Arvada, Colorado.

Acquisitions Editor: Arthur Pomponio
Editorial Assistant: Veronica Novak
Fictional Youth Narratives: Michelle L. Tolar
Contributions in Research and Lesson Design: Michelle L. Tolar
Editorial Management and Project Coordination: Karen R. Storck
Illustration: Erica Jacobs
Graphic Design and Layout: Erica Jacobs Design

TABLE OF CONTENTS

LIST OF WORKSHEETS

LIST OF FIGURES

LIST OF TABLES

WELCOME!

Welcome to *PATHWAYS TO SELF-DISCOVERY AND CHANGE*. You have been selected because you have expressed concern about your past experiences with crime and substance abuse and a willingness to explore the possibility of change. As many as 90% of people in the criminal justice system have substance abuse problems. There are programs that work with people with criminal problems, and there are programs that work with substance use problems, but this program is different in that we are *combining* criminal activity with substance use problems. We understand that there is a part of you that may not want to be here, which views treatment as a form of punishment. Yet there is another part that has a genuine concern about your future, the people you care about and a desire to change the direction of your life. That is the part we want to support and help grow.

Thinking, Freedom and Change

The *PATHWAYS TO SELF-DISCOVERY* program helps us to gain *freedom and strength* by learning how to control the most important part of our mind: *our own thoughts*. Thoughts about ourselves, the world around us, and the feelings that come from those thoughts, decide our behavior and actions. This program is designed to provide you with the knowledge and skills to become clear about how people and situations affect us and to *gain control over our own thoughts and feelings*. Then it is possible to *change and adjust our actions*.

To some extent, things that happen outside of us are not in our control because we are not of age and we have lost some freedom because of our actions. But the actions that got us here in the program are *completely in our control,* and only by *changing our thoughts* can we avoid having our freedom and choice taken away. The idea is *not to tell* you *who and what to be*, but to help you to gain a better understanding of the *events in your life and the workings of your own mind*. Then you can begin to feel the *power of self-improvement*, doing positive things for yourself and others.

What Does This Program Have To Do With Me?

Crime and drugs can be *very exciting*, and in the short run they can bring a lot of benefits. They get the adrenaline moving, prop up our courage, and allow us to do things that set us apart from the crowd. Sometimes they seem to help us to get things that we think we deserve, for our friends or even our families. But there are a lot of *negative consequences* from participating in those actions, as most of you in this program already know.

So what this program is really designed to do, is to show you that you can be different, have personal strength, feel good and gain respect from those around you, *without* using substances or committing crimes. There are a lot of things in the world that are just as, if not more, exciting—without the negative outcomes—as drugs and crime. Our goals are to see you increase your personal power, gain the freedom of making your own choices, become all that you can be, and to feel self-respect while earning trust from those around you.

PROGRAM DESIGN

This program is different from most others in that it is specially designed to be of interest to people who are in situations like yours. Notice that there are comics as well as full-page stories of youth who have struggled with problems concerning substance abuse and crime. Although they are artistically interesting, the main purpose of the comic strip drawings is to help you understand the ideas within each session. The illustrations are *artistic ways to explain* the stories, and they contain details that help the stories come to life. They convey very serious content in picture format, not to be at all confused with a lighthearted comic strip in the Sunday newspaper. Within each session is a *section of the full story*, which can be applied to the *specific ideas* that are contained in the session. You do not have to read the full-page stories, although your counselor may find them helpful depending on the subject matter. We do suggest reading them, however, in order to help you develop a better understanding of the program and how it can be applied to your life.

Each session is designed to provide an engaging and meaningful learning experience. Your counselor will use role-playing, modeling, action skits and small group discussions designed to help you to *put into action and practice* life-skills that will be of great help to you in real situations. The activities and worksheet exercises will allow you to get a better look at what you are thinking and feeling in different situations, and to help you to decide on *your own programs for change*.

We will take one step at a time in the process of change. There are *three phases* to the program, with each phase separated into several *chapters*. At the end of each phase, we will take a moment to *look at how you are doing* and whether or not you want to continue on to the next phase. Some of you may be required to be here. If that is the case, then we will take a break between each phase to *give you feedback* as to how you are doing in the program. During the feedback, you will be given a chance to explain what you think and feel about the program, and we will talk with you about how you can better make the program work for you. Now, let's take a look at the phases.

PHASE I: WHAT?
CHALLENGE TO CHANGE
Deciding What to Change

There are *ten sessions* in this phase and *five* important things that we want you to do.

FIRST we want you to *build trust*: trust in the counselor or counselors who will be conducting the program, and trust in those who are in the program with you. Most importantly, we want you to build a *trust in the program itself*. The reason we want you to trust your counselor and peers in the program is because we want you to open up and share with us your feelings and thoughts, essentially your story. Being open to *sharing your story* and considering your options by *hearing what others have to say* is the *essential pathway to self-discovery and change*. It is important, though, that you start talking about your *alcohol and other drug* (AOD) use, your criminal activities in the past, your worries and fears, and your problems and troubles in your life. Some of you may be more open than others, and some of you may have a lot of distrust, but we just ask you give it a try.

SECOND, we want you to learn the facts about AOD (alcohol and other drugs) and about criminal behavior. We will teach you some important ideas, some of which you will already know. But we want you to learn about how you have come to rely on drugs and criminal activities to satisfy some of your needs and resolve some of the problems in your surroundings.

THIRD, we want you to become more aware of yourself, your relation with AOD use and criminal behavior, and your thoughts, feelings, and actions pertaining to both. We want you to make a commitment to a long-term change in your thinking, believing, and acting.

FOURTH, we will spend time helping you to understand the triggers that could lead you to *a relapse* (return to substance use) and/or *recidivism* (return to criminal behavior). We will teach you how to *avoid and prevent returning* to negative behavior, and this will be a very important part of this phase of the program.

FINALLY, we want to help you in developing a *Self-Portrait*, or view of yourself that is a mirror of your many strengths and the problems that you have had to face in your life. You will be using your counselor and peers help get an in-depth look into who you are and what you do. In this phase you will decide on specific targets of thinking, feeling and action that you want to change. We will work together to develop your own *Plan for Change*, that is the things that you can really do to gain your freedom, respect from others and most important-ly, your self-respect and optimism about your future.

PHASE II: HOW?
COMMITMENT TO CHANGE
Using The Tools For Change

The idea of *Phase II* is to *discover the tools* and *learn the necessary skills* to achieve the changes that you decided on in *Phase I: Challenge to Change*. This phase will allow you to get stronger in your desire and ability to remain drug and crime free and to improve the overall quality of your life. The sessions in *Phase II* are designed to improve communica-tion, deal with cravings and urges, develop a sense of responsibility to others, overcome prejudice, zero in on negative thinking, manage uncomfortable feelings—particularly anger, guilt and depression. Within the group setting you will test out and practice these skills, which will provide the foundation for living a comfortable, responsible and fulfilling life.

PHASE III: NOW!
OWNERSHIP OF CHANGE
Calling The Shots

Phases I and II of *Pathways to Self-Discovery* are preparation for *Phase III: Ownership of Change*. In this final phase of the program, you will be *putting the knowledge* that you gained in the previous phases *into use* within your own life situation. That means looking at how to *avoid relapse and recidivism* (avoiding AOD use and crime) by mastering the skills of problem solving, decision-making, and negotiation, as well as learning how to develop alternative lifestyles and activities that will help you maintain the changes you have made.

As a means to help you in real life, we will be taking some time looking at family, school and job issues. An important part of *Calling the Shot* is to develop a sense of personal identity and to understand the importance of intimacy in our lives.

At this time you will put together what you have learned, and in the end make those things work for you. The power of ideas, skill, thoughts, and action you have learned will become yours, as well as the freedom of choice over your thoughts and actions. At this point the change becomes you, and you *begin calling the shots* over your actions instead of letting your actions control you.

Program Guidelines

These rules are to help you have a safe environment in order for everyone to be comfortable sharing and thus making the program mean something to everyone.

Abstinence: To Be Alcohol, Drug, and Crime Free

While in this program, we expect your goal to be AOD free and crime free. You may relapse in your thinking, and you may even test whether or not you can use substances or commit crimes. But you are expected to stop at that lapse point. We are not saying that we want you to quit the program if you have a lapse, however you are not allowed to come to a session if you have been using drugs or alcohol. We may ask you to take a urine or breath sample, and if you are positive, you will be asked to leave after setting up an appointment with your counselor to discuss your relapse and how you can continue to be AOD free. You may have cravings or slips into AOD use outside of the group, and we want you to talk about these cravings and urges. You will probably have mixed feelings about all of this, but you will begin to feel the power of self-control if this is accomplished.

Be on Time and Attend All Groups

We ask that you are on time to the sessions, and if you must be late or absent, you are asked to let your counselor know ahead of time. You will be expected to attend all sessions, and if you are having some problems in attending, you will be asked to talk with your counselor and the group.

Taking an Active Part in the Program

You are expected to be an active member of the group, as this program is about your need to change. This means you take part in the discussions, activities, and your own learning process. By doing this, you show you want to change.

Confidentiality: Keeping What is Said in the Group, In the Group

This is one of the most important guidelines for the program. In Phase I, we spend a great deal of time trying to build and develop trust between the members of the group and with the counselor, as well. What is said and heard in the group is to stay in the group at all times. The counselors of this program will be held to the same confidentiality as the group. The only time the counselor can break the promise of confidentiality is if the counselor is concerned about your safety or the safety of others—if you are in danger of hurting yourself or another person or if there are people who need to be held accountable for child abuse.

Eating and Smoking in the Sessions

Smoking is not allowed in the group, and it will be left up to the group and counselor whether or not snacks and beverages will be allowed and what kind of breaks you will have.

It is now time to start the program. Good luck!

PHASE 1

WHAT?

CHALLENGE TO CHANGE:
Deciding What To Change

Chapter One:

Building Trust and Motivation to Change

GOALS OF THIS CHAPTER
- To discuss the program
- Getting to know each other
- To learn how thoughts affect feelings and actions
- To recognize the importance of change

JEB'S STORY

I never thought I would end up here. I started smoking weed when I was 12 years old. By the age of 15, I was a full time pusher.

By 16, I was bringing in steady cash, which spent itself as quickly as I made it. I gave my mom money for food and bills. I also spent alot on my little sister. The rest I spent on me.

I was a satellite dealer, I got paged and delivered. There didn't seem to be any risk involved.

Slowly, I began to lose my clients. I came home one night to my mom yelling. My little sister had been caught using weed. Mom was blaming me.

I sat at a corner, wondering if it was my fault, when a car rolled up and asked if I had anything. Falling into old habit, I asked what they were looking for. Before I could even blink, I was manhandled and slapped with handcuffs. So here I sit......

... not knowing what's going to happen tomorrow.

I wonder...
where did I go wrong?

SESSION 1: GETTING STARTED

Objectives

- Discuss the purpose of the program and why you are here
- Cover program guidelines and rules
- Discuss program outline and the goals of Phase I
- Learn the purpose of change
- Get to know each other
- Build trust in each other

Jeb's Story

I started smoking weed when I was twelve. I didn't really listen to my mom when she gave me her anti-drug lecture. After all, what did she know? She was always at work anyway. So I started hanging out with the people around my block, and realized that there was a potential job scene. People wanted drugs, but they couldn't get them on a regular basis. That is when I became a drug pusher. I could make money, they could get their drugs, and I wasn't hurting anyone by doing it. After all, these people already chose their path in life.

Things were going good until some other dealers moved into the neighborhood. They were selling cheaper drugs, and I had to struggle to keep up with my old customers. I started pushing on the streets instead of just quitting the game. Ended up trying to sell to an undercover, and now I'm here in jail, waiting to be tried as an adult.

What is this program about?

Alcohol and drug use, and doing things we're not supposed to, can make us *feel good* and are *exciting* when we first do them. Why else would we do them? The excitement goes away, however, and leaves us with feelings that are *not good*, such as worry, guilt, anger, or isolation from people we like. For some reason, almost all of us go back to the drugs or trouble even though we had the bad feelings. It probably has something to do with the *excitement* or the feeling of *being different* that we like.

Most of us don't even want to be here. After all, this may seem like a punishment and no one likes to be told what he or she can or cannot do. This program is not meant as punishment; rather this is about seeing our own special **talents** and **strengths** so that we can make good decisions on our own, without someone telling us what to do.

Why are we here?

- To **learn** how to recognize thoughts that can cause us to do harmful things
- To **build** skills that will help us to change our thoughts so we can do things that are positive

This program has **three phases**, each of which is meant to help us gain power and control over our thoughts. You are expected to take part in some exercises as well as be a part of the group. At first this may seem like a waste of time, but the purpose is to help you be a great person to know. We would like you to be a part of the group and give it a try.

Basic Ideas About This Program

- Our thoughts, beliefs, and feelings can cause us to do things that have negative outcomes or are bad for us.

- We have the ability to control our thoughts, beliefs, feelings and actions.

- By sharing our experiences, thoughts and feelings with people that we trust, changes become easier.

Activity: The Power Of Thought

A volunteer participates in a skit in which the group leader thinks that he or she is being **disrespected** by the youth. Your counselor **becomes overrun** by feelings and the situation turns out negative. The situation is **redone**, but this time the counselor talks about their thoughts as the skit is acted out, emphasizing that **we can change and control our thoughts and feelings** and ultimately our actions.

What This Program Has To Offer

- Getting **control** of our thoughts and beliefs can help us change.

- Putting **changes** into action can help us stay out of trouble.

- Staying out of trouble means **freedom** and getting things we want, which gives us an even better reason to stay out of trouble.

> *We can change and control our thoughts and feelings!*

Activity: Jeb's Negative Thinking

Break into groups of three or four. Take a look at Jeb's story. What were his **thoughts** about selling drugs? He only smoked marijuana, and sold drugs. How did doing this **bring problems** into his life? How could Jeb have stayed out of trouble? Use **specific examples** from the story to support your opinions. Then get back together with the larger group for a discussion.

Activity: Beginning To Share

Now it is time for us to get to know each other. Tell us one thing about yourself for each piece of candy you take. Here are some suggestions for things we would like to know about you:

· How old are you?

· What is your favorite music or sport?

· What do you want out of the program?

Building Trust

Let's talk a moment about trust. How do you *begin to trust* someone? How does trust work with getting into trouble, or does trust have nothing to do with trouble? How can trusting the people around you help you to change?

Activity: The Real Me

You are asked to write three stories about yourself, two of which **are true** and one of which is **a lie.** Tell your stories, and then as a group we will **ask questions** to determine which ones are true. After a certain amount of time, tell the group which stories are true. Does getting to know the truth about someone help to build trust?

Activity: Whom Do We Trust

We have probably all played a game called **telephone.** The difference, though, is that we are going to apply the idea to **trust.** Tell something **about yourself.** As the story gets passed around, the information becomes different. When you trust someone who does not deserve your trust, the information about ourselves gets **messed up or distorted.** When you trust someone who deserves your trust, the information only gets passed once. This helps us feel comfortable with the person, and the information does not get distorted or ruined. You feel **good about the person** and **good about yourself.** Who did Jeb trust in his decisions? Who should have Jeb trusted?

What we're going to talk about right now is *why we are here* and the *different programs* we might have already gone to. This may seem scary, but talking about ourselves and getting feedback leads to change.

We will talk to each other about *what we think about alcohol and drug use, getting into trouble, and being punished for our actions.* You may not want to tell strangers about personal things. But we want you to get know each other, and we have to start somewhere.

Thinking About Change

Let us each take a second to think about how we got here, sitting in this room. Then ask yourself, what is my goal of change? Use the list below to help decide what you want.

· I really haven't thought about changing anything in my life.

· I've thought about change a little bit.

· I think I want to change, but I'm not sure.

· I want to change.

We talked earlier about how thoughts can lead us to feelings and actions. Can you give the group an example of when your thoughts lead you to feel and then do something? *Something negative? something positive?*

Talk with your counselor or the group about how thinking about drug use and criminal acts might have gotten you into trouble.

Putting It Together

· Jeb sold drugs to make money, and because he saw a job opportunity. How did Jeb's lack of trust play into that? Wat could Jeb have done to stay out of trouble?

· Why is it important to stay out of trouble and why is it that drugs and alcohol are not good for you (even though they seem lie fun)?

· Discuss how taking control of your thoughts instead of letting your thoughts control you can make you happier -- and you can trust that it wil.

· What is expected of you, and what do you expect of yourself, to complete *Phase I*?

SESSION 2: THE POWER OF THOUGHT

Objectives

- Review *Session 1: Getting Started*
- Discuss how attitudes, beliefs, and thinking patterns control our actions
- Realize that we may have mixed feelings about change
- Know that people who search out drugs and get into trouble often keep themselves from change
- Discover that change is something exciting and use your freedom of choice to begin the change process

Jeb's Story

It wasn't like I was hurting anyone or getting anyone hooked. My customers had already chosen their paths in life, and I was merely meeting a demand. If I hadn't done it, someone else would have. And my smoking weed was no big deal. Everyone knows that weed is natural and can't really hurt you. There really wasn't any risk involved.

When I started losing my customers and the risk went up, I thought about getting out of the game clean. But then I realized how much I would have to work flipping burgers to get even one fourth of what I was making already. And pushing on the street wasn't that much more risk than delivering to the customer. I was living good, so why would I want to change?

Looking back before we move on

Last time we were together we began talking and thinking about what this program is about. We told you the *rules and phases*, and hope you began to think about your role in the program and why you are here. We also talked about how *thinking and feeling* get wrapped up in our actions, and how *changing our thoughts* can help us to change our actions.

We then spent a little time getting to know each other. Although this might not have been easy for you, we hope you know why it is important to build a level of trust within our group.

Now it's time to begin to take a look at how change is helpful in *giving us power.*

> ~ **POSITIVE CHANGE = FREEDOM & POWER** ~

Activity: Who Are We With?

Right now we are going to go around in a circle, and try to **remember one thing** about each person in the group. This is not a test, so you don't have to get everything right. We just would like to make sure everyone knows everyone else. If you are new to the group, tell a few things about yourself when it is your turn.

Six Building Blocks Of Change

1. Our attitudes, beliefs, and thinking patterns control us in everything we do.
We all like to think that no one and nothing controls our actions, and that is *exactly true* since these things are in our minds. *We can control what we think, feel and do.*

An **attitude** is an opinion that we hold about everything outside of us. Attitudes will cause us to act in a certain way to people or situations around us, and are usually affected by *feelings*. If your parent or an adult says they don't like your attitude, it usually means they don't like how you are acting or the feelings that are causing you to be like that. An example of an attitude is "school sucks."

A **belief** is an idea we use to judge the outside world and ourselves. A belief, or value, is a "truth" that we hold on to, sometimes with more strength than needed. It is these beliefs that cause us to have uncomfortable feelings or to have attitudes that might very well lead to trouble. The *belief* that adults or the system are *"just out to get you"* is probably going to make you feel *angry* and act mean when they try to talk to you.

A **thinking pattern or thought habit** is an immediate reaction within our brains without us even knowing it, and the thought habit likes to hang out with attitudes and beliefs. Let's say the kid across from you is laughing. Your *immediate thought* could be that they are *dissing* or making fun of you. This causes your feeling to be *anger*, and is probably based in the *belief* that people are always trying to put you down. But the reaction doesn't have to be bad….you could say to yourself, *"I'm going to check it out further,"* and might find out that the kid next to him just said something funny and it has nothing to do with you.

What could your constructive thoughts be if the kid actually was laughing at something about you?

Our attitudes, beliefs, and thinking patterns control how we act and behave.

Activity: Jeb's Negative Attitudes

Let's get in a group and **discuss Jeb** for a moment. What are some of Jeb's **attitudes** towards selling drugs and the people who buy the drugs from him? What is the **belief** that supports his **attitudes?**

2. Everyone likes to think they are in control.
We like to think we are the only ones who have control over our actions. And for the most part that is true. Whose thoughts are those in your head? *Yours and yours only*. But sometimes the thought is not something that has our best interests in mind. All three parts of our minds (attitudes, beliefs, and thought habits) *get together in our brains* when something happens to help us make a choice. The choice made, depending on our attitudes, beliefs, and thought habits, will either have positive or negative results for us. We *can* control our thoughts and actions.

To see a picture of what we are talking about, take a look at the *Figure 1*. This figure shows the *path your mind moves along* when an action takes place. After the choice of how to act has been made by your thoughts and feelings, the ending result can be positive or negative.

Activity: How Thinking Leads To Feelings And Actions

Break into small groups and discuss the chart that shows how **thinking leads to feelings and actions.** Discuss the situation that Jeb is currently in and show how **his thoughts** can lead to more negative outcomes. What thoughts might he choose to have that might lead to positive outcomes? Pick an event in your life that had a negative outcome and discuss how you could **change your thought habits** to lead to more positive results. Have different people **represent parts** of the *Pathways of Learning and Change, (Figure 1)*.

3. No one likes changing.
In fact, pretty much everyone doesn't like and is afraid of change. But when we fight against change, we are really sticking up for how we see ourselves. We've been ourselves, and probably have seen ourselves a certain way, for a very long time. And since we see our beliefs as part of our identity, it's really hard to think about changing. But change is not a bad thing, or even all that scary. *It's like an adventure.* And as we change, we don't become different people. Who would want to change if it meant being a completely new person? We become stronger people who have more *freedom and power* over our actions, because we went on the adventure that other people are afraid of.

Activity: Taking Control Over Our Thought And Actions

Sit in a circle and **choose one of the other participants** to be your leader. But don't tell that person or anyone else who your leader is. Close your eyes and when told to open them, copy your leader's pose. Each time the leader changes positions, **change in order to copy them.** Now imagine that the leader is **your belief.** We mold ourselves to our belief. But let's say you just stop doing what the leader is doing. You are still the same person, but **now you control** your own actions and choices.

4. We are confused and have mixed feelings about change.
Sometimes it's *really hard* to figure out why we should change. Sometimes we're tired of being in trouble and feeling down, but other times we're having so much fun and think we're not hurting anyone. Feeling confused about why we should change is part of the same scariness that makes us not want to change. Everything gets mixed up in our heads, and most of the time we like doing the things we are doing. Otherwise we wouldn't do them. But really those thoughts and choices we make are hurting us, more than we realize. And when we gain freedom over our thoughts, we really begin to see how good it feels and how good we feel with ourselves.

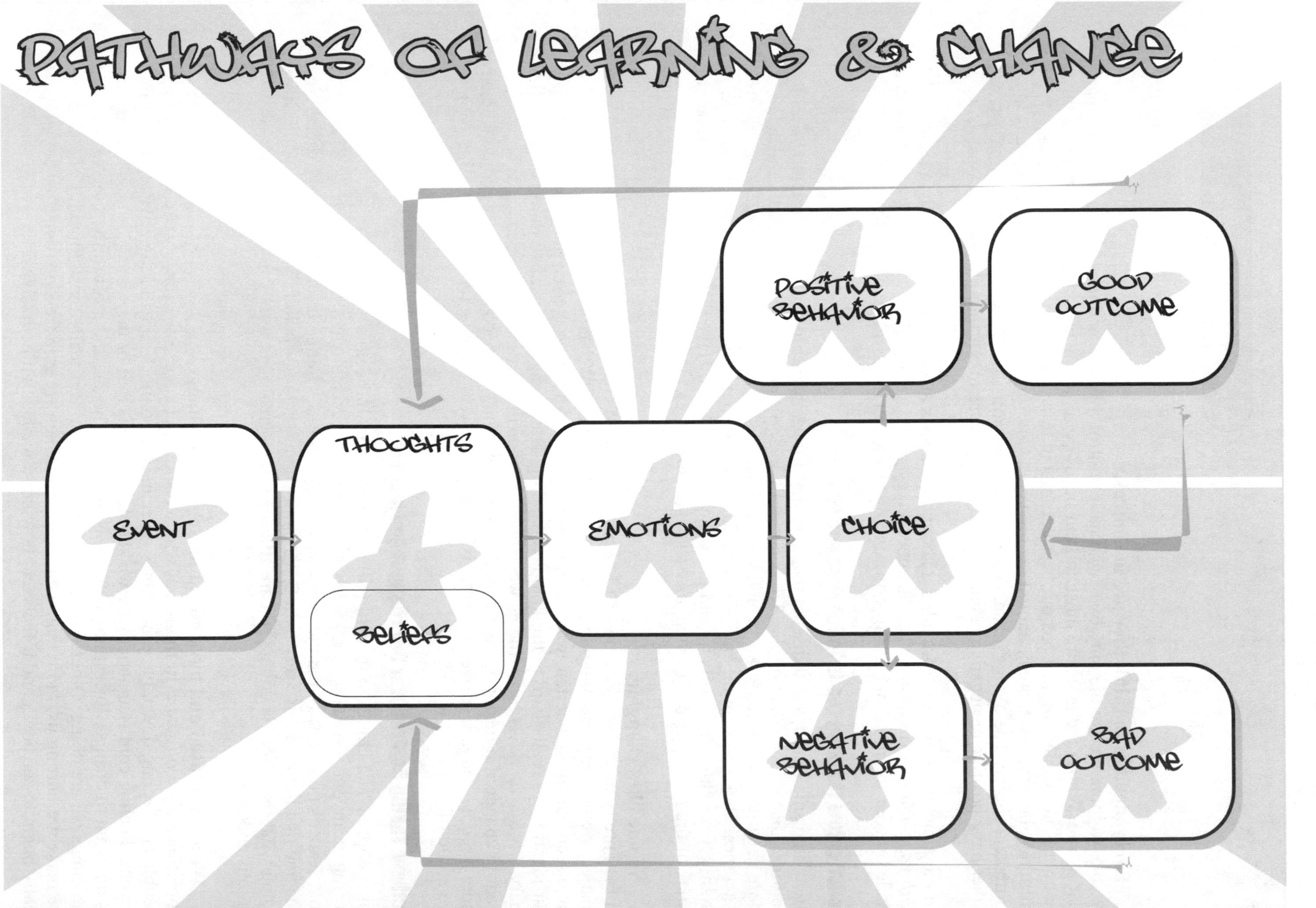

PATHWAYS OF LEARNING & CHANGE

EVENT → THOUGHTS / BELIEFS → EMOTIONS → CHOICE

CHOICE → POSITIVE BEHAVIOR → GOOD OUTCOME

CHOICE → NEGATIVE BEHAVIOR → BAD OUTCOME

Figure 1

Activity: Jeb's Mixed Feelings

Group discussion- Give an example of Jeb's **mixed** feelings about changing. How were his choices hurting him? How could he have changed to avoid being put in jail?

5. We are responsible for bringing about change in our lives.

Unfortunately, change does not happen while we sleep. Change does not happen *all at once.* If there were a pill we could take or a sentence we could read in order to change, then everybody would be changing and it wouldn't be so special. Changing, however, *is special* and so are the people who are able to change. Change happens slowly in different steps that we have to work at. Here are the *three stages of change* in our program:

· **WHAT: The Challenge to Change** is something that begins in our minds. We may even be ready to change or even talk about and do some changing. We *target* some aspect of our life that we intend to alter.

· **HOW: Using the Tools for Change** is our pledge or commitment to make a difference in ourselves. Our *second step* is that we make the choice to change. We become *committed* to the change process. We put *time and effort* into the program, learn the skills to change, and we even begin to feel freedom and power in being ourselves.

· **NOW: Calling Your Own Shots** means *taking responsibility* for the changes we made and our new thoughts, and being proud and powerful in those changes. *We* own the change! The third step is to learn ways to keep the change going. We learn about *what it means to go back* to our old lives. We realize that the changes, the skills, and the power of change are ours and belong only to us. The postitive changes that we have made become a regular part of our *everyday life.*

Activity: Setting Goals For Change

Let's take a moment to individually write down one goal for each of the above steps. How will you keep your goals in mind while you progress through this program? How might you achieve the goals you have set for yourself?

6. Keep the future in mind.

When we drink or do drugs, or even do something that will get us in trouble, we don't usually spend any time thinking about it. Why think about tomorrow when the party is tonight? *But not thinking about tomorrow makes us weak.* Before we even know it, we are being controlled by our actions and not even doing the things we like to do. It's like being in a pool, and at first the swimming is easy and fun. But as time goes on, *we get tired and weight gets added to our shoulders*, making the swimming not so fun and a lot more work. Before we know it, our head slips below the surface and we have *lost all control.* Instead, we should just get out of the pool and find something else that's fun too.

Activity: Visualizing The Ideas

To better understand how change happens, we are going to participate in a role-play of the **different parts of your mind.** We would like five volunteers to play the parts of:
· attitude
· thought habit

· belief
· block to change
· urge to change

We will set up a negative situation for the first three, with the attitude being the feelings about the situation, the thought habit being the reaction to the situation, and the belief as the reasoning behind the situation.

The **urge to change** will then begin saying things to convince the thought habit to change, while the **block to change** will tell the beliefs things that will keep them from changing. As a group, make a suggestion to help get rid of the block to change. How are the attitude, belief, and thought habit different when they can listen to the urge to change?

Putting It Together

· What were Jeb's beliefs, thoughts, and feelings about selling and doingdrugs? How did they change? What were the other choices Jeb could have made?

· Think about how your beliefs or view of yourself has led to some choices that may have gotten you in trouble.

· Think about a choice you've made. What were your thoughts and beliefs? How did they help you make your choice? If you had thought something different, what would the choice have been?

JEB'S STORY

I never thought I would end up here. After all, I was merely doing business that would have been done by someone else if I hadn't.

I had started smoking weed when I was twelve years old. Just to pass the time. I never even thought about my mom's drug lecture since weed's not a drug, as everyone knows. Around fourteen I began to buy directly from a dealer. There was more consistency in how I got my stash this way, and there wasn't as much waiting around and wondering. Slowly, kids began asking me if I knew someone who could get them what they wanted, and without even trying I stepped into being a middle man, getting smoke for other people when they couldn't find any.

My mom, a woman with two too many kids and not enough time, was usually working at one of her jobs, so for the most part I was left to my own devices. My friends' parents made sure they had after school activities, so most afternoons I would sit on the porch or wander the park smoking a joint. Slowly I got to be known by the locals, most of who had jobs but usually at night or part time, and we would sit and smoke as the larger world ignored us. As conversations flowed, I began to get a glimpse into a possible job scene. These people had a demand that was not being met. Namely, most of the people wanted drugs, usually pills or speed, yet their connections were not consistent enough to meet the needs of these paying customers. It was that realization that began my career in pushing. I was already running for most people I knew when their guys fell through, so I waited until I had several orders and then I would buy at the bulk rate. I pocketed the change, got my smoke for cheaper, my man was getting more money without exposing himself to more people, and the customers were getting the regular rate plus reliability. For everyone involved it was a win.

By the age of fifteen I was considered a full time pusher. I had a steady clientele, restricted to those I knew and those who knew the game (no street pushing for me), with posted business hours which guaranteed I would get home before my mom. As I was what I call a satellite dealer, meaning I got paged and then I delivered, there didn't seem to be any risk involved. And it wasn't like these people were my friends. The dozen or so in my client base had already chosen their life courses. Although my friends and I partied once in awhile when there was nothing else to do, I made it a rule to not sell my hard merchandise to my friends. The way I figured it, I was merely meeting a demand for a product. It wasn't like I was getting kids hooked, and if I wasn't there to push the drugs and take the money, someone else would have.

By sixteen I was bringing in steady cash which spent itself almost as quickly as I made it. I gave my mom a large amount each month to help with food and bills. I'm pretty sure she suspected how I got my money, yet she took the cash anyway. I also spent a lot of money on my little sister. I wanted her to have everything that I went without when I was younger. The rest was spent on me. I was living my life in the fast lane, the life of a celebrity, the life I never knew existed. It was just after my seventeenth birthday when things began to go wrong. Suddenly there were new pushers in the area offering a quicker and cheaper high. Slowly I began to lose my clients to crystal and crack. At first it was not big deal, as I am not greedy. I even thought of getting out of the game clean. Then I figured how many hours I would have to work at some greasy joint to make a fourth of the cash. So after school I started wandering the streets, not necessarily pushing but just getting a feel and seeing if I ran into anyone desiring some merchandise.

Things were going all right, despite the higher risk and not as much flow, when I came home one night to my mom throwing things at me and yelling. Slowly it came out that my sister had been caught smoking weed behind the gym at her school. My ten year old sister, the kid I took care of and adored, the one who wasn't going to be like the rest of us and who would get out of this dump. I was in a rage. I would kill the scum that sold her that bag. I would make sure she never saw her so-called friends again. And then I realized my mom was still yelling at me, blaming me. I went cold inside, as if a stake of ice was shoved through my heart. I left right after that to wander around and clear my head. I knew I had no business being out on the streets, but I couldn't get through the cotton that had my mind numb. Pondering, I sat at a corner, wondering if it was my fault, if I shouldn't have quit while I was ahead, if clothes maybe weren't what my sister needed from me, when a car rolled up and asked if I had anything. Falling into habit, I asked what they were looking for. Before I could even blink, I was manhandled and slapped with handcuffs.

So here I sit, not knowing what's going to happen tomorrow. My mom's been in to see me once, just to let me know there was no way she was going to bail me out and that I could sit here and rot. The lawyer the state gave me said they could easily charge me as an adult since I'm so close to eighteen, and that could mean a sentence of years. As I stare at my twisted reflection in the stainless steel sink stare back at me, and as the frigid coldness of the cinder block walls seeps into my bones, **I wonder where did I go wrong?**

NOTES

Chapter Two:
Building a Knowledge Base

GOALS OF THIS CHAPTER
- To learn how thinking and feeling affect our actions
- To learn basic facts about drugs and addiction
- To understand how getting in trouble is connected with doing drugs

JARROD'S STORY

I feel so lonely here. This is not where I belong. I have always felt lonely ... isolated, like I was trapped in a glass box. Then I met Mary. The sun came out and her hair was like a golden halo. She smiled and said she would like to take me to a party this weekend. Mary picked me up around eight. While we were in line, Mary took a couple of pills out of her pocket and gave me one.

I didn't care, what would one pill do? I was the happiest I had been for as long as I could remember. Mary and I spent pretty much every day together. Slowly, we began doing pills more often. One weekend, there was this huge party. To make it extra special we both took a couple more pills than usual.

Mary was pretty out there and begged me to drive. I would do anything for Mary. So I began driving. Somehow, I ended up on the left shoulder.

We crashed into another car. I had to sit there in pain as Mary slowly died. The passenger of the other car wound up dying, too

A young mother with two kids.

And now I'm back in my box, except this time it's metal with iron bars, while I wait out my sentence for manslaughter. I cry every night, and I have never been lonelier in my life.

SESSION 3: HOW THOUGHTS & FEELINGS AFFECT BEHAVIOR

Objectives

- Review *Chapter 1: Building Trust and Motivation to Change*
- Learn how thinking helps us to learn and change
- Understand and learn five principles about thinking and doing
- Know and use the concepts of how we learn behavior
- Understand how learning behavior works with change

Jarrod's Story

I have always felt lonely, isolated, like I was the only person in the world who thought and felt like I did. Until I met Mary. And then suddenly I belonged with someone. Because she took me out of my glass box and made me feel wanted, I would have done anything for her. Her wish was my command.

That's how it was with pills, too. They made me feel good, and I liked that feeling. Being with Mary and taking pills allowed me to belong. And I wanted that feeling more than anything.

Thinking back

In *Session 2* we began to learn the ins and outs of our minds and how change can help us as well as be exciting. We talked about what attitudes, beliefs, and thought habits were, and how we can change how our mind thinks in order to have more freedom in our actions and choices.

Activity: Remembering As A Group

Let's take a moment as a group to remember these concepts. What is a **thought habit**? What is a **belief**? What is an **attitude**, and how are those affected by our beliefs? Go around the room and give an example of each. Who is responsible for change? How do we change?

THE PRINCIPLES OF THINKING AND ACTING

There are certain principles that guide our thoughts and actions:

Principle 1: Our beliefs, attitudes, and thoughts control our actions and feelings.
We usually think it's the other way around, that what happens outside of us is what controls our actions and thoughts. It is actually *being able to control your thoughts* that can help control your actions, leading to freedom of choice.

> *Our beliefs, attitudes, and thoughts control our actions and feelings.*

Activity: Fly By Design

Everyone will receive a piece of paper to make a **paper airplane**. Use any design for your airplane. Standing along a single line, throw the airplanes and see whose plane can fly the farthest. Go back and make another plane, preferably with a **different design**, and see how far the second plane can fly. Your **thoughts** are like the design of the plane, and the distance is the action that you take part in. The design of the plane controlled how far the plane flew, just as your thoughts control your actions. By changing your design, or thought, you are able to control the plane, or action.

Principle 2: Everyone sees themselves and the world from different points of view.
How you see the world and how the person sitting next to you sees the world is *different* because our *thoughts and beliefs are different*. This also means that what we feel about the situation is different. One of us may think that a sunny day means a good thing, while another may feel upset because it's going to be hot. The concept of *seeing things differently* pushes us towards certain concepts:

We have certain ideas (beliefs) about what we think about the world.
Our thoughts and actions are based on those ideas.

There is no right or wrong way to look at the world.
But some of us do have some common ideas or beliefs. This forms a group in which the beliefs become rules of belonging to the group. If one belief is that the sky is gray, then everyone in that group has that common belief. But if one of us were to say the sky is blue, that concept would go against the group belief. It is *when you go against* the common rules of a larger group that your *thoughts and actions can cause problems*.

Activity: Rules Of A Group

By now we've gotten to know each other. **Without speaking** to each other, get into small groups according to what you think are some **common rules** of the group. An example of a group would be people who listen to heavy rock or dress the same. Talk about **what everyone thinks** are the common rules. Now rearrange the groups, with one person from each previous group in the new groups. Try to get in a group with **completely different** people. Are there common rules the new group can agree on?

Principle 3: Our ideas and thought habits (the ideas that pop into our head automatically) about everything around us and ourselves can become warped or bent.
Imagine sitting outside without sunglasses on, and think about the different colors and images that can be seen. When sunglasses with let's say green lenses are put on, suddenly certain objects come out more than others do and yet everything has changed. This sometimes happens to our thoughts and can cause us to act out or have feelings that cause problems.

Principle 4: Our thoughts, emotions, and actions are not separate.
It's like that meeting we keep talking about. All three parts of our mind are at the gathering talking and having fun together. How we feel can lead to thoughts; actions can change how we think and feel; our feelings about a thought can cause actions. If we take a look at *Figure 2*, we can see how all three are connected.

Figure 2

Interaction of Thoughts, Feelings and Actions

Keep in mind **Principle 1**. Things outside of you *do not* control your actions and feelings. Your *beliefs*, *attitudes*, and *thoughts* control your feelings and actions.

Activity: A Meeting Of Difference

Divide into three groups of about the same number of people. Take a couple of minutes apart with your group to come up with a collective **sound and a motion** that you think will make the other groups **laugh**, for example patting the top of your head while mooing like a cow. The sounds and motions should not be longer than a couple of seconds in length.

Once a sound and a motion have been decided upon, get back together with the other two groups and form a triangle, with each group facing the other two. Each group will then **demonstrate** the sound and motion they have decided on for the other two groups. After each group has presented their sound/motion, all three groups will try to **recreate and practice** the sound and motion they just witnessed. Have each of the three groups present and allow time for all the sounds and motions to be practiced.

Now comes the difficult part. You have just practiced three different sound/motion combinations. Separate into your groups and discuss **which sound/motion** you will do when you return to the triangle. The point is to **get all three groups to do the same sound/motion combination** at the same time **without discussing** it between the groups. Pay attention to what the other groups are doing, and keep repeating the last step until all three groups perform the same sound/motion in sync with the other groups.

You may have noticed that one or two particular groups **insisted on doing their sound/motion at all times,** or decided to not change according to what the other groups were doing. This group represents our **beliefs**, which often insist on not changing despite what is going on around us. The other two groups represent our **attitudes** and **thoughts**, which may change according to what is going on around us and often influence each other in what they do. All three, our beliefs, attitudes, and thoughts, **interact** with each other in our mind to help us make the choices we make. But when our **beliefs insist** on not changing, our attitudes and thoughts change to accommodate that belief.

Principle 5: What happens outside of us may cause thoughts that are based on our beliefs and attitudes.

These thoughts can make us feel a certain way, which may cause us to act or behave a certain way. Let's say a person offers you a hit of weed. In the meeting in your mind, the thought may be that weed can't hurt you because that's what you believe. So the thought offers your feelings the hit, which make your feelings mellow and happy. Since your feelings are good, your action is to take the drug. But the meeting in our heads also has us there, too. That means we have a choice in whether we take the drugs or not. Take a look at *Figure 3*.

When you have a thought, you have *the freedom to decide* whether to take the hit or not. *You can decide to change the thought* that automatically pops up into your head. Your choice of thought then decides the results you will have. The actions you choose will then affect your thoughts and emotions.

Activity: Jarrod's Principles

Break into smaller groups to discuss the **Five Principles of Thinking and Acting** and how they might apply to Jarrod's story. Here are some things to think about:
· What was Jarrod's thought about taking the pills?
· How did Jarrod's thoughts and feelings affect his actions?
· How may have Jarrod's beliefs about himself bent his view of doing pills?

One Step Further

Now let's take our action one step beyond the acting out. So the choice ended with you taking a drug. What happens after that? One outcome is that it was a onetime hit and it will never happen again. Another possibility is that we smoke weed again, but it doesn't happen all the time. The third result is that we begin smoking all the time, forming what we'll call an action habit. The action habit is *similar* to our thought habits, in that they happen automatically without much thinking on our parts.

So how do these actions become a *habit*? Well, we have results from the actions that we decide to take part in. Sometimes the results are positive for us, and sometimes the results are *not* positive. Whether the results are positive or not, there are certain *concepts* that help us to *decide* on the action again or not.

Learning Concept I -Turning On Positive Feelings
If an action that we participate in gives us a *good feeling*, then we are likely to do that action *again*. We may repeat it until it becomes a *habit*. When something causes us to feel good, then the action gets strengthened. If smoking weed results in excitement or happiness, then the smoking is strengthened and we are likely to do it again.

Learning Concept II -Turning Off Negative Feelings
If an action *stops* a negative feeling, such as pain or worry, that action gets *strengthened* and will become a *habit*. This is the *best way* to learn. When we feel pain, perhaps from *some memory* or even a *problem that we are now experiencing*, we may choose to deal with these *uncomfortable states of mind* by smoking weed (some people use other drugs for the same purpose). The *pain goes away* and drug use *gets strengthened*.

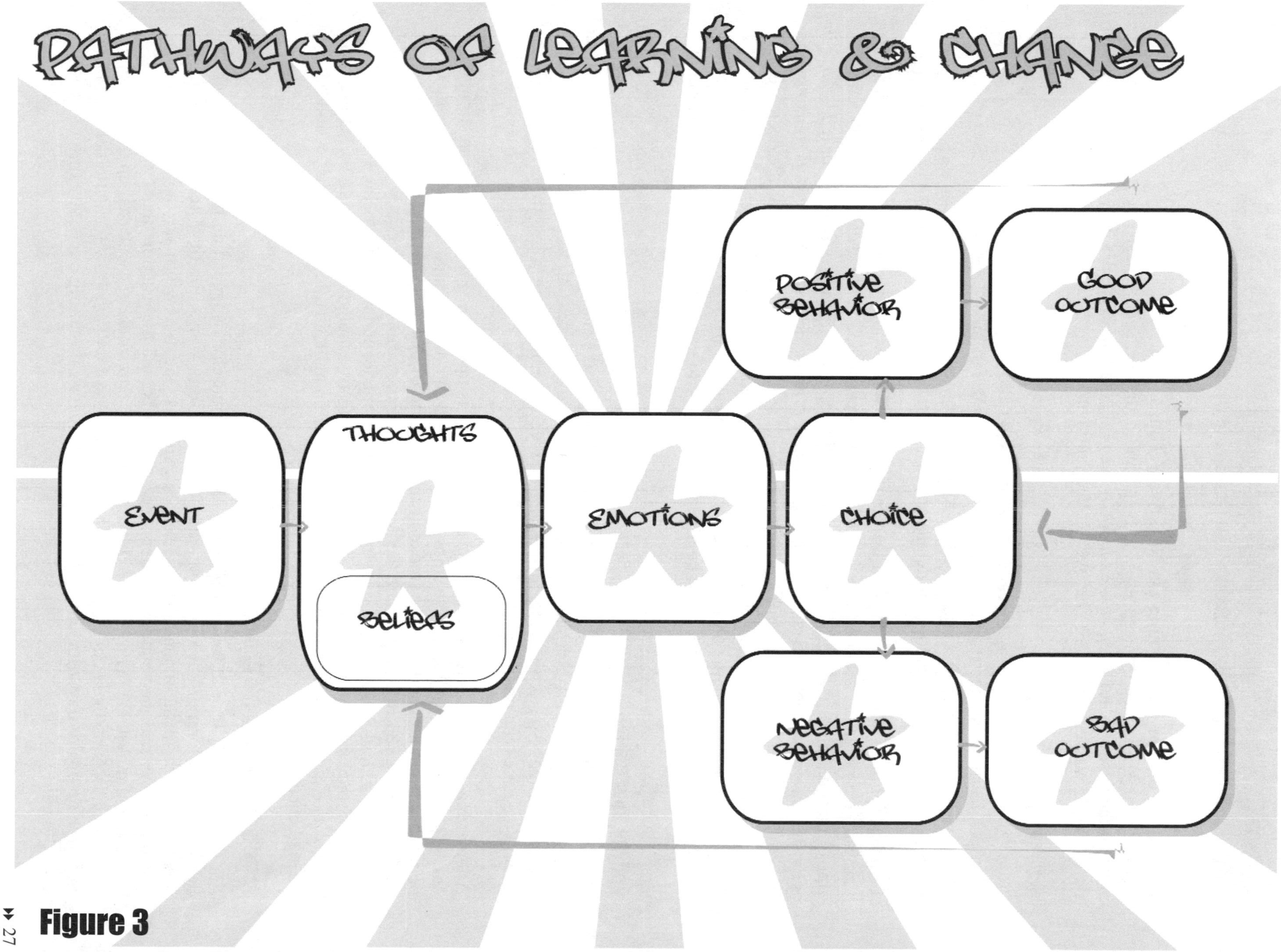

PATHWAYS OF LEARNING AND CHANGE

EVENT

THOUGHTS
BELIEFS

EMOTIONS

CHOICE

POSITIVE BEHAVIOR

NEGATIVE BEHAVIOR

GOOD OUTCOME

BAD OUTCOME

Figure 3

Learning Concept III -Turning On Negative Feelings

Let's say smoking marijuana causes us to be paranoid and confused. These *negative feelings* weaken the desire to get high, and it's *unlikely* we will continue to smoke. But sometimes we still do. Why do we keep smoking after we get bad feelings?

Activity: Jarrod's Learning

Take a moment to look at the **three learning concepts** above.

- Which learning concept(s) can be applied to Jarrod's use of pills?
- What are the feelings that might lead up to his use?
- Use examples from the story for details about the learning concepts and Jarrod's use.

Concept III *does not always work* in learning actions. Why would we continue doing something that causes us negative feelings? Well, sometimes **Concepts I & II** are *really strong*. When we smoke marijuana, for example, our immediate feelings are an *increase in comfort* or a *decrease in pain*. Just like what we were talking about in *Session 2*, about how we don't always think beyond the night of the party. The *reward* for our actions, either the positive feelings or the decrease in negative feelings, is something that happens right away while the negative feelings that come from *our choice* don't come around for awhile. The reward is *stronger* in our learning than the negative results from our actions. Take a look at *Figure 4* to get a better idea of how this might work.

Activity: Your Choice

Get into pairs and work together on *Worksheet 1*. Use a **real situation** and fill in the blanks about the **positive and negative results** of choices. How could the results affect the choice you will make next time? Spend some time discussing how you would change your **thinking** to arrive at a more positive outcome.

Another reason why **Concept III** doesn't always work is that the *negative* results can strengthen our *beliefs and thought habits*. We smoke weed, we get into trouble, and this may *strengthen* our belief that "I am no good." So we smoke again to get rid of that *negative feeling*. It becomes a cycle where we repeat and continue the actions despite the *problems* that occur. To see what we're talking about, look at *Figure 5*. Every time a *choice* is made, and negative feelings get turned on, the *action* may stop but it might also strengthen the negative thoughts that led to the choice. But if a *positive* outcome happens, then the action and the thoughts that lead up to that action become strengthened.

Activity: Who Makes The Choice?

For this skit we will need **four volunteers**. At your counselor's suggestion of an event, such as being offered a joint or having the opportunity to deal some drugs, the **first person** will state an *automatic thought* (the thought habits/reaction), such as "the joint will make me feel good." The **second person** will then state the beliefs and attitudes behind the reaction, that "weed isn't harmful and makes me happy." **The third person** will *choose an action* based on the beliefs and thought habits, like *take the hit*, and the **fourth person** will say how the action chosen had **negative or positive results**, either getting high and happy or getting caught by the cops and going to jail.

Figure 4

THREE ROLES OF LEARNING BEHAVIOR

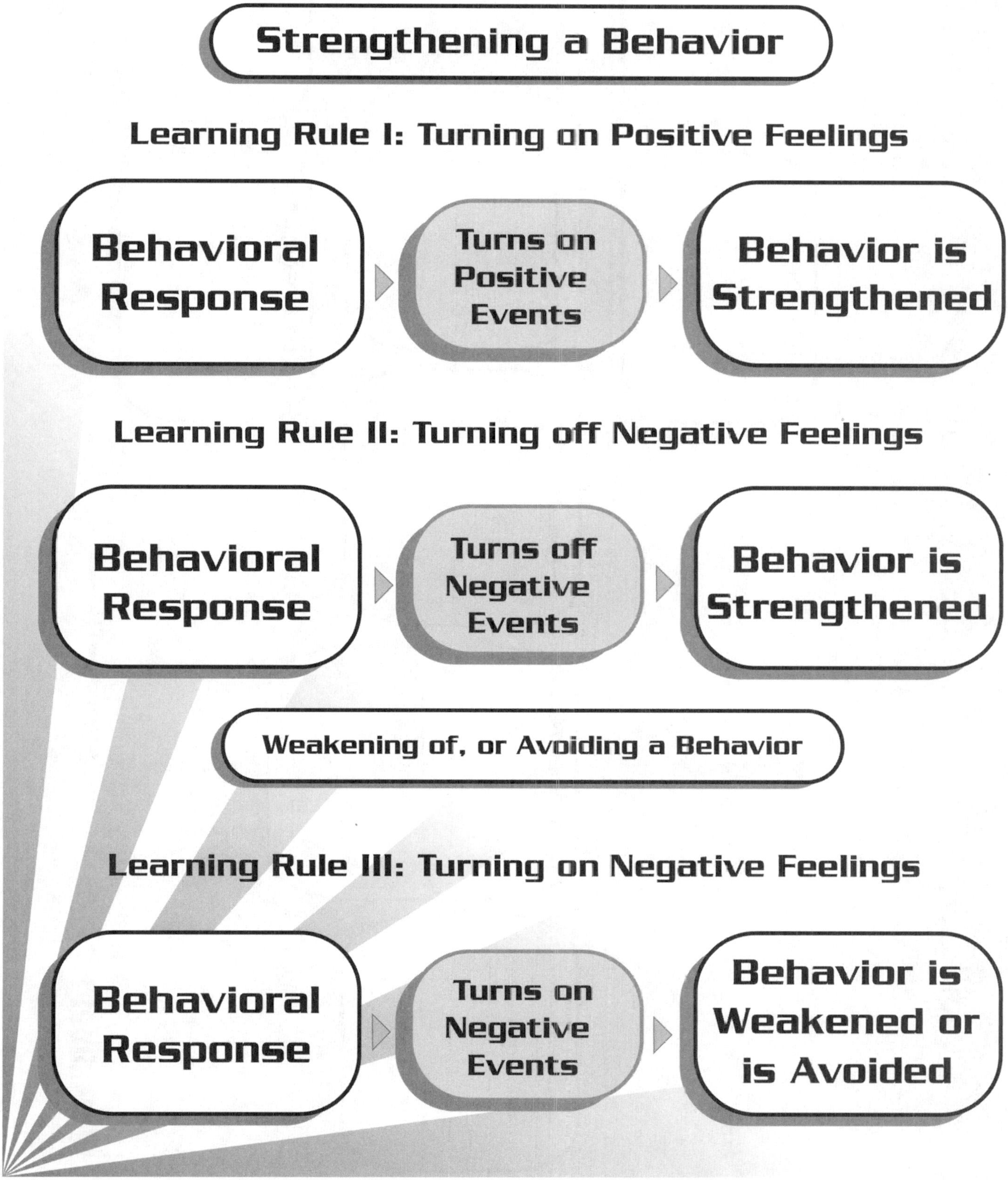

Strengthening a Behavior

Learning Rule I: Turning on Positive Feelings

| Behavioral Response | ▷ | Turns on Positive Events | ▷ | Behavior is Strengthened |

Learning Rule II: Turning off Negative Feelings

| Behavioral Response | ▷ | Turns off Negative Events | ▷ | Behavior is Strengthened |

Weakening of, or Avoiding a Behavior

Learning Rule III: Turning on Negative Feelings

| Behavioral Response | ▷ | Turns on Negative Events | ▷ | Behavior is Weakened or is Avoided |

PATHWAYS OF LEARNING & CHANGE

Complete this picture. Take an event that you recently experienced. Then note your automatic thoughts that came from that event. Then note your feelings and beliefs. What was your behavior? Fill in the rest of the squares. What might happen if you decide to change your thoughts and beliefs?

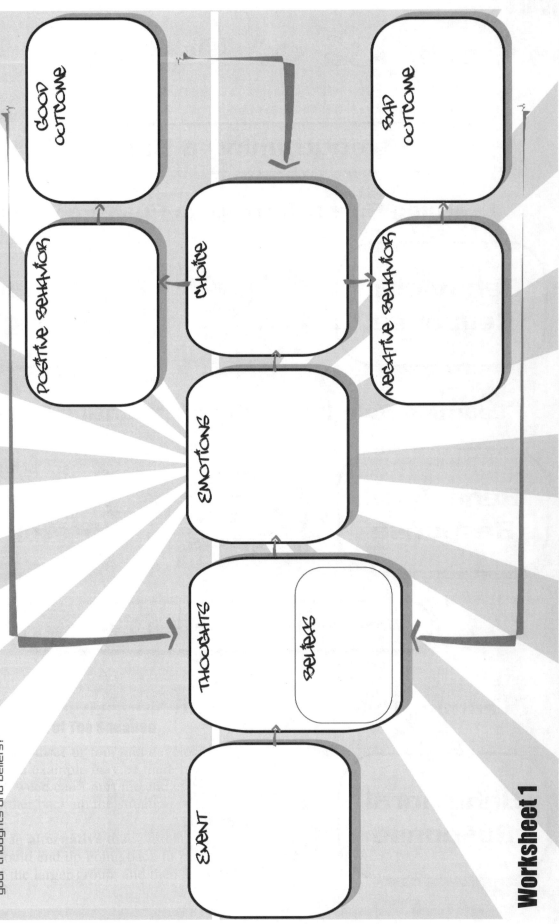

GOOD OUTCOME

BAD OUTCOME

POSITIVE BEHAVIOR

CHOICE

NEGATIVE BEHAVIOR

EMOTIONS

THOUGHTS

BELIEFS

EVENT

Worksheet 1

The group will then discuss how **each step decides** the choices given to the next step, and how the result could strengthen or weaken the **thoughts, attitudes, beliefs and feelings** that caused the reaction. The **thought habits** are that "weed will make you feel good," which are supported by deep-seated **beliefs and attitudes**.

How can this pattern of thoughts, beliefs, attitudes and feelings be altered?

Putting It Together

- Think about the principles above. How did the principles work together in helping Jarrod make his decisions?

- What are the specific thoughts and emotions that led up to Jarrod's decisions?

- Think about an action that led to a positive or negative feeling, and how that helped you make a choice the next time.

- Think about your thoughts, feelings, and emotions that led to a positive result, and how that made you feel.

- Which learning concept is likely the best way you learn?

Objectives

· Review *Session 3: How Thoughts and Feelings Affect Behavior*
· Talk about how we see substance abuse and drugs
· Learn some basic facts about substances and their effect on our bodies
· Discover the two paths to addiction
· Apply the paths and cycles to yourself

Jarrod's Story

We started doing pills all the time, pretty much every weekend. We didn't go to parties much because we couldn't afford it, but Mary and I were happy just being together. Just as long as we weren't with each other for a couple days after we had taken some pills. I needed and wanted the feeling all the time, the feeling of freedom and the ability to belong without the worry of rejection. Of course we started doing more pills at one time, trying to increase that good feeling.

I never really understood why I felt so low for a couple days afterwards. How could something that makes me feel so good end up bad for me? Every down I thought about how I didn't want to ever feel like that again, but then the weekend would come and Mary and I would party again.

Thinking back

Last session we began talking about how our thoughts, actions, and feelings are all sitting together in a meeting in our head, and how we are part of the meeting as well. Even though our thoughts and feelings control our actions, not the outside world, *we control our thoughts and feelings*. And although sometimes our thoughts can become distorted, it still means that we *have power and freedom over the choices* we make.

We also started talking about how we learn behavior. There were three concepts that we covered, all of which help to strengthen or weaken our responses the next time the same choice has to be made.

Activity: The Concepts Of Learning

Let's take a moment to remember what those concepts are and how they help learning. Separate into three different groups, each one representing a learning concept. Try to be in the group of how you think you learn best. Get together with your group and discuss how to **act out the learning concept**. Then act it out for the other two groups.

Now that we know how our thoughts and feelings can affect our actions, and how learning can sway whether we make that decision again or not, let's talk a little about drugs and addiction.

Thought and Discussion: What is addiction, and what causes it?

BASIC THINGS TO KNOW ABOUT DRUGS

1) Definition of drugs.
A drug is something we use to change how we feel, think, or act.

2) Drugs affect both our minds and bodies.
When we take drugs, it changes how our body talks to itself. It also changes and releases the chemicals in our brains that help control our thoughts and feelings.

Activity: How Much We know

We'll stop here for a moment so that you can take the drug knowledge test. Discuss your answers and why you chose them.

3) There are four categories of drugs that people take to get high.
- Drugs that s*low down* our brains are called *sedatives or downers*. Drugs like alcohol, Quaaludes and Xanax are downers.
- Drugs that reduce pain while providing an intense sense of pleasure and euphoria are called *narcotics*. Some drugs in this category are heroin, Demerol and Percodan.
- Drugs that *speed up* or excite our brains are called *stimulants or uppers*. Some uppers dramatically speed up our bodies and minds, like cocaine and speed, while others like caffeine speed us up in a less obvious manner.
- Drugs that *alter our perception* and sense of reality are called hallucinogens. Marijuana, mescaline, peyote, LSD and PCP are placed in this category.
- To see the different classes of drugs, look at *Table 1*.
- How about cigarettes? Cigarettes, which contain *nicotine*, combine some of the properties of stimulants and depressants.

4) Drugs affect us directly and indirectly.
- The drug effect during use (*the direct effect*) is what happens *when we are on the drugs*, which may be physical or mental. Smoking marijuana can make us feel physically tired or drained while it causes us to laugh.
- The *indirect effect* is what happens after the drug is gone. Our bodies begin to start missing the drug when it's gone, like not being able to sleep when we haven't used in awhile.

5) Different drugs have different effects (direct and indirect) on us.
- How a drug affects us depends on the drug, and the direct effects are usually *opposite* of the indirect effects. Cocaine speeds us up, so that when we are not on cocaine our system slows down and we are tired and depressed. Alcohol slows us down, but when we aren't drinking our system speeds up and we can't sleep.
- Both effects can cause problems.

Activity: How Drugs Affect Jarrod

Take a moment to look back at Jarrod's story. What were some of the direct effects of the pills? What were the indirect effects? Which category of drug do you think the pills that Jarrod took belonged to?

Table 1

DRUG CATEGORIES & WITHDRAWL EFFECTS

	Physical	Psychological
NARCOTICS * **Heroin** * **Codeine** * **Morphine**	watery eyes tremors runny nose chills cramps sweating nausea loss of appetite yawning	irritability panic anxiety
STIMULANTS * **Meth** * **Cocaine** * **Caffeine**	cravings tiredness headaches	depression anxiety paranoia irritability disorientation aggression apathy (meth)
DEPRESSANTS * **Alcohol** * **Barbs** * **Xanax,** **Valium, etc.**	loss of appetite muscle tremors insomnia sweating hyperactivity	anxiety delirium psychosis altered perceptions
HALLUCINOGENS * **MDMA** * **Marijuana** * **LSD**	hyperactivity (marijuana) loss of appetite	depression anxiety irritability delirium paranoia
NICOTINE * **Cigarettes** * **Chewing** **Tobacco** * **Pipes**	cravings fatigue headaches coughing indigestion nausea diarrhea insomnia sore throats increased appetite	irritability anxiety depression restlessness feelings of frustration and anger lack of concentration

6) When we take drugs, our bodies become toxic.

Drugs poison our bodies. When the drug (and that does include alcohol) leaves the body, the body has to try and return to normal. Sometimes this can cause the body *shock*, which is what we call *withdrawal*. The reaction can be only in our minds, but more often it is also our physical body that is in shock. Depending on the drug and how much was in the body, the reaction can be so strong that the body quits or goes into seizures.

7) Tolerance for drugs can increase, causing you to become physically and mentally dependent.

As we keep doing the same drug, we may need more and more just to get the same feelings, or the same amount will give us less of the feelings we want. This is called *tolerance*. The ability to grow tolerant depends on the drug, but all drugs can cause us to need more. You used to get a buzz off of one beer or a couple of hits, but now it takes two or three beers or a whole joint to get the same positive feelings. This is called tolerance and is one reason why we become dependent on drugs.

8) Mixing drugs at the same time can increase the strength of one or both.

One drug we take may get stronger because another drug is in our body. Drinking alcohol and smoking weed together causes our minds to become much more confused then if we used one drug alone.

SPECIFIC DRUGS AND THEIR EFFECTS

Nicotine/Tobacco

· Found most commonly in cigarettes and other smoking items, tobacco is grown and harvested.

· Symptoms of use can include smelly hair, clothes, and breath, coughs, shortness of breath and poor athletic performance.

· Consequences include addiction, emphysema and chronic bronchitis, heart disease, cancer of the lung, voice box, throat, bladder, pancreas, kidney and mouth.

Marijuana

· Known as weed, pot, grass, skunk, Mary Jane, and reefer, just to name a few, marijuana is a drug that is grown and has distinct leaves.

· Symptoms of use can include mood swings, euphoria, slow thinking and reflexes, increased appetite, dry mouth, and in some cases delusions and hallucinations.

· The consequences of smoking marijuana are memory impairment, weight gain, increased risk for cancer, lower sperm counts and increased infertility.

MDMA

· Known as ecstasy, E, X, and by a number of brand names, MDMA is part mental enhancer and an upper that releases serotonin in the brain, and is often in pill form.

- Symptoms of use include trance-like states, euphoria, increased pulse rate, and excitement of the senses, usually touch, taste, and smell.

- Consequences of use can include impaired judgment and coordination, deep depression and anxiety, sleep disorders, and states of confusion.

LSD

- Lyseric Acid Diethylamide, often going by the name of LSD, acid, or whatever the substance is taken on such as blotter or pez, is a chemical substance which is often found in its original form as a liquid.

- Symptoms of use include trance-like states, excitation, euphoria, hallucinations, insomnia, and often increased sense sensitivity, especially of visual stimulants.

- Consequences of use can be violent behavior, impaired judgment and coordination, self-inflicted injury, paranoia, depression, anxiety, and unpredictable flashbacks.

Methamphetamine

- Most commonly known as meth, crystal, or ice, this drug can be found in powder or rock form and is an upper.

- Symptoms of use include tremors, excitability, insomnia, sweating, dry mouth and lips, weight loss, paranoia, and in some cases hallucination.

- Consequences can be weight loss, nutritional deficiency, chronic sleep problems, paranoia, anxiety or nervousness, severe depression, violent behavior, and death from heart failure or suicide.

Activity: Passing The Buck

Get in a circle, if you aren't in one already, and pass around the ball your counselor will give you. The first person will begin by **saying which drug of abuse they are**. For example, "I am heroin." Then hand the ball to the **next person** who will say what **direct effects** can come from the drug. The next person will be the **indirect effect**. As the ball goes around, more drugs will be added together, showing how toxic drugs can be when added together in our systems.

Alcohol

Alcohol is considered a drug, and it's one of the most used and most dangerous drugs, so we'll get a little in-depth about alcohol. Drinking and driving is *the leading cause of death* in the 15–20-year-old age group. Just one drink is enough to be convicted of driving while impaired, which means you are put on *probation, lose your license* as well as have to *take classes* for your drinking. How many of the group knows someone who has gone through the experience of a DUI?

1) Alcohol is a *downer*, which means it *slows down our system* and makes us tired.
2) One drink contains about one-half ounce of pure alcohol. One can of beer, one small glass of wine, and one mixed drink are all considered one drink, despite the differences in size.
3) Although the alcohol level depends on the weight of the person, the number of drinks, and the time it took to drink the drinks, it takes about half of one percent of alcohol in the blood to kill a person.
4) Alcohol dissolves in water, so about 98% of alcohol is broken down by the digestive system and the rest leaves through breath and urine. That means most of the alcohol does not leave your body when you go to the bathroom.
5) Adult drinkers are classified by how many drinks they have on one occasion:
    a) Light drinker: one drink
    b) Moderate drinker: 2-3 drinks
    c) Heavy drinker: 4-5 drinks
    d) Excessive drinker: 6 or more
6) How many times we drink is also grouped:
    a) Infrequent: Less than once a month
    b) Occasional: Less than one time a week
    c) Frequent: 1-3 times a week
    d) Consistent: 4-5 times a week
    e) Daily: 6-7 times a week

Activity: A Glance At You

Take a moment to look at the above labels, and assess what kind of drinker or drug user you think you are. How many drinks does it take for you to begin to get a "buzz"? Go around the group and share how much you think you were drinking or taking drugs before treatment. Why did you drink as much as you do? What do you get from alcohol? What are your thoughts about drinking and driving?

Activity: Passing The Buck For Alcohol

Refer to **Activity: *Passing the Buck*** for instructions.

7) Females, people who weigh less, are tired or haven't eaten, tend to get more drunk. That doesn't mean that if you are fatter, you can drink more. *More body fat actually keeps the alcohol from breaking down*, and may *increase* the amount of alcohol in the blood. Because *females have more body fat*, sometimes it's harder for their bodies to get rid of alcohol. But just because *you don't act as drunk* as your friend does not mean you don't have the same level of alcohol in your system. Some people develop ways to act more sober than they are; this is called *behavioral tolerance*.

DRINKING AND YOUR BODY

Liver: When you drink a lot, or even moderately, *fatty tissue builds up* in your liver. The fatty tissue gets itself between the healthy cells and cuts off the blood supply, leading to *dead cells* throughout your liver. The body replaces the dead cells with *scar tissue*, and when that happens it's called *cirrhosis*, which stops your liver from working right.

Stomach and Guts: Have you ever gotten a cut and someone put alcohol on it to clean it out? It made your skin and the cut burn really badly. Well, this is what alcohol does to your stomach. The alcohol *burns holes in the lining*, which gives your stomach what we call *ulcers*.

Heart and Blood: Heavy drinking, especially when you drink and smoke together, can *increase your blood pressure*, the amount of pressure on your veins from the blood moving through them, and can cause *heart problems*.

Brain and Nerves: Your brain has a way of keeping small bits of alcohol out of it. But when there is a rush of alcohol, the fence is broken and the brain cells can be *hurt or killed* by the alcohol. How your nerves feel can also be affected when damaged by alcohol.

Activity: A Chain Of Destruction

Form **two teams** and sit down **facing each other** on the floor. All but the first people in each line have their eyes closed. The counselor flips a coin as many times as necessary until it lands on heads. Then the race begins. The first people (who have their eyes open) tap the next person and so on until the tapping reaches the end of the line, at which time the last person to get tapped raises his or her hand. The first team done is the winner. This is how our brains work when they send information. Only the messengers are electrochemical signals rather than hands.

Next let's see what happens when the brain is **compromised by alcohol or some other drug**. After your counselor secretly designates one person in line who can't function or do their job the coin is flipped and the race begins. Only this time, the impulse stops, and the "nerves" at the end of the chain do not get tapped. This is what can happen when too much alcohol gets into the brain - the brain connections become damaged.

PATHWAYS TO ADDICTION

Since everyone is different, there are also different ways to get addicted or hooked on drugs.

The mind-action cycle

Remember the *concepts of learning* that we talked about in *Session 3*? Well, **Concepts I & II** play into this idea of addiction. If we believe that marijuana *will make us feel good*, and it does, then we will do it again. If we believe that *marijuana will take away negative feelings*, such as pain or worry, and it does, we will do it again. Check out *Figure 5* to get an idea of how this looks.

Figure 5 : **AOD Use Increases Problems in Thinking and Behavior**

If you expect, or believe, that positive feelings will come from using a drug *and it happens*, then the *drug use* and the *thoughts about the benefits* of taking drugs have *been strengthened* and become what we called earlier an *action habit*. Positive feelings can include feeling powerful, relaxed, or happy.

But say you expect to turn off a *negative feeling*? If you do a drug with that belief, and the negative feeling gets turned off, then that also can lead to an action habit. An example of that may be *you can't deal with the worry of the future*, so you smoke marijuana. For a while it makes you forget, and you feel better.

The harmful cycle of abuse and dependence
So far what we've explained is shown by **Points A-C** on *Figure 7*. And many people stop at **Point C** with the *action habit*. But sometimes we have problems because of our drug use. You get caught smoking marijuana **(Point D)**. So you have to go to court and your parent(s) is really upset with you, which causes worry about what's going to happen.

When you get home from court, you go to your room and smoke a joint to *deal with the stress from the adults who are now on your back* **(Point E)**. This gets you more in trouble **(Point F)**, which gives you *more to worry about*, and causes you to want to smoke even more **(Point G)**. Now you're smoking marijuana because you smoke marijuana.

The mind-body cycle
Earlier in this session we talked about the direct and indirect effects of drugs. We may use alcohol or weed for the *direct effects*, which are *relaxation and reduction of pain*. But when the drug leaves our system and our bodies go into shock, we begin to feel the *indirect effect*, which is the opposite feeling. We call this the *rebound* effect. For alcohol and marijuana, the indirect or rebound effect would be lack of sleep, stress, and tension, which is likely the reason why we did it in the first place. Because these feelings are uncomfortable, we *may use the drug again* to reduce the negative feelings, almost as if the drug were a medicine that could cure the indirect effects. In order to keep yourself on balance you have to keep taking the drug. It seems as if the only other option to doing more drugs is to wait out the discomfort until your body can return to its normal, pre-drug state, which sometimes can take awhile.

This cycle also works for uppers as well as downers. After coming off an upper, you will likely get really *tired and depressed*, and crash. To keep yourself from getting tired, you keep taking the drug. The cycle of use continues until an addiction is formed. *Figure 6* shows us how that might look.

Figure 6 **Mental-Physical Addiction**

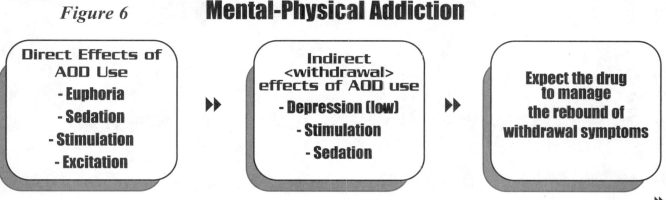

Direct Effects of
AOD Use
- Euphoria
- Sedation
- Stimulation
- Excitation

▶▶

Indirect
<withdrawal>
effects of AOD use
- Depression (low)
- Stimulation
- Sedation

▶▶

Expect the drug
to manage
the rebound of
withdrawal symptoms

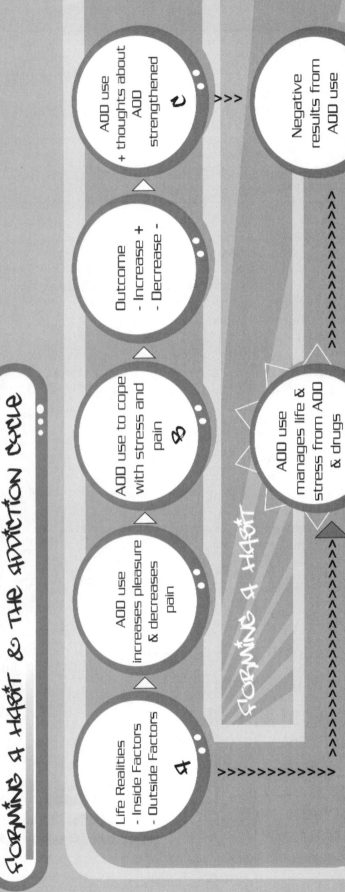

FORMING A HABIT & THE ADDICTION CYCLE

Adapted from Wanberg/Milkman, (1998).

Figure 7

The next activity is designed to show how your brain becomes damaged through repeated use of a mood-altering drug, in this case, cocaine.

Activity: Cocaine In The Brain

There are eight volunteers. One person represents **cocaine**; three represent the **pre-synaptic neuron**; three represent the **post-synaptic neuron**; and one person represents a **beautiful sunrise**. A container (clear bowl or glass) of small packages of sugar symbolize the **synaptic vesicle**, which contains many molecules (the sugar packets) of the **neurotransmitter dopamine**. The six people who represent the neurons arrange themselves in two lines of three with a three-foot space between them (the synapse). The sensation is a beautiful sunrise.

BEAUTIFUL SUNRISE					COCAINE			
pre	1	2	3	synapse	post	4	5	6

At one end (pre-synaptic terminal)—triggered by sensations from the sunrise—person #1 makes a motion and taps person #2 on the shoulder, who taps # 3—who is standing at the synapse. Then #3 **reaches into the synaptic vesicle** and takes out one of the sugar packets (dopamine) and **moves it across the synapse** giving it to person #4 who then taps #5 who taps #6 who exclaims **"Whoa!"**—waving his or her hand in ecstatic delight (showing a natural sense of joy that might come from seeing a beautiful sunrise).

When #4 sends the message on, s/he hands the neurotransmitter (sugar packet) back to #3 who replaces it in the synaptic vesicle. Then # 1 at the pre-synaptic neuron starts the process again. Practice this for two to five times until it runs smoothly.

In comes cocaine ... The message comes in normal fashion; that is #1 taps #2 and so on. The dopamine (sugar packet) crosses the synapse; however this time when #4 attempts to give it back to #3, cocaine steals the sugar and hands it back to #4 (blocks the re-uptake of the dopamine) and, #4 sends the message in the usual fashion by tapping #5. As soon as #4 taps #5, #4 **attempts to return the sugar packet to #3 but again cocaine takes it and hands it straight back**. #6 is saying, "whoa!" "whoa!" "whoa!" --- real fast (excess dopamine).

Then #3 is just sitting there with the remaining sugar packets in the synaptic vesicle (the container) and **s/he doesn't need them anymore**. So #3 **empties the cylinder** and dumps the sugar packets (dopamine) on the floor. The police officer then removes the cocaine and then the neurotransmitter (sugar packets) can no longer be accessed from the cylinder. Withdrawal comes when the cocaine is no longer available, and the pleasure derived from the excess dopamine is no longer there because the nerve cells felt that the dopamine molecules were **no longer necessary**. This leads to **cocaine withdrawal**.

With some slight modifications the same model could be used to explain withdrawal from other drugs like caffeine, methamphetamine, Ecstasy, or nicotine. Now let's do one more exercise, this time showing the various ways that people deal with the rebound or withdrawal effects of various drugs.

Activity: Dealing With Drug Rebound Or After-Effects

For this role-play, we will need 3-9 participants, who will play the part of **direct effects**, **indirect effects**, and **withdrawal managers**. Everyone will line up, with the **direct effects** in line first, followed by **indirect effects** and **withdrawal**. A drug will be chosen, and **the direct effects** will each say one belief about the drug. The **indirect effects** will then say what happens when coming off the drug. The **withdrawal managers** will then give one or two solutions as to how to deal with or prevent the indirect effects.

Putting It Together

· What were some of the *direct and indirect* effects of the pills on Jarrod?

· What cycle of addiction do you think Jarrod fit into the best? Did how the drugs made him feel affect his decisions?

· How do drugs affect your mind and body now and how will drug use affect your mind and body in the future?

· Which pathway to addiction might be closest to your use?

· How do the learning concepts play a role in addiction?

SESSION 5: CRIMINAL CONDUCT & THE INFLUENCE OF DRUGS

Objectives

- Review *Session 4: Basic Knowledge About Drug Abuse and Addiction*
- Understand the thinking habits that can get us in trouble
- Understand the cycles of negative behavior
- Understand how drug use and negative behavior work together

Jarrod's Story

One night there was a huge party that we went to. Of course we took some pills, but we took more than our normal amount because it was a special event. Boy, did we have a great time that night.

When it came time for us to go home, Mary was still really messed up. She asked me if I could drive us home since we both were going to get in trouble if we were late. I didn't really think that I was all that messed up, and besides, I would have done anything for Mary.

I was too messed up to drive. I got us into an accident and ended up killing Mary and a passenger in the other car. Now I sit in this metal box, waiting out my sentence for manslaughter.

The Discussion of Drugs

In *Session 4*, we talked about the *four different types of drugs* and how they can affect our bodies. We also began talking about the effects of alcohol (also a drug) on our bodies and our minds. *What are the four types of drugs?*

After we learned more about drugs in general, we discussed how drugs are used to either *give us positive feelings or get rid of negative feelings*. But it is when we apply the concepts of learning to drug use that we begin to understand how addiction can occur. When drugs give us feelings we want, or get rid of feelings we don't want, we begin to do them more. But problems, and negative feelings, come out of drug use, so we continue to do them to get rid of the negative feelings. The learning concepts *don't just apply to drug use*, though. They can also apply to getting into trouble.

Getting Into Trouble And How It's A Cycle

Just like drug use, *getting into trouble is a learned process*. Getting into trouble and having problems is a way to deal with our worlds inside and outside of our mind. Stealing something from a store *may cause positive feelings*, because we now have something we want and we've gotten away with something. But it can also be used to *turn off negative feelings*, like skipping school because it stresses us. In turning on positive feelings or turning off negative feelings, *our actions get strengthened* and form *thought* and *action habits*, like "I don't need money; I can just steal it." Just as smoking marijuana can lead to problems and smoking more, actions that we do in the world around us can lead to problems. How could *Figure 7*, be applied to developing a habit of crime and violence?

As shown in **Learning Concept III**, when we get in trouble for problems we cause, we sometimes stop doing those actions. But remember that we talked about how negative results can *strengthen our negative thought habits and beliefs?* The same idea applies to getting in trouble. If we're always getting in trouble, our thought may be that "the world is against me." That thought will help choose our actions (because remember our *thoughts, feelings, and actions* are always together in the meeting in our minds), and if the action turns out negative, then it just makes the thought stronger. If we rely on *old negative thought habits* to deal with the problems from our actions, we are likely to get into even more trouble.

Activity: How Negative Thoughts Lead To Bad Outcomes

Form a circle, facing inwards towards each other. You will be given two objects, spaced evenly in the circle. You will pass the object to the person next to you. **One object represents beliefs**, and the other represents **negative results**. The purpose is to get both objects in one of your neighbor's lap while avoiding having both objects in your lap. When a person finally has both objects in their lap, they will give one example of a **negative result and the belief that led to the action** and was **strengthened** because of the negative result. Then start passing the objects around again.

An example of this is the **belief** that "smoking marijuana is good for me and won't cause any harm." Because of this belief you smoke marijuana, and the **negative result** is getting into trouble with the system, your parents, or other adults. Then you might **strengthen the belief** that "I am being treated unfairly and smoking more weed is the best way that I can find to deal with my frustration and anger."

What Do We Mean By Negative Behavior?

Getting into trouble means putting yourself at risk of becoming a focus of the legal and criminal systems.
- **Legal trouble** means going against a law of a city, state, or country, and also means going to court, like doing drugs.
- **Moral trouble** means going against what people or a religion see as right or wrong, like having sex before marriage.
- **Social trouble** means going against something a culture or community believe in, like treating elders with respect.
- **Psychological trouble** is when we do something that causes us to have negative thoughts or feelings about ourselves.

Activity: Jarrod's Trouble

Jarrod got in trouble because of a **bad decision** he made. What kind of trouble do you think best fits Jarrod's situation? Are there **more than one type** of trouble that could apply? In what way is just doing drugs getting into trouble?

Risk Factors

There are certain situtions, thoughts and patterns of behavior that we have participated in during past situations or in the present that are considered *risk factors* for continued problems with AOD abuse and the law into adulthood. Some of the things we can control, and some of the things we cannot. But *we can always control how and what we think about the actions and situations*. The first six things on *Worksheet 2,* have *already happened to us*, while the others are present needs or parts of our personality and life situation that put us at risk. These are the things that we can *really do something about.*

Activity: Your Own Risk Level

Fill out *Worksheet 2* with your level of risk, and then discuss with the group how you may be able to deal with the risks. What risks are stronger in their influence in your actions? Are there risks that everyone has in common?

Errors In Thinking

Remember the green sunglasses that distort our thoughts? When we get into trouble, it is usually because we have thought habits that have become distorted, or are errors in our thinking. *Worksheet 3* lists some of the distortions in reality that we may have which led to problems.

Activity: Errors of thought

Fill out *Worksheet 3* and discuss how the **errors affect your life**, and how you may use your thoughts and freedom of choice to change the errors. Do you have some errors in common with someone else? How do the errors in thought affect your choices and your actions? Can you think of some **different ways** of thinking that might lead to more positive outcomes?

Cycle of Trouble

Just as there is a **cycle of addiction**, there is also a **cycle of problem behavior**. There are *external* forces (e.g., influence of group leaders and friends) and *internal* pressures (e.g., hurtful past memories) that lead to problems and trouble. We make our *mental choices* according to those events. The choice gives us a positive or negative reaction or response, and then we make a decision as to how we are going to act. Let's say you see something you want, but you don't have the money for it. An *internal event* may be that you think, "I will never be able to afford this thing." This makes you feel frustrated and angry because you can't have it, so you decide to steal it. This is an example of how an internal event has led up to *legal trouble*. *Figure 9,* shows us how this cycle begins and where it likely ends. But there are ways *you can change* the cycle:

· The first thing you can do is to *change your mental reaction*, or thought habit, about what is going on around you. Instead of thinking, "I can just steal it," it is more positive to think, "I would rather pay for it because I would feel better." This change makes your thought more **pro-social**.

· The second thing you can do is to *change your actions*. Choose not to do something you know would get you in trouble. You may think about stealing something, but instead you just walk away.

RATING SELF ON RISK FACTORS

Check or Rate the Risk Factors as to How They Apply to You

RISK FACTORS THAT CAN'T BE CHANGED	NONE	LOW	MODERATE	HIGH
Past Involvement in Crime				
Negative Family Situation				
School Problems				
Early AOD Use				
Involved with Delinquent Friends				
Isolation From Peers				

RISK FACTORS THAT WE CAN CHANGE	NONE	LOW	MODERATE	HIGH
Antisocial/Criminal Friends/Peers				
Have Criminal Role Models				
Self-Centered Thinking				
Criminal Thinking				
Criminal Beliefs				
Lack Social/Relationship Skills				
Have Angry/Aggressive Attitude				
Have Angry/Aggressive Feelings				
Act on Spur of the Moment				
Don't Have Family Closeness				
Go Against Authority/Rebellious				
Get Rewards Through Doing Crimes				
Blame Others for Your Actions				
Lack of Good Logical Thinking				

Worksheet 3

ERRORS IN THINKING CHECKLIST

| Checklist for Your Use in These Errors in Thinking |

ERRORS IN THINKING	DON'T USE	USE SOMETIMES	USE A LOT	USE ALL THE TIME
Power Thrust: Put People Down				
Seeing Things Only Your Way				
Blaming Others: Victim Stance				
Feel Superior to Others				
Lack Concern for How Others Affected				
Think: Can't Trust Anybody				
Refuse Something You Don't Want to Do				
Want What You Want Right Now				
Take What You Want From Others				
Refuse to Lean on Other People				
Put Off Things Until Tomorrow				
I Don't Have to Do That				
Won't Change Your Ideas				
Think in Black and White Terms				
Mountains Out of Molehills				
Feel Singled Out				
Think: They Deserve It				
Think: I Feel Screwed				
Tune Out What You Should Hear				
Think About Forbidden Things				
Demand From Others, But Don't Give				
Thinking About Criminal Things				
Lying or Exaggerating the Truth				

Figure 8

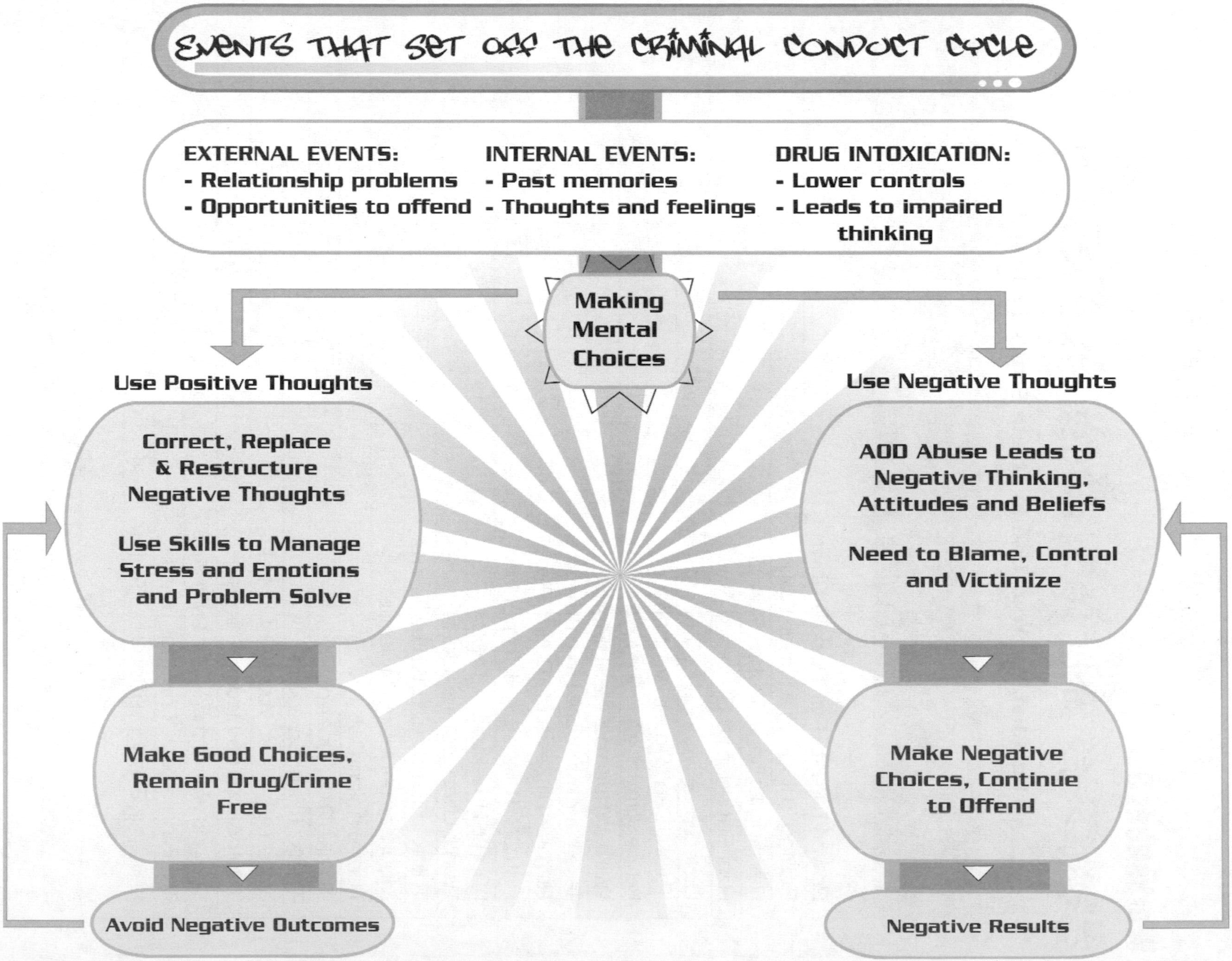

EVENTS THAT SET OFF THE CRIMINAL CONDUCT CYCLE

EXTERNAL EVENTS:
- Relationship problems
- Opportunities to offend

INTERNAL EVENTS:
- Past memories
- Thoughts and feelings

DRUG INTOXICATION:
- Lower controls
- Leads to impaired thinking

Making Mental Choices

Use Negative Thoughts

AOD Abuse Leads to Negative Thinking, Attitudes and Beliefs

Need to Blame, Control and Victimize

Make Negative Choices, Continue to Offend

Negative Results

Use Positive Thoughts

Correct, Replace & Restructure Negative Thoughts

Use Skills to Manage Stress and Emotions and Problem Solve

Make Good Choices, Remain Drug/Crime Free

Avoid Negative Outcomes

· Third, you can *avoid putting yourself in the situation*. If you know smoking weed will get you in trouble, then don't hang around places that have weed. This is considered *preventing the action*.

Activity: An Avoidable Situation

You will be given a situation by your counselor that could have negative results, such as vandalizing property. Think about the **thoughts and actions** involved with the situation. One by one give an alternative to the negative thought or action, such as "instead of thinking it doesn't matter, I could think…" or "instead of breaking that window, I could…," or give an example of how you would avoid the situation. Keep doing this until everyone has had a chance to offer an alternative, and then discuss how you can put the **alternatives** to use in an actual situation.

We are not able to hide ourselves from all situations, though. So keep in mind that true change comes when you *handle the mental habits and reactions*. Change can only happen when you *take control of your thoughts and feelings*, and make the choice out of your free will. This can lead to postitive outcomes.

Using Drugs And Negative Behavior Have Strong Effects On Each Other.

Using drugs and drinking alcohol are illegal, but there is also a connection between the two actions in which one causes the other. There are several ways using drugs can get us into trouble:

1) Using drugs *lowers our self-control, stops good judgment*, and gets our *thoughts into distorted views* (like seeing with green sunglasses on).

2) Drugs are often found in situations that can be *problematic* (like someone might be carrying a weapon).

3) Drug use can stop us from having positive mental habits and often can lead to losing control over our thoughts.

4) Drugs *can distort how we think and feel*. They can stop us from feeling guilt or fear before doing something we know is negative and could get us in trouble.

Activity: Seeing How Distortion Works

For this exercise you will need to get in pairs or groups of three. Take a moment to look at the following phrases. As a group, **try to figure out what the phrases say**. Write the reorganized phrase below in your workbook, and then get back together as a large group. How did the change of spaces within the phrases change the meaning? Did the phrases make more sense before or after you rearranged them? How does distortion rearrange your thinking?

Ifi tswo rthd oing, I tswor thdoi ngri ght. _____

Yo urmi ndc anma ket hewh olew orl dch ange. _____

I fiam tole arn, the nimu stbe sho wnhow. _____

Putting It Together

- Out of the four types of trouble (*legal, moral, social, and psychological*), which one(s) do you think most applies to Jarrod's situation?

- How did the drugs affect Jarrod's ability to make decisions? How did they distort his thinking?

- How do drugs affect your thinking and behavior?

- What are some of the ways your thoughts can become distorted?

- How might you be able to avoid drugs and trouble by controlling your thoughts?

1. (T or F) Alcohol is a deadly poison.

2. (T or F) A can of beer, a glass of wine, and a mixed drink all have the same amount of alcohol.

3. Define a "drug."

4. How do drugs work?

5. What are the general kinds of drugs?

6. Define "tolerance."

7. (T or F) Mixing two drugs in the body at the same time may increase the strength of one or both drugs.

8. Of the following, who will get more drunk: The person who just ate or the person on an empty stomach?

9. (T or F) Bigger people, or people with more fat, can drink more alcohol before getting drunk.

10. Define "drug addiction."

11. List three negative effects marijuana has.

12. What are the dangers of using ecstasy?

13. What are long term effects of acid use?

14. (T or F) Coffee and cold showers can help you sober up.

15. (T or F) It's more dangerous to drive drunk than to drive high.

16. (T or F) "Natural" drugs like pot and shrooms are less dangerous than chemical drugs made in labs.

17. (T or F) You feel more depressed when coke wears off than you did before you used it.

18. (T or F) Children in families with alcoholic parents are 3 to 5 times more likely to become alcoholics themselves.

19. (T or F) Smoking cigarettes relaxes you even when you aren't used to smoking.

JARROD'S STORY

I feel so lonely here. I shouldn't be here. This is not where I belong.

I have always felt lonely…isolated. Maybe it has something to do with my dad leaving when I was really young, or maybe that my mom never has time for me because she's always working. Or maybe it's because I just never really felt like I belonged with anyone my age. I've had friends, but I've always been on the outside. Or better yet, like I was trapped in a glass box.

Up until my freshman year, I thought that's how everybody felt. But then high school started. Suddenly everyone else was involved in a whole different world. I was still in my glass box as all my old friends grew and met new friends and left me behind.

Then I met Mary. She was sixteen, older than me, but really friendly. I was sitting on the lawn at school, in my own thoughts, when she walked up and asked me for a light. I didn't really smoke, but I had this thing for fire so I had a lighter I let her borrow. Next thing I knew she was sitting down and talking to me. We talked for only a couple of minutes, and then she ran off to join her friends, but for a moment I felt like I was a person.

I hadn't seen her for a couple of weeks when I ran into Mary again. I was downtown, sitting in the park and staring at the grass, when I looked up and saw her smiling down at me. The sun suddenly came out, and her hair was like a golden halo. She sat down and stared at the people walking around for a minute. Then she looked at me and asked me if I partied. I looked back at the ground before I quietly admitted I didn't have friends I could go out with. She smiled and said she would like to take me to a party this weekend, if I didn't think my parents would mind. My heart stopped as I watched her open the door to my glass box, and I said yes.

That Friday night Mary picked me up at my house around eight. I had told my mom I was staying at one of my old friend's houses, and she didn't really ask much more. Mary's car was crowded with her friends, and we all squeezed in tight to drive to this party out in the middle of nowhere. Despite the crowd in the car, I felt isolated and alone until we got there and then Mary took my hand. While we were waiting in line, Mary took a couple pills out of her pocket and gave me one. I knew what it was, but at that time I didn't care and besides, what would one pill do? So I took the pill and waited. I was in a corner, isolated from everyone around me, when gradually my body began relaxing and my mind began feeling free. Mary, who was watching me closely, laughed and grabbed my hand, pulling me into the crowd. And for the first time in my life, I didn't feel like I was somewhere I didn't belong. Everybody was happy, and they let me know that I was deserving of love.

I was the last one to be dropped off the next morning, and all I could do was sit in Mary's car in a daze. We hadn't rubbed backs, or made out, but I'm pretty sure we had held hands the entire night. With a "see ya later" I was on the curb in front of my house, watching as she drove away. And despite feeling sweaty and sleep deprived, I was the happiest I had been for as long as I could remember.

Although it was hard to remember that a day later. Suddenly I felt as if the world was ending, like I was on a roller coaster through the pits of emotional hell. My mom noticed something was wrong, and tried to talk to me a couple times, but then she just left me to myself in my room.

From then on Mary and I spent pretty much every day together, just hanging out after school. It wasn't like we were dating, we were just really close to each other. It was about a month or so before the next party, and once again there were pills. But we were happy and together, and feeling comfortable and relaxed around people was important to me. And being with Mary was the most important. I didn't think about the down.

Slowly we began doing pills more often. We began doing them in small groups, and sometimes it was just Mary and I, listening to music and talking about worldly things while we held each other's hand. We always made sure to stay away from each other the two days following, though. No one wants to be around another person going through a down, especially if you are too.

One weekend there was this huge party that we decided to go to. To make it extra special we both took a couple more pills than usual. It was about five in the morning when we had to go home. Mary was pretty out there and told me she couldn't drive and begged me to drive for her. I thought I could do it, and I would do anything for Mary. So I began driving. Somehow I ended up on the left shoulder and we crashed into another car. I had to sit there in pain as Mary slowly died.

The passenger of the other car ended up dying too, a young mother with two kids. I couldn't stop crying during my court, but it didn't matter. Two people had died, one of whom was the most important person to me in the world. And now I'm back in my box, except this time it's metal with iron bars while I wait out my sentence for manslaughter. I cry every night in pain, emotional and physical, and **I have never felt lonelier in my entire life.**

Chapter Three:
Talking About Yourself and Listening to What Others Say

GOALS OF THIS CHAPTER
· Learn the importance of developing good communication skills
· Begin using tools to help you become aware of your thoughts, feelings, and actions
· Share some deeper stories with each other

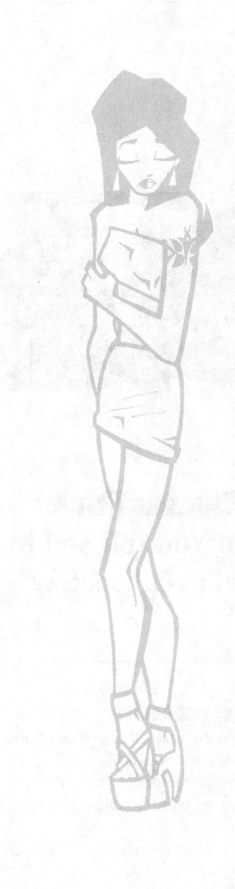

CYNTHIA'S STORY

SESSION 6: LEARNING COMMUNICATION SKILLS

Objectives

· Review *Chapter 2: Building a Knowledge Base*
· Understand the importance of good communication
· Learn how to talk about yourself and how to be open to receive feedback
· Learn how to make it easy for others to talk to you and to hear your feedback
· Learn the tools of awareness: autobiography, journals, and thinking reports

Cynthia's Story

My dad used to beat me, and beat me bad. My mom tried to protect me when she was home, but she wasn't always home. Besides, she got beat too and when she didn't have her alcohol she was likely to throw me out of her way. My brothers were never home, so I never really had anyone to talk to or tell about the beatings.

I used to dream of being an actress or doing something special to get away from my family. But I ended up running away from them, and now I'm out on the street making a lousy twenty bucks to let some old fat and sweaty man touch me. The memories of my dad and my mom don't seem so bad now. I used to try to save money to get out, but then I realized that there is no point to goals and that this is the life I'm stuck with.

Up to this point

So far we have learned about change and how our *mind* controls our actions. Although our *attitudes, thought habits, and beliefs* are what control our actions in the outside world, we are the ones who have control over our thoughts. *We have freedom* in the choices we make and the actions we take. Everyone sees the world differently because of their past and their opinions, but *everyone has control* over the thoughts that come from how we see the world.

We then learned about drugs and alcohol, and how these can *poison our bodies* and gain *control over our thoughts*. Of course, using substances usually doesn't occur all by itself. Getting in trouble and negative actions are tied to using drugs, even if it's just the fact that drugs are illegal. By taking part in these *negative* actions, doing drugs and committing crime, sometimes we are enforcing or strengthening the negative thoughts that got us there in the first place. By using the learning concepts we talked about in *Session 3*, we begin to get an idea of how behavior *continues* despite negative feelings and results.

So now that we have gotten to know each other a little bit and we have an idea of the basic concepts and principles behind learning, substance use, and negative behavior, it is time to start *sharing something* about ourselves with each other, as well as be able to see ourselves from another person's view.

What Is Communication?

Talking to another person is considered *communication*. But there are actually *two kinds of ways* that we use to show our feelings and thoughts to others:

1) The first is *non-verbal communication*, also known as *body language*. This is how we "talk" without using words. The *tone* of our voice, the way we *move* our body and hands, and the *expressions* we have on our face are all part of non-verbal talking. Sometimes our body language is *different* than what we are saying with words. This causes us to be misunderstood, and to be clearly understood we should use the body language that *agrees* with our words.

Activity: Let Your Body Talk

Get into **groups of three** and sit in slightly separate parts of the room. **Attitudes** and **situations** will be handed out, and as a group come up with a way to get the other groups to **guess what the attitude and situation is**. You **cannot** use words to talk about your situation, only **body language** and **facial expressions**.

For example, the group situation might be getting arrested with the attitude as anger and unfairness. While acting out the arrest, use your **facial expressions** and **hand movements** to betray the anger and frustration of being innocent. Then take a moment to talk about some of the wrong guesses the groups may have come up with. What could have made the other groups think that? What could your group have done to get the message across clearer?

2) *Verbal communication* is how we talk when using words. When using words, though, we have to make sure that the other people understand what we mean. Remember **Principle 2** in *Session 3*? Everyone sees the world *differently*, meaning we have different opinions, attitudes, beliefs and values, so that what we *assume* to mean one thing may mean something very different to *another person*. Opinions are often not right or wrong, but they do affect how we see and understand.

Clear and *honest verbal communication* can help others understand the point we are trying to make as well as help us to understand our own thoughts. When we understand ourselves, we can begin changing the thoughts that hurt us.

Activity: Building Blocks Of Communication

One person will stand up and **choose** from a bag a piece of paper that has some shapes drawn on it. Then, with **words only** and no hand or body movements, the person will **describe** what is drawn on the piece of paper. Each person of the group will **draw** what the person standing up is describing without asking questions. Then have a **second person** stand up and describe **the same drawing**, with each person making a second drawing based on the second description. **Compare** the two drawings with the original shape. How do different words and descriptions aid in drawing the picture? How would you have described it differently? Notice that, depending on the words chosen, the picture can turn out differently. It is important to choose your words when trying to communicate with another person.

Opinions Are Not Facts

Sometimes the same words can have *different* meanings, like music. Music is defined as *arranged sounds to create something that has a beginning and end with a pattern of rhythm*. But when someone says music to us, we may think of different things. One of us may *think* of rap while another may hear heavy guitar. The definition of music is the fact, while what we think is music is *opinion*. In order to communicate clearly, you would not only say, "Music makes me feel good," you may want to say, "When I listen to rap music, it makes me feel good." Even if the other person's opinion is different, they will still understand what you mean.

Let's See Ourselves Through Communication

There are *two ways* that we participate in talking with other people, *talking about you* (self-oriented) and *talking about them* (other-oriented). Both are important in talking with other people to *understand and be understood*.

ACTIVE SHARING: TALKING ABOUT YOU

When talking about *you* with another person, there are actually two things involved: *self-disclosure and receiving feedback*.

Self-disclosure means *talking about yourself* and not the other person. It involves using "I" when talking and sharing with someone--your counselor or group—about *your* past and current thoughts, feelings, and actions. Self-disclosure does *three things* that can help you change.

- It puts your *thoughts into words* so that you can hear them. By saying the words out loud, you are really disclosing to yourself, making you more aware of what and who you are.

- It allows others to see *who you are*, and also allows them to give you *honest feedback* about how they see you.

- It opens *channels of trust* and helps others disclose to you.

It is important for us to remember to use "I" when we are self-disclosing, and not "you." When we use the word "you," we are really talking about *the other person* and not our own thoughts and feelings. When we are in an argument with someone, the sentence usually begins with "you" because we want to *blame* or tell the other person what he or she did to upset us. But the whole point of self-disclosure is to talk about us, so we want to avoid using "you."

Activity: Cynthia's Sharing

Get into pairs or groups and take a look at Cynthia's story. Did Cynthia have anyone she could share her story with? Are there people at school or outside of her home that she could have talked with? Was running away her only option?

Receiving Feedback means listening when someone else is talking to you about you and how he or she sees you as a person. *Feedback is the other person's opinion and not necessarily true*, and we want to keep that in mind so we can *avoid* getting defensive. When we get defensive about what someone else's opinion is, feedback becomes blaming and then both people end up getting hurt. The point is to *see ourselves* from outside, not to get angry or hurt with another person.

Take a look at *Figure 9*. This is a picture of how talking about ourselves can help us to change. When we share ourselves with another person, that person gives us feedback as to what they see and think about us. We not only hear ourselves talk, but then we hear ourselves in the other person's feedback. This helps us to talk more about ourselves and to become more *aware* of who we are.

ENCOURAGING OTHERS THROUGH ACTIVE LISTENING:

This means getting people to talk to you and then you share how you see them. There are two skills involved to encourage others to talk with you.

· *The open statement or question:* An open question allows for the person to give us more than a "yes" or "no" answer. Instead of saying, "So, do you like rap music?" you might say, "What are some of your thoughts about rap music?" This opens the lines of communication so that other people may feel open to telling you about them. An example of this is "tell me how you feel," or "how are you today?" We know we hear people ask others, "What's up?" and then not even wait for the answer. The important thing here is that we do wait for an answer and we listen to what the person actually says.

· *The feedback listening skill:* This is when we say to the other person "I see you as angry," or "I can see that something's wrong." These are *active listening skills* where we hear what the other person says and then *reflect back* what they are saying. We serve as a kind of *mirror* so the person can hear what they were telling us.

Activity: Hearing Ourselves

Pair up and use the skills of **self-disclosure** and **feedback** to talk to each other about a situation that is **important** to you. First decide which one of you will be self-disclosure and the other feedback, and after a couple of minutes, switch roles. Then get back into the large group. One at a time have the feedback person say what **they heard** about the situation, and then have the sharer tell the group what they heard about themselves. Does hearing what another person has to say change what you think? Does it help to hear what others say?

UNDERSTANDING OUR OWN THOUGHTS

Becoming *aware* of ourselves does not happen just by talking with other people and hearing what they have to say about us. We also have to *become aware* of what we are thinking at any moment in order to have *choice* over our actions. There are *three* tools that will help you with the process of *controlling your thoughts and actions*.**1) Autobiography** (telling your story); **2) Journal**; **3) Thinking Report.** These tools will help you in *gaining awareness* of yourself and your thoughts. One of the most important parts of understanding your own thoughts is to recognize thinking errors.

Figure 9

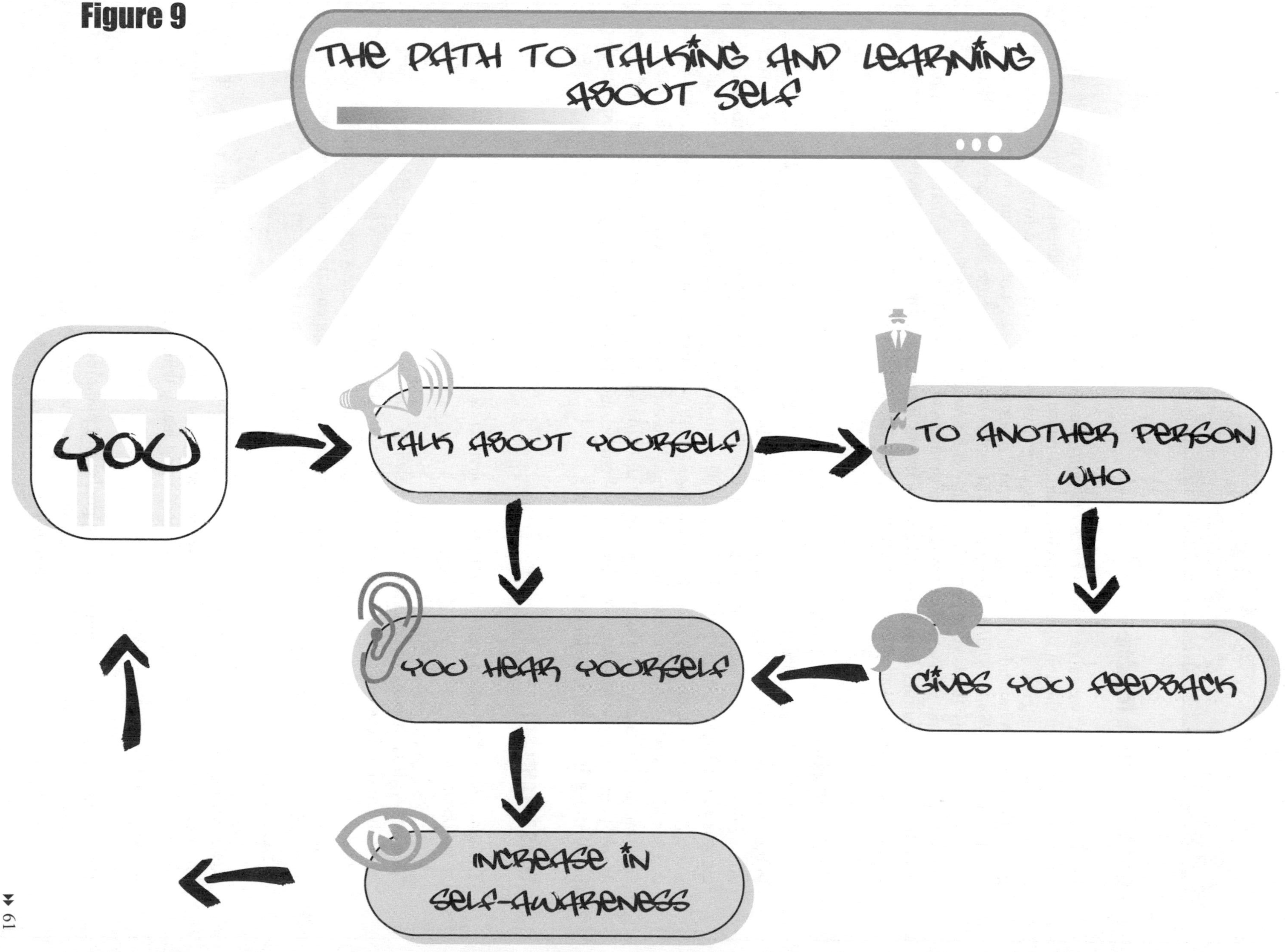

THE PATH TO TALKING AND LEARNING ABOUT SELF

YOU

TALK ABOUT YOURSELF

TO ANOTHER PERSON WHO

GIVES YOU FEEDBACK

YOU HEAR YOURSELF

INCREASE IN SELF-AWARENESS

But First—Errors In Thinking:

Earlier in *Session 2* we talked about *thought habits*, how they are *automatic* even if there is an error in them. Even though these thoughts are not based on fact, we *use* them to help us through hard times and problems. If your parent looks angry when they come home from work, your first thought may be "What did I do wrong this time?" Your parent may not be angry with you at all, but that was your *thought habit*. These *errors* in our *thinking* can cause a lot of problems though. If you automatically think your parent is angry with you and for no reason, then you are more likely to act hurt and angry with them. Take a moment to look back at *Work Sheet 3* in *Session 5*. Which of these thoughts do you consider to be errors in your thinking. We all have them, and the quicker we become aware of our *particular errors*, the sooner we can make positive changes in our lives.

Activity: Whose Error Was That?

One at a time **choose a situation** out of the bag. Once everyone has a situation, **read** it out loud to the group. Within each situation there is an error in thinking that causes the action to end as it does. For example, one situation could be a kid walks into a store. There isn't anyone around, the clerk is in the back, and the kid is by himself. The kid originally came into the store to buy a soda, but when he didn't see the clerk his thought habit was to just take the soda. The clerk catches him, and he gets arrested for shoplifting. You are to **pick** out the **error** in thinking in each situation, and then give an **alternative** way of thinking so the situation ends better. The kid thinks of just taking the soda, but then decides that is wrong, and he should just pay for it. He spends the dollar to get the soda, and doesn't get arrested.

TOOLS FOR CHANGE

There are *three* important parts to our minds: *memories, responding to now, and our dreams about the future.*

Memories: It is through our memories that we write our story about ourselves. But our *memories* come from our daily experiences, so our memories are decided by how *we choose* to live each day. It is true that things happen to us outside of our control, but we always have a choice in how we handle what happens. So how *we choose* to handle what happens also decides our memories. The *autobiography* will help us to understand where we have been so we can choose our paths in present and future.

Responding to now: The *journal and thinking reports* will capture our responding to now. Three important parts of responding to the present are *thinking, feeling, and speaking.* All three of these are the glue of our mind that help us to reason and learn, which then *help us to organize* our present and awareness of now.

Dreaming the future: Imagining, setting goals, and planning are how we map out our future. But to make the map possible, we have to *know* where we've been (memory) and where we are now. Our journals and thinking reports help us *keep track* of our future.

Activity: Cynthia's Memories

Take another look at Cynthia's story. How did her future dreams affect her decisions, if at all? What were her memories before she ran away, and what are her memories now because she ran away? How are her memories decided by her actions? Use as specific detail as possible when answering the questions.

Activity: Dreaming Of The Future

Take a moment to write down a future goal of yours. How will that goal be made possible? What can you **do** or **avoid** in order to obtain that goal?

We will use three tools in trying to become *aware* of ourselves in the past and present, and give ourselves something to look forward to in the future. The three tools are *writing your story* (autobiography), *keeping a journal*, and *using a thinking report*. During the remainder of the program we are asking that you use these tools to describe your life experience and to record your current thoughts and dreams for the future. You may be asked to discuss the *progress* that you are making on *your autobiography* at the beginning of each session.

Writing Your Story

We will write our stories over the next couple of weeks. This story *represents* our history and is made up of our memories and past experiences. We can't really know where we are now unless we *understand* and *know* our history. There may be experiences that you may not want to share with the group. If something comes up that is troubling or upsetting to you, it would be a good idea to talk privately with your counselor.

We realize not all of our history and past are pleasant, but it is important to see that both our negative and positive experiences have *come together* to make us who we are. It is not easy to write your history, but it is important in order to *take control of your change*.

Though you won't have to write your story from scratch. Here is an outline we would like you to follow.
· Describe the family you grew up in.
· Describe your childhood from your first memory through now.
· Describe your education, job, and relationship experiences as well as your hobbies.
· Write your history with substance use and/or getting into trouble.
· Describe what brought you into this program.

Your Journal

You will use your journal to write down your *thoughts, feelings and actions* on a daily or weekly basis. This will help give us an idea of how we think and feel over time. It is helpful to include the situation, your feelings, your thoughts, and what you did in the situation. Did you handle it well or could you have done it differently? It is important to be *honest* and use the journal as a way to express yourself. Once again, if something comes up that is upsetting, it would be wise to ask for some individual time to discuss this with your counselor.

The Thinking Report

A thinking report will help you to pay *attention* to your thoughts and actions. The *first step* in taking control and changing is learning to pay attention to our own thinking.

Here are some basic things to include:

· **Event:** *Describe* in a few words the situation. Try to follow the *facts* and describe what you see, but not what you thought or felt.

· **Thoughts:** Describe and write down any *thoughts* you might remember. Don't worry about explaining, blaming, or making excuses, just write down what you thought at that moment.

· **Feelings:** Make a list of all the *feelings* you had: nervous, angry, excited.

· **Attitudes and Beliefs:** What attitudes and beliefs are *related* to this event?

· **Outcome:** Write down what your *action* and *behavior* was as a result of the event. Then think about and write down the thoughts, feelings, beliefs, and attitudes that all added up to your action.

> ***The first step in taking control and changing is learning to pay attention to our own thinking.***

Putting It Together

· Cynthia ran away because she didn't feel like she could talk with anyone. How did her future goals, or lack of direction, affect her decision?

· How did Cynthia's life, memories, and goals change with that one choice of running away?

· Think about some opinions you have. How might those opinions affect your actions?

· Remember one situation that turned out negatively for you. How did thinking play a part in the decision made? How could have changing your thoughts changed the results of the situation?

SESSION 7: SHARING YOUR STORY

Objectives

- Review *Session 6: Learning Communication Skills*
- Share a deep emotion that you have been holding onto
- Share your thinking report about your past substance use
- Retake the tests you took when you entered the program and compare your scores from then and now
- Increase your awareness of past criminal offenses by logging them all and relate this with your recorded legal history
- Review the thinking report that dealt with one offense
- Share a deep emotion that you have been holding onto

Cynthia's Story

It really hurt me, being beaten and thrown about by my parents. It was like I was a rodent or some unwanted pest that should be punished for existing. I used to be close with my older brothers, but then they got older and started hanging out and staying at their friends' houses. I felt abandoned, by my parents, my brothers, and the world. .

So when it came time for me to start selling myself to make money, I didn't really think too much about it. After all, there really wasn't much to me. Don't get me wrong, I still dream of something different. But my reality is this, and there isn't anything that can change that.

A look at last time

Last session we spent some time learning about communication, both *verbal* and *non-verbal*, and how it is important to communicate *clearly* to others. How do the two kinds of communication differ from each other? Which is most effective in getting across our point to another person? We also learned about *active sharing* and *active listening*. We then learned about how *our choices* can decide what our *memories* will be later on in life. It is also important for us to keep our *dreams* in our minds, so that our choices will be in our *best interest* and those who we *love and care* about. Finally, we learned about the three tools for becoming more aware of the thoughts and events that shape our feelings and actions: the *autobiography, journal and thinking report*.

Activity: A Skit In Time

Get into groups of three or so, and create a skit in which memories and future goals interact with the thoughts, feelings, and choices made. Have one person represent **memories** and **future goals**, one person represent **thoughts and feelings**, and the third person will represent **choices**.

The **first person** will mention a memory or future goal. Then the **second person** will state the **thoughts and feelings** that come from the memory or future goal. The **third person** will then say the **action chosen** based on what the other two people have said. For example, one future goal may be to go to college. The thought may be "I need to study in order to get a scholarship," and the feeling may be excitement over what the future might bring. The action is then to study and focus on school to make the goals a possibility. Is it better to make choices from memories of the past or goals of the future?

Dig A Little Deeper

Although we discussed *trust* in *Session 1*, it's now time for us to dig deeper and *trust* each other a little more. This will not be easy for most of us, and a lot harder than the sharing games we've done up to this point. But it is really important for us to get an *honest look* at ourselves, in terms of our thoughts and feelings, as well as our choices. In *Session 2* we talked about how it is hard to change because *we hold on to our view of ourselves*. At this point, we may continue to hold on to some parts of our old views of ourselves. But this can cause thinking errors and often makes us ignore our past errors in action. But *you have decided* to be here, to continue on with the program, and now *you are ready* to move to the next level.

Activity: Cynthia's Pain

Cynthia speaks in her story about the feelings she had while living with her parents and later when she was living on the streets. What do you think is Cynthia's **view of herself**? Why is it hard for her to change that? What feelings and emotions does Cynthia have and how do they affect her decisions and goals?

Sharing a deep emotion

Now we will ask you to take a look at a *deep emotion* that you have carried around with you. The emotion might be hurt, anger, betrayal, or deep sadness. Take a moment to think about that emotion.

Activity: The Pain Of Me

Get into **pairs** or **groups of three**. Share with the others a **deep emotion** that you have carried around with you. **Describe** how that emotion has helped you to make choices, such as anger at your parents has made you want to fight everybody. Be sure to use your best communication and listening skills from the last session. Take a moment to **listen** to what the other person is saying to you. What emotions do you have in common? How can talking about and sharing this emotion help ease the pain and help you make better choices?

An honest look at substance use

Take some time and *look honestly* at your substance use. You may be asked to retake some of the questionnaires that you took when entering the program. The counselor will assist you in making *your profile*. Use *Worksheet 4,* to compare the scores from before you entered the program and now. How are they different, or are they the same? Then take a moment to fill out *Worksheet 5* about *negative results or problems* that have come out of your *substance use*. These should be specific episodes of your life with a tie to substance use.

A walk down memory lane

We all *want* to feel like we are *good people*, doing good things. Even some of us who have long histories of getting into trouble have a hard time looking at our past offenses. Most of us haven't even looked at how substance use and criminal conduct have worked together in our past.

Worksheet 4

YOUR TEST SCORES

NAME OF TEST	1ST SCORE	2ND SCORE	HOW ARE THE SCORES DIFFERENT?
1.			
2.			
3.			
4.			
5.			
6.			

Worksheet 5

RECORDING PROBLEM EPISODES COMING FROM AOD USE

DATE	DESCRIBE THE PROBLEM OR NEGATIVE EPISODE

Keeping in mind the *honesty* of this session, fill out *Worksheet 6, Criminal Conduct Log*. Right now you are only to fill out the *first four columns*. Review this log in class as well as compare it with your recorded legal history.

After you have compared and reviewed, fill out the *last column* of the worksheet. Write **NO** if *substances were not involved* in the situation. Write **(B)** if you used before the offense; write **(D)** if you used during the offense; write **(A)** if you used after. If all three apply, write **BDA**.

Activity: An Unfinished Thought

Sit in a circle and the first person **chooses an incomplete sentence** out of the bag. The person has to **complete the sentence** with their own thought or experience. Go around the circle until everyone has completed two to three sentences. Remember to **listen** to what the other group members are saying, and possibly what you have in common with them. Which sentence was harder for you to finish? Which sentence was easier for you to finish? Is it harder to share deeper emotions, or is it easier to pretend you don't care?

Putting It Together

- Cynthia's lack of self-worth was created by her feelings about the situation at home. How do those emotions control her actions now?

- Deeper emotions often cause us to choose actions that are negative. How do your emotions influence you?

- Why is it hard for us to talk about our deeper emotions? What emotions did you have a problem sharing?

Worksheet 6

CRIMINAL CONDUCT LOG WORK CHART

ARREST DATE	NAME OR TYPE OF CHARGE	CONVICTED	PROBATION	TIME SERVED	RELATIONSHIP WITH GOD

For the last column, use the following:

Put **(B)** if you drank or used other drugs before the offense.

Put **(D)** if you drank or used other drugs during the offense.

Put **(A)** if you drank or used drugs after the offense.

Put **BDA** if you drank or used drugs before, during and after the offense.

Don't touch me. I hate it when people touch me. I know that's my job, you don't have to tell me that. Just do what you have to do and leave me alone.

Did you know I was once a princess? I had my sparkling tiara, a long silky dress, nice shoes, and jewelry. Okay, actually it was a cheap Halloween crown, one of my mom's worn-out night gowns, her scratched high heels that I nearly broke my ankle in, and plastic crap my mom bought at some drug store. But in my mind, I was a princess and I controlled my whole world. I never noticed the dirty floors of our trailer or the fact that my brothers rarely came home when I was in my world.

But that was when my dad wasn't home. Because when he was home, I was a mouse. And not even the kind that squeaks. I was a mouse that hid in my room behind my dolls. It wasn't so bad when he came home sober. For the most part he would ignore me and yell at my mom because the house was a mess and yell at my brothers for being lazy pieces or something like that. But when he came home from drinking, he would shake the trailer with his yelling and throwing things. For the most part he beat on my mom, since she usually pushed me into my room when she heard him coming. But sometimes she was gone when he came home. And not even my door would stop him from coming in and hitting me while I cried and screamed.

Tell my mom? What good would telling my mom do. She got beat more often and harder than I did. Besides, when she had her alcohol, she was a zombie that didn't even know who I was. Sometimes I couldn't even stand to look at her, to have her turn those vacant eyes my way. When she wasn't drinking, though, she turned into some demon from the pits of the underworld and was worse than him. If I didn't want to get thrown at a wall, I had to be quiet in a corner far from her eyes. Telling my mom was not something I could even attempt to do.

So I dealt with it. As far as I knew, everybody's daddy did this to them. Just a normal event in a normal family that does the normal things that we did. I dealt with it until I was twelve and I couldn't deal with it no more.

One night, after my mom passed out but before the monster came home, I stuffed my backpack with my most treasured things, and I left. I only meant to be gone for the night. Spend the night away and then maybe go back when everyone was sleeping. But as I sat and shivered on a sidewalk not too far away, I got scared. I would probably get beat by both of them, and beat bad, if I went home because I had been out all night. That scared me even more so I stood up and started walking. I didn't really know which way to go, so I just started walking towards the lights and kept walking. Ideas and dreams of getting a job and my own place or becoming an actress or marrying a prince and never seeing my parents again floated through my head and lulled me into not feeling the cold or the pain.

A week on the streets taught me that no one wants to hire a twelve-year-old girl. Once again my world was shattered, and so I settled down into begging and feeling like the scum I am. One night I was walking around an all-night convenience store, hoping for some food, when I bumped into a girl who looked like she was looking for someone. I mumbled sorry, cause I didn't really have the energy to do much more, when she stopped me and said I looked hungry. She asked how long I had been on the streets, at that point I think it was around a month, and she took me back to her hotel room. She gave me a little something, a candy or something, and told me she was looking for a roommate if I was willing to work. I told her that no one would hire me, I had already tried and besides I had no clothes or anything. And she said I didn't have to work a regular job to make money. I had in my possession something that men would pay for.

So the next night I was standing on the corner with her. At first I didn't know what to do. But then I noticed it didn't seem to matter whether I knew what I was doing, and it seemed that me being really young made me more money. So now I had a place of my own and a job to pay for it. For a time I tried to save every dollar, except what I had to pay for my room and the little I ate. But after awhile my dreams began to fade, just as the memories began to fade. Being beat by my dad didn't seem as bad as doing what I had to do for some twenty dollars. But I can't go back now.

And every time some dirty man touches me, I shudder and cringe. I hate when people touch me. But it pays the bills and **I have no where else to go**.

NOTES

Chapter Four:
Backsliding to Drugs and Crime

GOALS OF THIS CHAPTER
· Learn what relapse and recidivism mean
· Discuss the process of relapse and recidivism (RR)
· Learn the warning signs to RR

TYLER'S STORY

The world is a painful place, and I am filled with that pain. I liked being a loner. That's not to say I didn't have friends. A couple of friends and I were partying. I was sticking to smoking the occasional bowl, I'm not much of a drinker. My ex-girlfriend was there, life is just depressing enough as it is, so I was just about to leave when a friend suggested we go smoke a joint.

The guy who lived in the house offered us some powder. I took a bump. Later I learned it was heroin, but by then I thought I had seen a little bit of heaven. Until the next morning. That was when I found out just how much pain there can be in one human body, mind and soul. But the high was too perfect to think about the low. Next thing I knew, I was free-basing just to get high. Of course, that was when my parents took me to rehab. And it worked.

About six months later, I ran into one of my old friends. We decided to hang out again, but the next time her boyfriend, who was there the first night, was there. I thought he would never do anything to put me at risk. Except that he did. And I fell. Stoned out of my mind, I took a bump. I thought that I was strong enough to control it this time. So the next time, I did it again. Until one hit turned into another. And now I will buy more, just to avoid the pain of living and the pain of my body letting go.

SESSION 8: IDENTIFYING TRIGGERS & YOUR HIGH-RISK SITUATIONS

Objectives

- Review *Chapter 3: Talking About Yourself and Listening to What Others Say*
- Develop skills to identify warning signs for negative or criminal behavior
- Develop skills to identify warning signs for substance use
- Increase your understanding of the connection between substance use and negative behavior

Tyler's Story

I'll admit it, I started doing heroin at a party. I didn't know exactly what it was, and I didn't really care. I feel that you only live once so I try different things, and besides, my ex was at the party stressing me. What I didn't realize was how hard it was going to be for me to get off heroin.

So finally I was clean after months in a program, when I ran into an old friend. I wasn't too worried because she had nothing to do with my using. But her boyfriend did. I started hanging out with him again, and before I knew it I was back at that house, stoned out of my mind, and taking a bump.

Sharing our stories

In our last session, we spent some time sharing a deep *emotion* that we have been carrying around for awhile. We then took a moment to see how that emotion may have led us to act out *negatively* or make choices that did not end well for us.

You were also asked to retake some of the admission questionnaires you had already taken, and to record a log of your negative behavior. The point of this was to not only show the possible changes you have *already started*, but also to share how *substance abuse* (drug and alcohol) and *negative behavior* (criminal actions) tend to *work together*.

Although we have all participated in negative behavior, most of us tend to avoid or pretend the past did not happen. Just as there are *errors in thinking* which cause us to make the wrong choices, there are also errors in *how we look at the past*. The criminal log is an effort to remind us the things we did wrong, and how they went wrong, so that we may *make the choice* to not go back to that life.

With our *past* in mind, it's time to move *forward* in our change and focus on how to live comfortable and responsible lives without the use of drugs or participation in criminal activities.

What Are High-Risk (HR) Situations?

In *Session 5* we discussed certain things in your life that are *risk factors*. For a memory jog, take a look at *Worksheet 2, Rating Self on Risk Factors*. These factors cause a person to be *high-risk* (HR) for substance abuse and criminal conduct. But *situations* can be high-risk as well. These high-risk situations are usually the *HR events* that have led us to use alcohol and drugs in the past.

The events may even trigger your old patterns of *thoughts and feelings* about needing the substance in order to deal. An example of this may be that after a hard day at school when you think everyone is stressing you, you may feel like you *need* a joint just to relax.

The craving and urge from a situation like this may lead us to a thought like "I cannot deal without the use of substances." These *stressful situations*, or even happy situations, like when you do something well and feel the *urge to celebrate*, can lead us back into our previous use.

The *high-risk situations* do not just apply to substance use, though. It can also apply to criminal or other behavior. This type of situation makes you think or feel like you want or need to be involved in getting in trouble while it increases your impulse. Situations like this could be just hanging out with old friends that you used to get in trouble with. Another could be allowing your-self to be in a situation that has led to you committing a criminal act.

Activity: The Situation At Risk

When looking at Tyler's story, what were some of the **high-risk situations** he was put in? Did he have a choice to be in the situations or not? What could he have done to avoid the situations?

So Then What Is High-Risk Thinking?

High-risk thinking for substance use involves the *thought habits*, the thoughts that automatically jump into our head that lead to the use of substances. The thought habits can be *set off or triggered* in high-risk situations, or it could be the other way around, where the thinking leads you into high-risk circumstances. The *thinking* often takes place when we feel scared or like when we believe that we aren't being treated fairly, and may also be tied with *cravings* and *urges* to use the substance. An example of a thought habit may be "I'm stressed so I need to smoke a joint" or "No one cares anyway, so I may as well drink."

Just as high-risk situations are *similar* for criminal conduct and substance use, high-risk thinking for crime is similar to HR thinking for substance use; it involves using the old thought habits that lead you to participating in negative behavior, and usually takes place before the behavior itself. They may even be set off by HR situations, or could lead you to HR situations. "I deserve better" or "it doesn't matter anyway" or "nobody's going to get hurt" are thought habits that lead us to fall back into negative behaviors. Even thinking about participating in negative or criminal behavior is an example of HR thinking.

Activity: The Thought Of The Situation

Get into groups of three or four and develop a skit in which the **HR thoughts interact** with the **HR situation**. An example may be there is marijuana smoking going on at a party. The HR thought is that "weed can't hurt me and everyone is doing it anyway." Think about how the **thought** can either back up the situation or change the situation.

Come up with an **alternative** thought that might counteract the high-risk situation, such as "If I smoke pot, I could end up going back to jail" or "If I smoke, then I will get in trouble." Do your skit in front of the larger group, and then ask if they can distinguish between the positive or HR thought.

Relapse And Recidivism: What Are They?

Sometimes we think that *relapse*, or going back to using substances, only occurs once we start *using* again. But that's not necessarily true. Relapse actually *begins* when we put ourselves in a situation that has led to use in the past. Relapse also can mean *going back to thought habits about using substances* as an option for dealing with HR situations. Let's say you get angry at the school system and want to break some windows or pull a prank, and your friends are egging you on. Instead, you begin thinking that smoking a joint will help you calm down and forget. To deal with your friends pressuring you to act negatively, the *thought habit* is "I need to smoke a joint." But just because you think the thoughts does not mean you have fully *relapsed*. Just as with everything, there are *stages*. The *early stage of relapse is thinking about using* but not going back to your habit of use. A *full relapse* is when you go back to your previous level of use, which led to problems.

Recidivism means re-offending. Recidivism happens when we start having the thought habits that lead to *destructive behavior*. It also happens when we start to put ourselves in situations or act a certain way that in the past has led to negative behavior. Recidivism does not mean getting caught, or even choosing the action. Just as with relapse, recidivism happens in *stages* with the *full recidivism* happening when you *commit a crime*. It is important to remember that recidivism begins when you allow any of the risk factors from *Worksheet 2* to play a dominant role in your life.

The Causes Of Relapse/Recidivism

Relapse usually begins when we feel like *we don't have the power or strength* to deal with a feeling or problem. Try to find out what situations cause you to want to use the substance, and what you are *thinking and feeling* at the time. This allows you to *take control away* from the drugs and *have the strength* to do it without a substance that changes how you act, think, or feel. By understanding how we *think and feel* about these high-risk situations, we can figure out what causes us to use substances and participate in negative behavior. Then we can figure out ways to deal with these situations without being *weakened* by the problems that come with substance use and criminal behavior. Here are some possible triggers, or causes, for relapse/recidivism:

· **Conflict with another person**

· **Social pressure, or hanging out with peers involved in substance use and trouble**

· **Unpleasant feelings: stress, depression, anger and guilt**

· **A change in self-image** from being a person who doesn't use to being a user; change from the image of living free of trouble to one who gets involved in trouble; change from a person who is incarcerated or in a restricted living situation to someone who is back home or in the community.

Activity: A Discussion About Tyler

Something triggered Tyler the **first time** he tried heroin. What was his **trigger**? What was the **trigger** when he **relapsed back into his heroin** use? Were the triggers similar or different in how they affected Tyler? How could he have avoided his first use and his relapse episode?

Activity: Your Own Triggers

Let's take a moment to fill out the **Relapse/Recidivism Log** in *Worksheet 7*. Take each of the triggers above and write down a **specific event** that applies to you. Then write your **thoughts** and **feelings** and your **response**, either positive or negative. Then use *Worksheet 8, Coping Skills* to write down how you dealt with or **would now deal with** each of the events.

Activity: Once Again --- A Cycle

Just as there is a pattern to substance use and getting into trouble, there is also a **pattern to relapsing or going back to negative behavior**. There is a way to gain control over the pattern of our relapse/recidivism, though. *Worksheet 9, The Relapse/Recidivism Calendar* is meant to help you understand your pattern of substance use and criminal behavior. You will not only be able to see the patterns of your problems, but you will also be able to see further into **how substance use and crime go hand in hand**. In filling out the worksheet, use **straight lines** to show sober and positive periods of your life and use **wavy lines** to show when you were using substances or committing criminal acts. Hold onto this worksheet because you will be doing more work on it in the next session.

Putting It Together

· What was the HR situation for Tyler, and how did it affect his decisions? What were Tyler's triggers?

· What are some of your warning signs for getting into trouble with criminal activities?

· What are some triggers that cause you to want to do substances?

· How will knowing your pattern of use and negative behavior help you to change?

· Describe how relapse and recidivism are gradual processes of erosion.

Worksheet 7

RELAPSE/RECIDIVISM LOG

Below are four situations that are often seen as high-risk situations which can lead to relapse or reoffending. Write in specific situations that apply to you. Then write down your thoughts and feelings. What was the action you took? Discuss the positive and negative outcomes. Describe at least one situation in each category. What thoughts would lead to better outcomes?

TRIGGERS	THOUGHTS/ FEELINGS	BEHAVIOR + −
1 : CONFLICT WITH ANOTHER PERSON		
2 : SOCIAL OR PEER PRESSURE		
3 : AN UNPLEASANT FEELING		
4 : A CHANGE IN SELF-IMAGE		

Worksheet 8

Write a short description of how you have coped or now cope with the situations outlined in Worksheet 6. Write a statement for each of the four situations.

    1) Conflict with another person
    2) Social or peer pressure
    3) An unpleasant feeling
    4) A change in self-image

Worksheet 9

The Relapse/Recidivism Calendar [Adapted from Gorski, 1993]

Use this exercise to examine your AOD abuse and criminal activities. You will gain insight into how your AOD and legal problems are related. Write in the dates of your first serious attempts to stop AOD abuse and criminal behaviors. Use a **straight line** to indicate periods of sober and resposible behavior. Use a **wavy line** to indicate periods of relapse or recidivism. When you come to the next session, describe the series of events that led to AOD relapse and to criminal involvement.

Year	Jan Feb Mar Apr May Jun Jul Aug Sep Oct Nov Dec
AOD	
Crime	

Year	Jan Feb Mar Apr May Jun Jul Aug Sep Oct Nov Dec
AOD	
Crime	

Year	Jan Feb Mar Apr May Jun Jul Aug Sep Oct Nov Dec
AOD	
Crime	

Objectives

- Review *Session 8: Identifying Triggers and Your High-Risk Situations*
- Understand the idea of relapse/recidivism (RR) erosion
- Understand the mind and actions that lead to RR
- Learn to avoid RR by seeing the thoughts, feelings, and attitudes that trigger your use and criminal conduct

Tyler's Story

I didn't really want to do heroin again. I remembered the pain I went through while I was on it and while I was trying to get off of it. But I started hanging out with my old friends again. After awhile I went to the house with my friend, and when I was smoking weed I took a bump. I didn't really think it was a big deal. I thought I could control it, and besides I knew it would make me feel good. But then the next morning, while I was withdrawing, I became confused and angry. I wasn't clean anymore. I no longer had the months of sobriety at my back. The next time I was offered a bump, I took it. After all, I had already used once, what would one more bump do? I would quit after this one. But one turned into another, and another. If I wasn't clean anymore, then I was a user. So I might as well use and enjoy myself. But I still felt like crap.

High-Risk, triggers, and you

In the last session we spent some time learning what *relapse and recidivism* (RR) mean, which is *going* back to the actions or thoughts that either lead us to use substances or cause criminal behavior. Remember, relapse and recidivism *do not* happen all at once, but occur in stages that begin with the *thought habits* first and then end with a return to our old harmful and destructive patterns.

There are also *triggers* that can make the *old thought habits* come back to us. The triggers can be anything from *outside conflict and pressure* to *inner feelings and changes* in our self-images.

But because there are *stages* and different *triggers* to relapse and recidivism, that means the process happens slowly. Since the process occurs in stages, that means we can *change* or *stop* the relapse before it becomes full blown. But to stop the relapse, we have to be *aware* of how and why it begins in the first place. That is what this session is about, *learning* the how and why so you can have *control* over stopping RR.

Activity: Tyler's Trap

Tyler started falling into some **high-risk situations** and **high-risk thinking**. What were the thoughts that helped Tyler to fall back on his old habit? What were Tyler's triggers and what stage of relapse is Tyler in now?

What is RR Erosion?

Because RR is a *process* that means there is a sort of erosion within our mind that happens with RR. Just as rain *erodes* away the topsoil, which contains the good stuff for growing and nurturing plants, RR begins the erosion of the topsoil of our mind which contains the good stuff for us to grow and mature. But this doesn't happen quickly; rather, relapse and recidivism erosion can happen over a long period, even *years*, so that we can't really see it happening, even if a relapse episode seems spur of the moment. *Figure 10, The Relapse/Recidivism Erosion Process*, gives us some idea of how the erosion happens. It's a slow *decline* in our positive selves until the relapse episode happens. It is then a *choice* of whether we continue back to our old selves in a full relapse or if we stop the relapse. But it is in *your control* whether you decide to relapse or not. Fill in the lines on *Worksheet 10* to describe Tyler's RR process and how he might have stopped the erosion before reaching a full-blown RR episode.

Activity: Your Own Path

Take a moment to think about some possible RR episodes in your life. **Draw** on the right half of a piece of paper an **action that you were participating in when you relapsed**. Now **think** about what happened **before** the action. For example, you were hanging out with some friends at the park and ended up smoking some marijuana. Before you relapsed, you may have been thinking you were bored, or you were stressed out about something.

Think about your own situation and these questions:

Did someone say something, or were you going somewhere?

Write the thought or feeling that led up to the relapse in front of it (left side of paper).

What led to that thought or feeling? Did something happen? Draw or write that event.

Try to trace back your thoughts and feelings to the initial choice that led to your being in a high-risk situation. Notice how many things happened before the action of relapse. This is the **erosion of relapse and recidivism**. It doesn't start with the actions, but rather the thoughts, feelings, and choices before the action. Create an **Erosion skit** where a person gradually loses their resources and returns to drugs or crime. Re-run the skit and model how the situation can be prevented.

STEPS TO RR

Just like the steps to change, there are *steps* for relapse/recidivism. But unlike the steps to change, the steps to RR are *negative* and move us *backwards* rather than forwards. We have to keep in mind what we talked about in the last session, RR does not mean committing the act. RR starts with the thought habits that lead to the actions. Take a look at *Figure 11, The Relapse/Recidivism Model*, which shows the following steps to RR:

High-Risk Situation and High-Risk Thinking

We talked in the last session about the high-risk situations and thinking which can cause you to

Figure 10/Worksheet 10

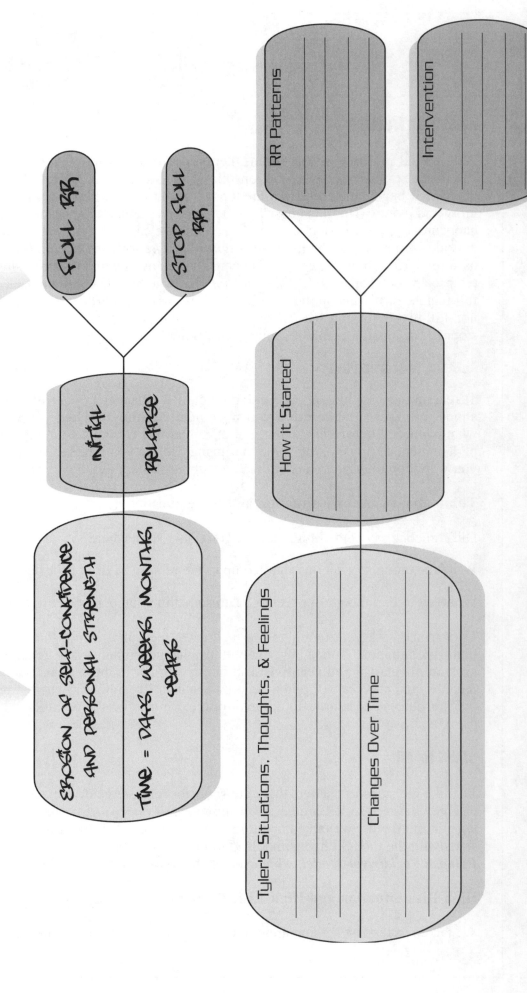

THE RELAPSE/RECIDIVISM EROSION PROCESS

[Adapted from Daley and Marlatt, 1992]

Figure 11

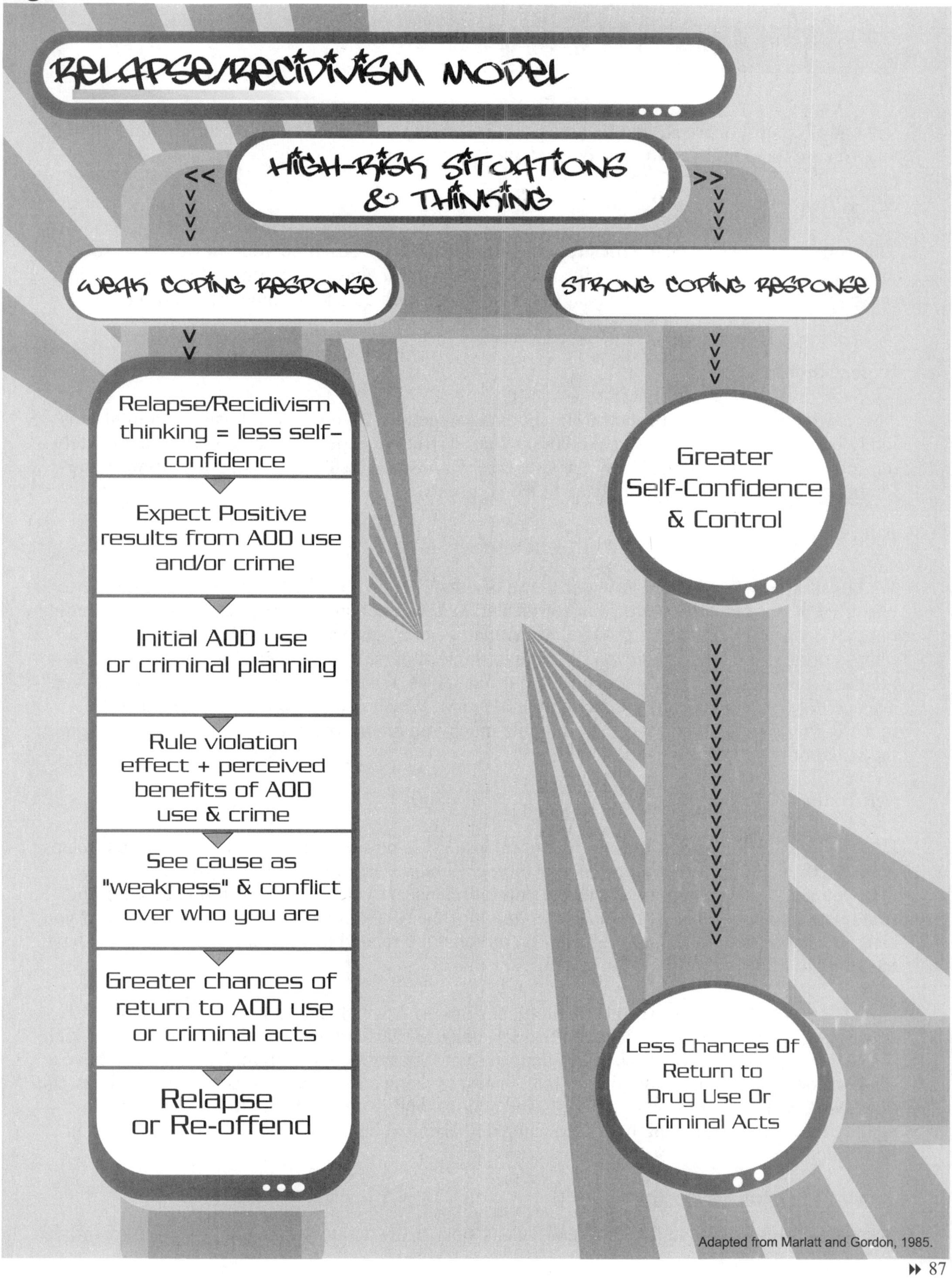

RELAPSE/RECIDIVISM MODEL

HIGH-RISK SITUATIONS & THINKING

<< >>

WEAK COPING RESPONSE

STRONG COPING RESPONSE

Relapse/Recidivism thinking = less self–confidence

↓

Expect Positive results from AOD use and/or crime

↓

Initial AOD use or criminal planning

↓

Rule violation effect + perceived benefits of AOD use & crime

↓

See cause as "weakness" & conflict over who you are

↓

Greater chances of return to AOD use or criminal acts

↓

Relapse or Re-offend

Greater Self-Confidence & Control

↓

Less Chances Of Return to Drug Use Or Criminal Acts

Adapted from Marlatt and Gordon, 1985.

feel out of control or weak, and by doing that increasing your risk for RR. Keep in mind, though, that you are the only one who has *control* over your actions.

Self-Efficacy or Sense of Personal Power

This is how we cope or deal with stressful situations. This is *based* on your *memories* of success or failure, how *others* judge and influence you, and your *feelings* at the time. It is your *personal sense of power* or ability to manage a given situation, such as asking someone out or being straight at a party where everyone is drinking or doing drugs.

Expected Outcome

This is what we *expect* to happen from choosing an action. If you *choose* to smoke a joint, it is likely because you *expect* it to make you feel good. But the expected results may be completely *different* than the actual results. When you expect a *positive* result from using a substance, the likelihood of relapsing, or going back to using, goes way up.

Rule Violation Effect

We talked in *Session 2* about how our views of ourselves can be *challenged* when we decide to change. But our new views are *good* for us, and *help* us to choose the right actions. But in setting our new views, we set *rules* for ourselves so that we don't go back to our old identity. When a relapse occurs, it causes *confusion*. We like to think of ourselves as "clean" or "honest," but a relapse means getting back in touch with our old selves, which was "using" or "a trouble maker." This *conflict* often makes us go back to the *old view*, which is the rule violation effect. How much *guilt* you feel about relapsing and how much you *blame* yourself will decide the *strength* of the violation.

Self-Blame

How we think of ourselves and our role in relapse gives power to our choice after the first relapse episode. If you believe the relapse is due to your *personal weakness* and that you *lost control*, then you are likely to *continue down* the path of relapse. If you are able to stop yourself at the first relapse episode (that is, the *initial violation* of the rule you have set for yourself), and if you can see clearly the *internal and external factors* that are related to your fall, then you might have the strength to get off of the relapse path.

Now is probably a good time to take a look at *Figure 12*, which shows how giving in to seemingly unimportant urges can lead to a RR episode. Earlier we showed you *Figure 10*, which shows how relapse and recidivism can happen after years of being straight. But once you have a RR episode, it does not mean you are forever lost to using substances and committing crimes. *You have the ability to control* your thoughts and actions, and *you can choose* to move towards a healthy life instead of falling back into using and criminal behavior. We will cover this idea in more depth in future sessions.

Activity: Tyler And His Erosion

Look at the steps above and then reread Tyler's story. How do any of the above steps play into his

Figure 12

Road to Relapse & Recidivism

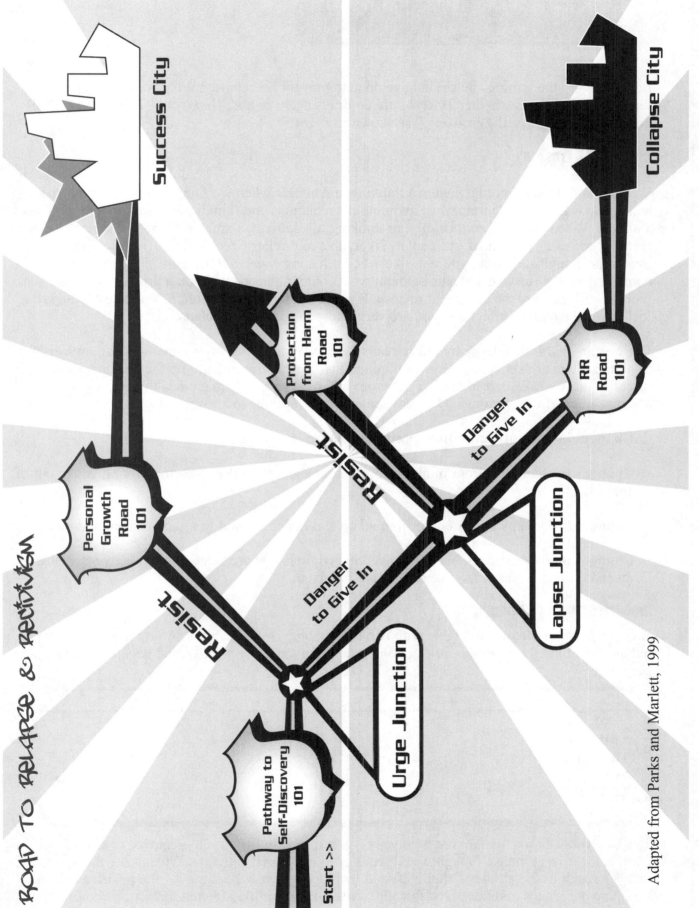

Success City

Collapse City

Protection from Harm Road 101

RR Road 101

Danger to Give In

RESIST

Personal Growth Road 101

Danger to Give In

RESIST

Lapse Junction

Urge Junction

Pathway to Self-Discovery 101

Start >>

Adapted from Parks and Marlett, 1999

relapse? Were there things he could have done to prevent his relapse? What was the step that had the most influence in whether Tyler would do drugs again or not? How could Tyler have stayed on the "Pathway to Self-Discovery," as shown in *Figure 12*?

Clues To RR Erosion

We tend to fall back into the *negative* thinking and beliefs when we find ourselves in high-risk situations. But more important than avoiding the situations and thinking is how you *deal* with the situation. When you take *control* of your thinking to *deal* with a situation, you will begin to feel a *sense of power* in your decisions and are likely to avoid relapse/recidivism. If you *lose control* over your thoughts, though, you will likely begin feeling *weak and insecure*. The weakness, combined with positive expectations about what could happen if we took a drug or got some fast money, will increase the chance of relapse. If you don't have control, once you relapse you will feel the *rule violation* effect and you are very likely to continue to relapse.

But we can *avoid* the relapse by pulling ourselves away from high-risk situations and high-risk thinking. There are skills and ways of thinking that we can use to build up the nurturing topsoil of our mind. We take part in *healthy* activities and *trust* people who are healthy, and we are always *aware* of the warnings. Here are some of the warnings to keep in mind.

· **Changes in your attitude:** from positive to negative.

· **Changes in thoughts:** from thinking confidently about your decisions to thinking you're out of control.

· **Changes in feelings and moods:** from an up and hopeful mood to a sad or depressed mood.

· **Changes in actions:** from being involved in activities that are healthy and positive to being involved in activities where substances are involved.

Activity: Charting A Change

As a large group, **draw** out a table with two sides that everyone can see. Along the left side **write** out attitude, thoughts, feelings, and actions. Along the top write positive and negative next to each other.

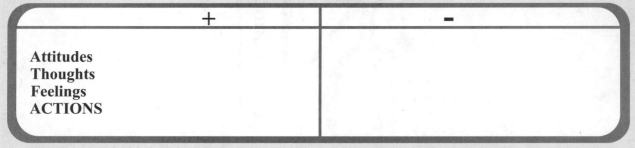

+	-
Attitudes Thoughts Feelings ACTIONS	

Together **think** of a situation that involves relapse or recidivism. In the **negative column** write out the negative attitudes, thoughts, and feelings in a high-risk situation. Then write the **action** that is a result of the attitudes, thoughts, and feelings. Now do the same for the **positive column**. Compare the results and how each thought, attitude, and feeling affected the action chosen.

Discuss the different ways you can control your attitudes, thoughts, and feelings in order to prevent a negative outcome (i.e. relapse or recidivism). Now do the same for the other, for example if you did a chart for relapse the first time, now do a chart for recidivism.

Putting It Together

- Tyler's relapse began by hanging out with old friends. Can you trace Tyler's story through the different steps? How might Tyler have changed his relapse in each step?

- What were some of the thoughts that lead to Tyler's relapse?

- Relapse and recidivism are processes that can happen over a period of years. Do you recognize yourself in any of the stages?

- What are some of the thoughts that can lead to RR? What are some of the thoughts that can prevent RR?

TYLER'S STORY

The world is a painful place to be. And I am filled with that pain.

When I was younger, I was never the person to stick out much. One look at me and people usually didn't look again, unless they were the type to search out people like me. And I liked that. I liked being a loner for the most part, staying home to write and play my guitar when everyone else was out drinking and being stupid. I didn't get involved much in the drama and shallowness of high school. I always considered it a waste of time.

That's not to say I didn't have friends. I had a few, just enough to be a normal kid, I suppose. I got along with everybody, and most people got along with me. I just didn't enter myself in any popularity contests, which was definitely different than my parents. But they had their agenda, and I had mine.

So one of the few nights I went out, a couple of friends and I were at some older guy's house partying. While most people were drinking, I was sticking to smoking the occasional bowl that got passed my way. I'm not much of a drinker. My ex-girlfriend was there and creating a lot of drama that I didn't want to be part of, life is depressing enough as it is, so I was just about to leave when my friend suggested we go in the back room and smoke a joint before I left. The guy who lived in the house came with us, after all you should share with the host, and while we were puffing it up he offered us some powder. Although I didn't know what it was, and I wasn't much of a user, I took a bump. I always thought you only live once so you might as well experience it all. Later I learned it was heroin, but by then I thought I had seen a little bit of heaven.

By the time that hit kicked in, I was swimming through the clouds of apathy. I didn't feel a thing, and I was better for it. I still left the party, that didn't change, but as I floated through the crowds and brushed past my ex, I was in a state of nirvana. I'm not sure how or when I got home, but I barely waved to my parents on my way down to my bedroom, closed the door, put on some music with a heavy bass beat, and was lost.

Until the next morning. That was when I found out just how much pain there can be in one human body, mind and soul. But that didn't stop me the next time, though, or the next. The high was just too perfect to even think about the low. Next thing I knew I was free-basing just to get a high. Of course, that was when my parents took me to rehab. A full three months in an in-patient treatment program, learning how to change my thoughts and actions. And it worked.

I went back to school, although a different one this time. Everyone decided I should make different friends to help keep me sober. I was deep into my guitar, and had started making plans to go to school for music theory. Life was getting back to how it was, and I was once again a clean guy who had dreams and goals. For awhile.

About six months later, I ran into one of my old friends. She asked me if I was okay, and we started talking about the old days. We hung out the rest of the afternoon, and I didn't think anything of it because she was not a friend who was involved in my using. We decided to hang out again, but the next time her boyfriend, who was there the first night, was there. I thought there was nothing to worry about. After all, I was strong and clean by now. But a couple of weeks later I ran into him again, and he asked me to come to this party with him. Not to worry, I thought, he would never do anything to put me at risk.

Except that he did. And I fell. It was at the same guy's house as before, and almost the same situation as before. Stoned out of my mind, I took a bump. I thought that I was strong enough to control it this time.

But I wasn't. The next morning, as I was withdrawing, I was confused and angry. I was no longer clean and sober for almost a year. I would not be clean for a couple of days. And I had enjoyed it. I wasn't sure who I was or what was going on anymore.

So the next time I did it again. I figured, hey, I don't have those months of sobriety anymore, so what would one hit do? Until one hit turned into another and another. And each time was an excuse to do it one more time. And one more time meant that I would do it one more time and then quit. But the quitting never came.

And now I sit here in the dark, plucking at strings that should have been changed months ago, never seeing the sun or my parents except to go out and buy more. **And I will buy more, just to avoid the pain of living and the pain of my body letting go.**

Chapter Five:

Making a Commitment to Change

GOALS OF THIS CHAPTER
· Begin moving from Phase I to Phase II
· Describe our targets for change
· Think about how far along we are in the change process
· What do we want from here on?

MIKE'S STORY

I've thought about changing. I really have. I started drinking when I was young, I can't even remember when. I never really thought my drinking was a problem, or something that needed to be changed. But then one night, I was at a party with some friends. We had all ditched school to start drinking early, and by 9 o'clock we were all hammered.

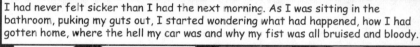

I had never felt sicker than I had the next morning. As I was sitting in the bathroom, puking my guts out, I started wondering what had happened, how I had gotten home, where the hell my car was and why my fist was all bruised and bloody.

I called the friend who I thought had gotten me home. I guess I had gotten a little too wild at the party, making a fool of myself, and as I was walking past the garage of the house, I guess I punched it. A cop had stopped us and I had a court date for MUI and public intoxication.

M.U.I.
Court date:
February 15
~~ge: $200

But I didn't think anything of it. So I kept drinking. And it kept happening. Almost every weekend was a blur or some non-existent action of my body.

My girlfriend broke up with me. She said she couldn't be with a guy who drank so much and made an ass out of himself and her. My friends avoided me.

I didn't want to drink anymore. My mom was actually kind of helpful. It was really cool to think that other people were willing to share and help me if I asked.

So I think I want to stop drinking. In fact, I know I want to stop drinking. Besides, pretty soon, they're going to put me on probation, then I'll have to take tests every couple of days. I don't get the warm and numb feelings anymore, and it's just not fun.

SESSION 10: DEVELOPING YOUR PLAN FOR CHANGE -- PFC

Objectives

- Review *Chapter 4: Backsliding to Drugs and Crime*
- Discuss the stages of change
- Discuss which stages of change you are in
- Learn the tools for changing your thoughts and actions
- Develop your *Self-Portrait* and *Plan for Change*

Mike's Story

I think I want to change. In fact, I know I want to change. Drinking just isn't fun anymore. I drink all day long, even at school because I bring in a pint and sip on it between classes and during lunch. My girlfriend broke up with me. I guess during my blackout periods I make a real ass out of her and myself. My friends don't like drinking with me anymore; I think they are embarrassed to be around me when I drink.

When it got really bad I decided to sit and think about what I get from alcohol, and why I drink so much. I don't know why, but the urge to drink until I can't drink anymore is really strong. My mom has been a lot of help, though. I guess she used to drink a lot, and now she's cut way back. I even asked my ex and my friends about what I do when I drink and how it makes them feel. I never realized there were so many people who were willing to help me.

Relapse/Recidivism: staying clean

Last session we spent some time talking about the *triggers of relapse and recidivism*. To review, a *relapse* is when we participate in the *thinking and actions* that lead to substance reuse. *Recidivism* is the *thoughts and actions* that lead to returning to criminal conduct. Remember, *just the thought itself* is considered part of the process of relapse/recidivism.

We talked about how triggers, usually high-risk situations and HR thinking, can result in urges and cravings to participate in destructive patterns of behavior. These triggers can be anything from *conflict and stress*—or *even good feelings* (like wanting to celebrate)—to being around *old friends and old situations* where we used to participate in the action we are now trying to avoid. Although it may not always be possible to stay away from HR situations, we do have *control over our thoughts*, and that in itself can help prevent relapse/recidivism.

Activity: Taking Charge Of Cravings And Urges

Break into groups of two or three and discuss possible **relapse/recidivism situations** that you have faced in the last month. Take some time to discuss what happened and how it may have been different **depending on your thoughts**. For example, someone may have offered you a drug or suggested doing a crime. The craving was to get high, to get money, to get even… or whatever, but your thought was, "I am already in trouble—been there, done that—and I really want my freedom." Because you have **power over your thoughts**, you resisted the drug or criminal activity and controlled yourself through the craving and urge. With your partner/group, **develop a skit** with the relapse/recidivism situation that you think shows the process the best.

After performing the skit, discuss in the large group about what was done right in the situation and what may have been done differently to have a better outcome.

RECOGNIZING YOUR STAGE OF CHANGE

In the first session, we discussed the three phases of this program: (*I—Challenge: Deciding What to Change; II—Commitment: Using Tools for Change; and III—Ownership: Calling the Shots for Change);* each of which is related to the stages that people experience when deciding to change a negative habit or destructive pattern of   behavior. Now it's time to look at where you are in the process of changing important areas of your life. We will complete a questionnaire to clarify where we stand on changing *AOD abuse and criminal activities.* Remember, you can be at different stages of change for different problem areas. For example, you may be 100% ready to stop criminal activity, but not at all ready to quit smoking cigarettes. We shall now review the stages of change.

WHAT—Challenge: Deciding What to Change
This is the phase where we start thinking about change and looking at ourselves to see *where and what changes need to be made*. In this phase you are open to *getting information* about yourself and your problems. The early phase of this stage is about *building self-awareness*, while the latter part is about taking greater risks in *talking about yourself* and your problems to others. You have met this challenge when you commit to *continued treatment* with the desire to learn how to be free of substance use and crime. The basic ideas are *thinking, self-awareness, sharing about you, and being willing to commit yourself to further help*.

HOW—Commitment: Using Tools for Change
You have made the commitment to work on improving the quality of your life, and are now open to talking about your problems and what changes need to be made. You are now making a *genuine effort* to change your *thoughts, attitudes, and beliefs*, and you have been able to go awhile without using drugs or getting into trouble. You are now involved in *learning and using the skills of thinking and acting* to keep yourself away from using substances and participating in criminal activities. It is in this stage when you begin to assert your *control* and *freedom* over the thoughts and actions that lead to problems.

NOW—Ownership: Calling the Shots for Change
When you reach this stage, you are now making changes because *you want* to and *not* because "they" (the system, parents, or others) want you to. You feel strong about your distance from substances and criminal behavior, and you have *replaced your negative thinking* with positive alternatives. The skills to control your thinking have become an important part of your everyday life. You can recognize when you are on the *road to relapse or re-offending*, but are able to stop the RR progression at the thinking part. You are here because you want to be.

Activity: Mike's Desire To Change

When looking at Mike's story, do you think he wants to change? Why? Is he ready for change? Do you think Mike will be successful in his effort to quit drinking? What **stage of change** is Mike currently in? What are some of the **specific signs** that Mike is ready to change his pattern of drinking? What things can Mike do that will help him to move forward in his effort to change?

THE MOMENT OF DECISION

You are now at the point where you have made a very positive decision—to continue on the road to change. You have learned and worked hard and are now ready to become committed to the action phase of treatment—*Using Tools for Change*.

How do you know if you are ready for change? That is a big question that we all ask ourselves, and we are the only ones who really know the answers. Some of us may still be here mostly because we have to be. That is fine, just be honest about how you feel concerning change. Here are a few signs that may show you that you are ready for change.

· You are open to people telling you (giving you feedback) about your drug use and criminal behaviors.

· You see that you have problems in your behavior and substance use.

· You talk about what you want to change, and often hear yourself say that you can change.

Change *does not happen all at once* nor does it happen easily. There will be times that you will feel that it's not worth it, or it's just too hard to change. But that is what you will be learning in *Phase II*, the *skills to deal with everyday situations* so that you aren't stressed or worried about what is going to happen and have confidence in dealing with your HR triggers in positive and healthy ways. Of course the first step in targeting and learning how to change is to focus on your thinking.

Activity: Where Am I In The Change Process?

Fill out *Worksheets 11 and 12, Self-Rating on Stages of Change*, to get some ideas on **where you stand** in the change process for AOD abuse and criminal activities.

A very important indication of your readiness to change is *successful completion* of your *Self-Portrait* and *Plan for Change*, which are to be finished as part of this session.

Activity: Looking At Yourself And Planning For Change

Fill out *Worksheet 13, List of Strengths and Problems*, **on your own** and then create your *Self-Portrait (Worksheet 14)* and *Plan for Change (PFC - Worksheet 15)* **together with your counselor**. The *PFC* will take some time and careful consideration, as it will involve **specific problems**, needed changes in **thoughts and actions**, and specific **treatment activities** that will helpful to you in changing the problem. Try to be complete, and identify as many problems as you want for each main area. Your counselor will give you examples on how to complete the *PFC,* which will set **important guidelines** for the next phases of your treatment. Your *PFC* **will change** as you discover more information about yourself and will help you to set your **goals** and **change targets** for *Phases II* and *III* of your program.

SELF-RATING ON STAGES OF CHANGE FOR AOD USE

Rate yourself on each stage of change.

CHALLENGE TO CHANGE

KEY ELEMENTS IN STAGE	Low			Moderate			High		
	0	1	2	3	4	5	6	7	8
Given thought to changing	0	1	2	3	4	5	6	7	8
Want information about myself	0	1	2	3	4	5	6	7	8
Level of self-awareness	0	1	2	3	4	5	6	7	8
Commitment to more treatment	0	1	2	3	4	5	6	7	8

USING TOOLS FOR CHANGE

KEY ELEMENTS IN STAGE	Low			Moderate			High		
	0	1	2	3	4	5	6	7	8
Pledge to change	0	1	2	3	4	5	6	7	8
Open to self-disclosure	0	1	2	3	4	5	6	7	8
Efforts to change attitudes	0	1	2	3	4	5	6	7	8
Efforts to change thoughts	0	1	2	3	4	5	6	7	8
Use relapse prevention skills	0	1	2	3	4	5	6	7	8
AOD thought-free for long period	0	1	2	3	4	5	6	7	8
Corrected relapse thinking	0	1	2	3	4	5	6	7	8
Learned skills to avoid AOD thought	0	1	2	3	4	5	6	7	8

CALLING YOUR OWN SHOTS

KEY ELEMENTS IN STAGE	Low			Moderate			High		
	0	1	2	3	4	5	6	7	8
In program because want to be	0	1	2	3	4	5	6	7	8
No desire for AOD involvement	0	1	2	3	4	5	6	7	8
Long time free of AOD thinking	0	1	2	3	4	5	6	7	8
Replace need for AOD use	0	1	2	3	4	5	6	7	8

Worksheet 11

SELF-RATING ON STAGES OF CHANGE FOR CRIMINAL THINKING & CRIMINAL CONDUCT

Rate yourself on each stage of change.

CHALLENGE TO CHANGE

KEY ELEMENTS IN STAGE	Low			Moderate			High		
Given thought to changing	0	1	2	3	4	5	6	7	8
Want information about myself	0	1	2	3	4	5	6	7	8
Level of self-awareness	0	1	2	3	4	5	6	7	8
Commitment to more treatment	0	1	2	3	4	5	6	7	8

USING TOOLS FOR CHANGE

KEY ELEMENTS IN STAGE	Low			Moderate			High		
Pledge to change	0	1	2	3	4	5	6	7	8
Open to self-disclosure	0	1	2	3	4	5	6	7	8
Efforts to change attitudes	0	1	2	3	4	5	6	7	8
Efforts to change thoughts	0	1	2	3	4	5	6	7	8
Use relapse prevention skills	0	1	2	3	4	5	6	7	8
CC thought-free for long period	0	1	2	3	4	5	6	7	8
Corrected relapse thinking	0	1	2	3	4	5	6	7	8
Learned skills to avoid CC thought	0	1	2	3	4	5	6	7	8

CALLING YOUR OWN SHOTS

KEY ELEMENTS IN STAGE	Low			Moderate			High		
In program because want to be	0	1	2	3	4	5	6	7	8
No desire for CC involvement	0	1	2	3	4	5	6	7	8
Long time free of CC thinking	0	1	2	3	4	5	6	7	8
Replace need for CC use	0	1	2	3	4	5	6	7	8

Worksheet 13

LIST OF STRENGTHS & PROBLEMS TO WORK ON

List problems that you need to work on for each of the focus areas.

A. Family issues and problems:

1. _____

2. _____

3. _____

4. _____

B. Emotional and psychological problems:

1. _____

2. _____

3. _____

4. _____

C. Involvement with negative and deviant peers:

1. _____

2. _____

3. _____

4. _____

D. School achievement and adjustment problems:

1. _____

2. _____

3. _____

4. _____

E. Problems with criminal thinking and acting:

1. _____

2. _____

3. _____

4. _____

F. Problems with alcohol and other drug use and abuse:

1. _____

2. _____

3. _____

4. _____

G. Community living environment and situations:

1. _____

2. _____

3. _____

4. _____

H. Thinking and feeling patterns and errors:

1. _____

2. _____

3. _____

4. _____

I. Physical and medical health problems:

1. _____
2. _____
3. _____
4. _____

J. My strengths and strong points:

1. _____
2. _____
3. _____
4. _____
5. _____
6. _____
7. _____
8. _____
9. _____
10. _____

Worksheet 14

SELF-PORTRAIT

1. Family and Living Environment

	Area of Assessment	Low				Moderate				High	
Family	Degree Family Disruption	0	1	2	3	4	5	6	7	8	9	10
	Lack of Family Closeness	0	1	2	3	4	5	6	7	8	9	10
	Lack of Family Support	0	1	2	3	4	5	6	7	8	9	10
	Parents Have Problems	0	1	2	3	4	5	6	7	8	9	10

2. Emotional and Psychological Problems

	Area of Assessment	Low				Moderate				High	
Emotional	Anxiety and Fears	0	1	2	3	4	5	6	7	8	9	10
	Depression	0	1	2	3	4	5	6	7	8	9	10
	Impulsive Acting	0	1	2	3	4	5	6	7	8	9	10
	Angry Feelings and Acting	0	1	2	3	4	5	6	7	8	9	10
	Concern About Self-Harm	0	1	2	3	4	5	6	7	8	9	10

3. School Achievement and Adjustment Problems

	Area of Assessment	Low				Moderate				High	
School	Conduct Problems	0	1	2	3	4	5	6	7	8	9	10
	Poor and Failing Grades	0	1	2	3	4	5	6	7	8	9	10
	Negative School Attitude	0	1	2	3	4	5	6	7	8	9	10
	Skip Classes/Dropped Out	0	1	2	3	4	5	6	7	8	9	10

4. Relationship with Peers

	Area of Assessment	Low				Moderate				High	
Peers	Negative Peers	0	1	2	3	4	5	6	7	8	9	10
	No Close Friends	0	1	2	3	4	5	6	7	8	9	10
	Criminal Associates	0	1	2	3	4	5	6	7	8	9	10
	Drug Associates	0	1	2	3	4	5	6	7	8	9	10

5. Criminal and Antisocial Thinking and Conduct

	Area of Assessment	Low				Moderate				High	
Conduct	Property Offenses	0	1	2	3	4	5	6	7	8	9	10
	Person Offenses	0	1	2	3	4	5	6	7	8	9	10
	Violent Crimes and Conduct	0	1	2	3	4	5	6	7	8	9	10
	Sex Offender Conduct	0	1	2	3	4	5	6	7	8	9	10
	AOD Impaired Driving	0	1	2	3	4	5	6	7	8	9	10

SELF-PORTRAIT

5. Criminal and Antisocial Thinking and Conduct, Continued

	Area of Assessment	Low					Moderate					High
Criminal Thinking	Antisocial Peers & Models	0	1	2	3	4	5	6	7	8	9	10
	Impulsive Thinking/Acting	0	1	2	3	4	5	6	7	8	9	10
	Cops Are Out To Get Me	0	1	2	3	4	5	6	7	8	9	10
	Planning Crimes	0	1	2	3	4	5	6	7	8	9	10
	Blame Others For Problems	0	1	2	3	4	5	6	7	8	9	10
	Take Victim Stance	0	1	2	3	4	5	6	7	8	9	10
	Lying And Not Telling Truth	0	1	2	3	4	5	6	7	8	9	10
	Angry/Aggressive Attitude	0	1	2	3	4	5	6	7	8	9	10
	Rebellious/Anti-Authority	0	1	2	3	4	5	6	7	8	9	10
	Seeking Out A Victim	0	1	2	3	4	5	6	7	8	9	10
	Want Revenge Or To Get Back	0	1	2	3	4	5	6	7	8	9	10
	They Deserve It	0	1	2	3	4	5	6	7	8	9	10
	Lack Of Empathy For Others	0	1	2	3	4	5	6	7	8	9	10
	Reckless Thinking	0	1	2	3	4	5	6	7	8	9	10

6. Alcohol and Other Drug Assessment

	Area of Assessment	Low					Moderate					High
Drug Choice	Alcohol Involvement	0	1	2	3	4	5	6	7	8	9	10
	Marijuana Involvement	0	1	2	3	4	5	6	7	8	9	10
	Cocaine Involvement	0	1	2	3	4	5	6	7	8	9	10
	Amphetamine Involvement	0	1	2	3	4	5	6	7	8	9	10
	Other Drug Involvement	0	1	2	3	4	5	6	7	8	9	10
	Poly Drug User	0	1	2	3	4	5	6	7	8	9	10

	Area of Assessment	Low					Moderate					High
Style	With Friends or at Parties	0	1	2	3	4	5	6	7	8	9	10
	Sustained & Continuous	0	1	2	3	4	5	6	7	8	9	10
	Compulsive & Obsessive	0	1	2	3	4	5	6	7	8	9	10

	Area of Assessment	Low					Moderate					High
Benefits	Cope with Social Discomfort	0	1	2	3	4	5	6	7	8	9	10
	Cope with Emotional Discomfort	0	1	2	3	4	5	6	7	8	9	10
	Cope with Relationships	0	1	2	3	4	5	6	7	8	9	10
	Cope with Physical Distress	0	1	2	3	4	5	6	7	8	9	10

SELF-PORTRAIT

6. Alcohol and Other Drug Assessment, Continued

Level of Problem Severity

Results

Area of Assessment	Low					Moderate				High	
Behavioral Loss Of Control	0	1	2	3	4	5	6	7	8	9	10
Emotional Disruption	0	1	2	3	4	5	6	7	8	9	10
Physical Disruption	0	1	2	3	4	5	6	7	8	9	10
Social Irresponsibility	0	1	2	3	4	5	6	7	8	9	10
Overall Disruption	0	1	2	3	4	5	6	7	8	9	10

Ready

Area of Assessment	Low					Moderate				High	
AOD Problem Awareness	0	1	2	3	4	5	6	7	8	9	10
Treatment Receptiveness	0	1	2	3	4	5	6	7	8	9	10
Motivation to Change	0	1	2	3	4	5	6	7	8	9	10

7. Assessment of Thinking and Feeling Patterns

Thinking and Feelings

Area of Assessment	Low					Moderate				High	
Put People Down	0	1	2	3	4	5	6	7	8	9	10
Narrow-Restricted Thinking	0	1	2	3	4	5	6	7	8	9	10
Personalizing Responses	0	1	2	3	4	5	6	7	8	9	10
Seeing Things My Way	0	1	2	3	4	5	6	7	8	9	10
Self-Defeating Thinking	0	1	2	3	4	5	6	7	8	9	10
Can't Trust Others	0	1	2	3	4	5	6	7	8	9	10
Self-Centered Thinking	0	1	2	3	4	5	6	7	8	9	10
Don't Need Anyone's Help	0	1	2	3	4	5	6	7	8	9	10
Feel Better Than Others	0	1	2	3	4	5	6	7	8	9	10
Feel Screwed Over	0	1	2	3	4	5	6	7	8	9	10
Mountains Out Of Molehills	0	1	2	3	4	5	6	7	8	9	10
Think In Black and White Terms	0	1	2	3	4	5	6	7	8	9	10

8. Other Areas

Other

Area of Assessment	Low					Moderate				High	
Health/Physical Problems	0	1	2	3	4	5	6	7	8	9	10
Job and Employment Problems	0	1	2	3	4	5	6	7	8	9	10
Gangs In My Neighborhood	0	1	2	3	4	5	6	7	8	9	10

SELF-PORTRAIT

9. Motivation and Readiness for Treatment

Level of Problem Severity

Rate Each Stage Separately	Low				Moderate				High		
Awareness of AOD/CC Problem	0	1	2	3	4	5	6	7	8	9	10
Acknowledgement of Need for Help	0	1	2	3	4	5	6	7	8	9	10
Willingness to Accept Help	0	1	2	3	4	5	6	7	8	9	10
Other's Perception of Need	0	1	2	3	4	5	6	7	8	9	10
Has Taken Action to Change	0	1	2	3	4	5	6	7	8	9	10

(Readiness)

10. Stage of Change

Rate Each Stage Separately	Low				Moderate				High		
Challenge to Change	0	1	2	3	4	5	6	7	8	9	10
Using Tools for Change	0	1	2	3	4	5	6	7	8	9	10
Calling Your Own Shots	0	1	2	3	4	5	6	7	8	9	10

(Stage)

11. Strengths and Resiliency

Strength Areas	Low				Moderate				High		
Relationship With Parents	0	1	2	3	4	5	6	7	8	9	10
Relationship With Family	0	1	2	3	4	5	6	7	8	9	10
Emotional and Mental Health	0	1	2	3	4	5	6	7	8	9	10
Positive Self Thoughts	0	1	2	3	4	5	6	7	8	9	10
Control Of Anger	0	1	2	3	4	5	6	7	8	9	10
Have Successful Friends	0	1	2	3	4	5	6	7	8	9	10
School Adjustment	0	1	2	3	4	5	6	7	8	9	10
Follow Rules/Regulations	0	1	2	3	4	5	6	7	8	9	10
Obey Laws Of The Community	0	1	2	3	4	5	6	7	8	9	10
Respect Rights Of Others	0	1	2	3	4	5	6	7	8	9	10
Physical/Medical Health	0	1	2	3	4	5	6	7	8	9	10
Able To Not Use Alcohol	0	1	2	3	4	5	6	7	8	9	10
Able To Not Use Other Drugs											

(Thinking and Feelings)

PLAN FOR CHANGE

PROBLEM AREA & DESCRIPTION	CHANGES NEEDED IN THOUGHT & ACTION	TOOLS FOR CHANGE	DATE WORKED ON
1. Family & Parent Relationships			
2. Emotional & Relationship Problems			
3. School Achievement & Adjustment			
4. Criminal Thinking & Conduct			

PLAN FOR CHANGE

PROBLEM AREA & DESCRIPTION	CHANGES NEEDED IN THOUGHT & ACTION	TOOLS FOR CHANGE	DATE WORKED ON
5. Alcohol Or Other Drug Problem Areas			
6. Thinking & Feeling Patterns			
7. Modifications or Other Areas For Change			

After you and your counselor have agreed on your *Self-Portrait (Worksheet 14)* and *Plan for Change (Worksheet 15)*, you will *share this information* with the group. When you accomplish this, it means that you have successfully completed *Phase I - Challenge to Change*. You have taken on the challenge of identifying what areas of your life are *specific targets for change* and how you will work on self-improvement for the remainder of this program. You are soon ready to begin *Phase II - Using Tools of Change*—Congratulations!

WAYS TO CHANGE

We have now completed the first steps in change by becoming aware of **WHAT** we would like to change and the **THINKING AND ACTION HABITS** that cause our problems. The most *important person* we talk to is *ourselves*, so now it's time to seriously begin to learn how to use the tools for changing the thoughts that lead us into problematic feelings and actions. These will become your *target thoughts* and *target actions*. These are thoughts and actions that you recognize as causing problems in your behavior, and that *you* want to change. Below are the basic steps for changing target thoughts and behaviors.

· **Pick the thoughts** that lead to feelings and behaviors that are problematic.

· **Describe attitudes** and beliefs behind the thought.

· **Set goals** on how you would like to think or act. To set a goal we have to stop and think what we want the new behavior to be. You may feel uncomfortable about changing, and that's okay, but once you have set a goal, live up to it.

· **Pick one or more action methods** you will use to change the thought or behavior. We will cover these next.

· **Change the target behavior**—if you really want to change, you will.

ACTION METHODS FOR CHANGING NEGATIVE THOUGHTS AND BEHAVIORS

When we talk to ourselves, we are really teaching ourselves new ways to do things. Here are four ways to teach ourselves to change.

Thought stopping
If we have an automatic thought, for example "I don't trust him," then we are able to *stop this thought* by thinking "I can be open to hear what he or she is trying to say … I am not going to think this way." We may still not completely trust the other person, but we have interrupted our thought and made ourselves think something different.

Their Position
By taking *responsibility for our actions*, and then placing ourselves in the *other person's position*, we can develop respect for the other person and a sense of control over our lives.

Positive thought

When you begin thinking negatively, replace the thought with something positive. Instead of thinking " I need that jacket," think instead, "I'm ready to graduate this phase of my treatment." If you train yourself to think positively, then your behavior begins to reflect that.

Arguing with yourself

Every time you have a thought that you know will lead you into trouble, argue with yourself. By saying "That's stupid" or "That's not true," you can stop yourself from thinking and then acting on negative thoughts by showing yourself how the negative thought actually doesn't make sense. For example, the thought, "I would like to get high and feel great" can be countered by: "Taking this drug will only make me feel worse in the long run."

Activity: Changing Together

Your counselor will hang some paper on a wall where everyone can see it. Then, as a group, think of one **thinking error** from *Worksheet 3* that is common to the group. Write down the thought on the paper and **underline the common thinking error**. Underneath the thought,   separate the paper in thirds, and on one side write down the **attitudes and beliefs** that are behind the thought or behavior that is going to be changed. On the other side of the paper write down a couple of goals and things that you would like to happen or what you would like to think. Then in the middle third, write down a **thinking or action method** that would be helpful in changing the thought or behavior. Use the example below as a model.

Thinking Error

I WANT WHAT I WANT RIGHT NOW

Attitudes and Beliefs	Methods of Change	Goals
"I'm entitled to take things that aren't mine because I've been abused."	**Their Position** **Arguing with yourself**	Freedom "I am trustworthy"

Change is promoted by sharing our story (self-disclosure) and listening to feedback

Now that we have reviewed the *stages of change*, decided we *want to change*, and began to cover *general ways* that we can change behavior and thought, let's take a look at how being in this group helps us to grow and change.

We have discussed how *talking* about our thoughts and feelings and the *feedback* we get from others are important parts of learning about ourselves, while they also help us to build *trust, friendship and support*. Yet there are many parts of our lives that we have still not shared. The part of our lives that *we know* about, but that *others don't* is called our *Hidden Area*. The part that *others see*, but *we don't* is called our *Blind Area*. The part that *we don't know about ourselves* and *others don't know* either is called the *Unknown Area*. Finally there are things that *we see and know* and that others *also see and know*—this is called our *Free or Open Area*.

The Johari Window in *Figure 14*, gives us a picture of what these areas look like. It is our goal to make the *Free Area larger* and shrink the *Blind and Hidden Areas*.

Figure 13

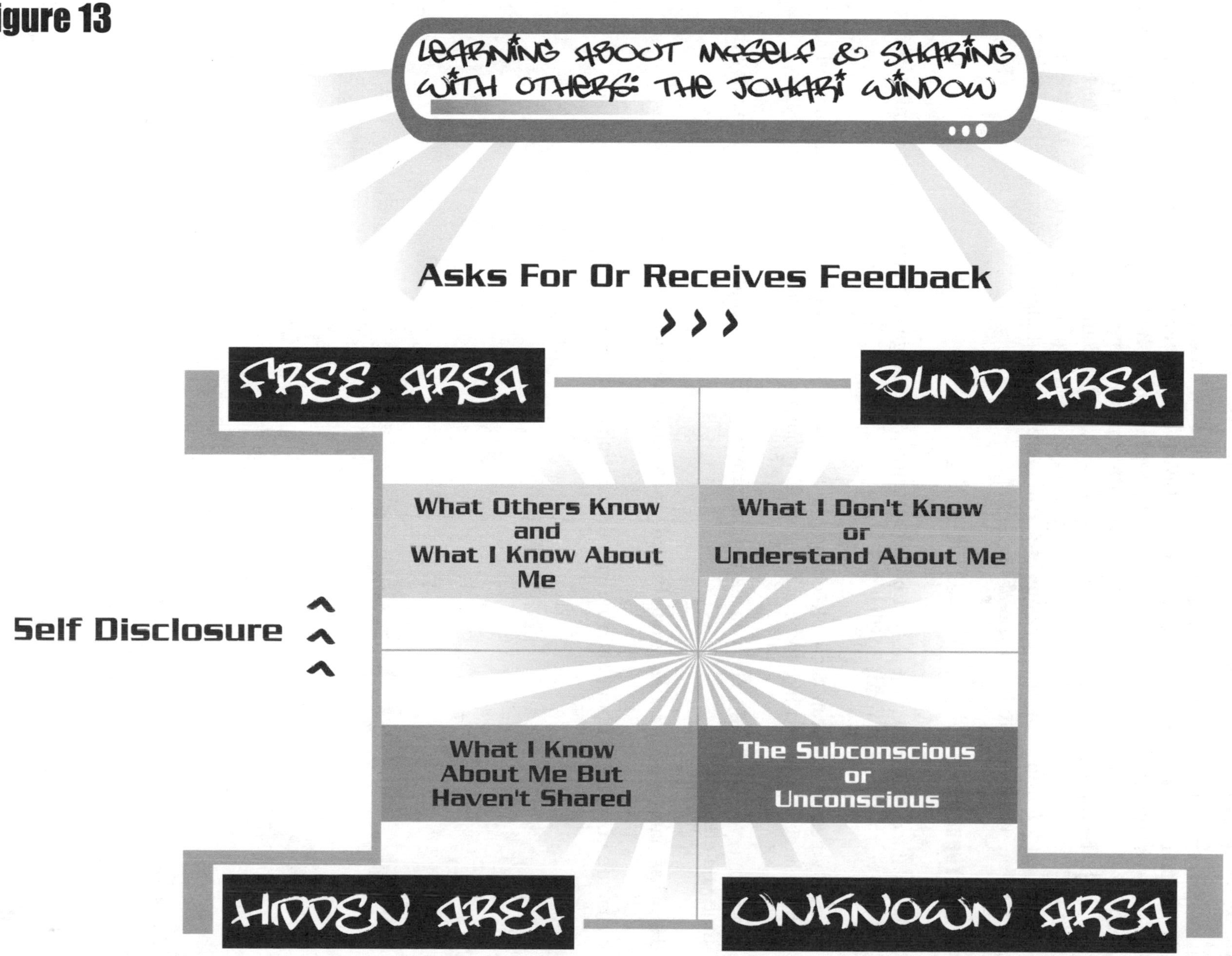

LEARNING ABOUT MYSELF & SHARING WITH OTHERS: THE JOHARI WINDOW

Asks For Or Receives Feedback

\> \> \>

Self Disclosure

\< \< \<

FREE AREA

BLIND AREA

HIDDEN AREA

UNKNOWN AREA

What Others Know
and
What I Know About Me

What I Don't Know
or
Understand About Me

What I Know
About Me But
Haven't Shared

The Subconscious
or
Unconscious

Activity: Building Trust And Freedom By Sharing And Receiving Feedback

On another piece of paper, next to the one used previously, draw a *Johari Window*. As a group write in some of the things that you have **shared with each other** in the *Free Area*. In the *Hidden Area*, think of some general things that people **tend to hide** from other people, and in the *Blind Area* write some general things that **only other people** may see. Then as a group think of ways to be able to move the things from the *Hidden and Blind* areas to the *Free Area* of the window. What about parts of your mind that **nobody is aware of** in the *Unknown Area?* Are the methods you are using realistic for your life? Are there certain things that you have hidden in the past that you would like to be in your *Free Area?*

Putting It Together

· Mike wanted to change, but at first he wasn't sure. What stage of change do you think Mike is in? Do you think he is ready to change?

· The only person who can decide to change is you. What stages of change are you currently in? Which stage would you like to be in? For AOD problems? For criminal activities?

· How have you changed since you started the program? How would you like to change by the time you are done?

· How has participation in the group helped you to grow and change?

· What are your views about entering into the next phase of treatment?

I've thought about changing. I really have. But sometimes it so hard to think about changing when all I want to do is have fun.

I started drinking when I was young. I can't even remember when. I'm sure I was drinking even before my first memory of drinking, but like I said, I can't remember. So everything was fine for me, I guess. I never really thought my drinking was a problem or something that needed to be changed. I liked how it made me feel, ya know? All warm and numb without a care in the world.

I still didn't think much about it when I started taking pints to school. I would steal them from my mom's liquor cabinet, or get my friend's cousin to get it for me. I kept it in my pocket, and since I preferred schnapps, I didn't really have to worry about the smell ratting me out.

But then one night I was at a party with some friends. We all had ditched school to start drinking early, and by 9 o'clock we were all hammered. All I remember was going to this one girl's house and getting myself a beer from the tap. The next thing I knew, I was stumbling along the sidewalk with one of my friends trying to hold me up. I sat down on the curb and then all the sudden I was home. I had never felt sicker than I had the next morning. As I was sitting in the bathroom, puking my guts out, I started wondering what had happened, how I had gotten home, where the hell my car was, and why my fist was all bruised and bloody. That was just the beginning of my nightmare.

When I called the friend who I thought had gotten me home, I didn't like what he had to tell me. My car was fine, I guess. Someone had driven it to my house while I was stumbling home, and it should be out on the curb. But I guess I had gotten a little too wild at the party, throwing things around and making a fool of myself. It took all my friends to drag me out of the party, which I insisted on not leaving because I wasn't done drinking, and as I was walking past the garage of the house I guess I punched it with all my strength. Mystery of the bloody knuckles solved.

Of course I couldn't remember any of this. But when he told me that a cop had stopped us and that I had a court date for a MUI and public intoxication, I thought he was just messing with me. I thought I would have remembered something like that. Until I reached into my pocket and pulled out a ticket. What a freaking night.

But I didn't think anything of it. I thought maybe I had some bad alcohol or because I hadn't eaten anything or something. So I kept drinking. And it kept happening. I needed to drink more in order to feel buzzed, yet I was still blacking out. Almost every weekend was a blur or some nonexistent action of my body with my mind gone.

My girlfriend broke up with me. She said she couldn't be with a guy who drank so much and made an ass out of himself and her. My friends started avoiding me. I would ask them if they wanted to do something, and they would I ask if I was going to drink. I usually said yes and they usually said no. And the truth was I didn't want to drink anymore. I couldn't remember if I had any fun, or if I met some cool people, or really anything.

I started talking to my friends and my ex about the things I did when I was drinking, just to get an idea of how I looked to other people. Then I spent a lot of time in my room, by myself, thinking about why I liked drinking so much and why I felt the need to drink to the point of blacking out. My mom was actually kind of helpful. I guess she used to drink a lot, that's probably where I got my first drink, but she had cut way back. It was really cool to think that other people were willing to share and help me if I asked.

So I think I want to stop drinking. In fact I know I want to stop drinking. Besides, pretty soon here they're going to put me on probation, and then I'll have to take tests every couple of days, and then I won't be able to drink. It's time anyway. I don't get the warm and numb feelings anymore, and it's just not fun. **I don't even know why I started drinking in the first place, even if I could remember my first drink.**

NOTES

PHASE II

HOW!

COMMITMENT TO CHANGE: Using the Tools for Change

Chapter Six:

Basic Communication Skills

GOALS OF THIS CHAPTER

- Review basic skills to communication
- Learn how to start conversations
- Practice the skills of active sharing and active listening
- Learn and practice assertive problem solving

CRYSTAL'S STORY

Life is not fair. I'm always getting into trouble for things I didn't even want to do, and when I try to explain myself...forget it. So this one time my friend and I were walking through the mall. We went into a Walgreens to get some candy when we decided to look at the make-up. So my friend started pulling some expensive make-up off the shelves, and with one glance around, she put it in her purse. I didn't really want to, but I ended up taking some lip gloss. I had a really bad feeling, but I figured she was probably right. The security guard stopped us and asked us to open our purses.

Needless to say, he pulled us into the security office and then began to call our parents. The guard didn't call the cops since he released us to our parents, but we weren't allowed back in that Walgreens forever. My mom was furious. She didn't talk to me the whole way home. When we got home, she sent me to my room to wait until my dad got home. And then the shit hit the fan. When I walked into the room, there was an eerie and dead silence. Calmly, almost too calmly for my tastes, my dad asked me why I took that make-up without paying for it. It was almost like something snapped in me....

And that was that. I guess eventually things got back to normal. Actually, I don't even know what normal is, or if it will ever be that way again. I just know that for some reason, I get into situations where I get into trouble when I don't even want to be there. And my parents, they never understand and they never will understand.

.....I was in a whirlwind of emotion and tears. Suddenly I yelled that they never spent any time with me and that I want so many things that I never get and that it wasn't fair that everyone else got to wear make-up and wear expensive clothes and get to drive their parents' car at fourteen and do whatever they wanted and I got stuck in a cage treated like a child. My mom stood up, and with a look that could kill a serviceman, called me an ungrateful brat and that I was grounded. I stomped up to my room and slammed the door.

SESSION 11: GIVE & TAKE WITH OTHERS

Objectives

- Review *Phase I* and *Developing Your Plan for Change*
- Review and discuss basic skills to communication
- Learn how to start conversations
- Practice how to give and receive compliments
- Learn and practice the skills of active listening and active sharing
- Share and receive feedback about a deeper part of yourself

Crystal's Story

My parents don't understand me. I don't think they'll ever understand me. I got in trouble for shoplifting, and all they did was yell at me. I tried telling them that they didn't pay enough attention to me, and that they don't give me the things I need to feel good about myself. But they got all upset and said I was blaming them for something that wasn't their fault. After all, I was the one who shoplifted.

It just seems like every time I try to talk with them we end up fighting. I try to tell them how I feel, but they get upset like I'm always blaming them. Or sometimes they try to tell me what they hear me saying. I know what I'm saying, and it's not like I blame them for everything, I'm just trying to get my point across. I don't think they listen to me...so I just don't listen to them.

The program so far

In the last session you were asked to make a decision about change. We spent some time covering the three phases of change, and then you were asked where you thought you were and where you wanted to go. We then had you complete your *Self-Portrait* in order to develop your personal *Plan for Change (PFC)*, which will be your goals and direction from this point on. Your *PFC* will change as you continue through this program because you will learn more about yourself and will develop improved ideas about how you wish to continue on your journey of self-discovery and change.

Many come to this program because they are court ordered or for some other reason, they have to be here. But you have all fulfilled the requirements for completing *Phase I* of *Pathways to Self-Discovery*. This means that you have made an active choice to learn and practice the *Tools for Change*. You have made a commitment to making change an important part of your life. In some ways the journey of self-discovery is similar to, though *much better than*, taking drugs. Understanding ourselves while gaining freedom and control over our lives is *extremely exciting* and you *feel different*—only this time in a very positive way.

> **You have made a commitment to making change an important part of your life.**

Activity: Thoughts About Change

Make a large circle in which everyone can see everyone else. Go around the circle and one by one **talk about** your **interests, desires, and concerns with change**. Some of you may still think that it isn't fair that you have to be in the program but most will agree that we have learned a great deal so far. Be genuine and tell everyone **what you think about being in the program** and it how it may or may not affect your life. Be sure to listen to each other, and when appropriate give some helpful feedback. Offer constructive advice about how that person may be able to achieve what they want from this program and life.

LET'S TALK: IMPROVING THE ART OF COMMUNICATION

In *Session 6* we took some time to learn about communication. After we discussed *verbal* and *non-verbal* communication, we took some more time to learn about the two sides to talking with someone: *self-disclosure (active sharing)* and *active listening*.

Active sharing, where we talk about ourselves to someone else, is a very important part of talking with another person. But *active listening* is just as important. After all, communication can't happen with just one person.

Active Sharing

Active sharing is when we share or talk about ourselves to another person. The sharing involves two skills that can help you communicate more easily.

The first skill is using the **"I" message**. This means talking about you, using four basic parts to talk about:
- I feel
- I need
- I think
- I do or I act

The purpose of using *"I"* when sharing with others is exactly that: we are *expressing ourselves* and not *talking down to, blaming,* or *talking about* the other person. This is not like bragging because you are *sharing something* about yourself. As shown in *Figure 9*, when we talk about ourselves we usually learn more about how we actually think and feel about important parts of our lives. *Most important* though, rather than saying things like, "You make me feel … or "You are so selfish… " we can improve our communication by taking *personal responsibility* for our thoughts, wants, needs, feelings and actions, instead of placing blame or making demands on others to take care of us.

The second skill when trying to actively share yourself with another is *being open to feedback from others*. Sometimes it's hard to hear what others have to say about us, but it is important to hear ourselves through their point of view. The important thing to keep in mind is to *not get defensive or angry*. People give you feedback on the basis that you have given them permission to tell you what they think. And although it's easy to get angry when we hear something negative, it is our responsibility to listen to what people are telling us and to *make our own decisions* (without becoming defensive or angry) about whether the information is true and helpful.

We always have *the options* of disagreeing with, or not believing, what is being said.

Activity: A Voice Of Blame

Crystal has a hard time talking with her parents. She thinks they are always repeating stuff to her without really listening to her point. How do you think Crystal could **improve communication** with her parents? How do you think she can better get her point across? What kind of **messages** does Crystal use when trying to talk with her parents? Does she use the **"I"** or **"you"** forms of communication?

Just as we tend to push away or *get defensive* (sometimes we *strike out* at the person who we think is being critical of us) about *negative feedback*, we often don't accept *positive feedback* either. We may push away the compliment because we might feel afraid of getting *too close* to someone, or sometimes we *don't think much of ourselves* so we think the compliment is a lie, or maybe we think the person is trying to *set us up* so they can get something from us.

Active Listening

Active listening is when we are on the other side of the conversation. That means we listen to what the other person is saying. There are *two key skills* in active listening:

· **Invite the person to share** by using open statements or questions such as "How are you?" or "Tell me about…" We don't want to use questions that can be answered with a "yes" or "no" answer because that does not tell us much about the other person.
· **Reflect back what you heard** the other person say: "I hear that you are saying you are upset."

It is important for us to keep an *open mind and channel* when actively listening. Our attitudes, beliefs, and feelings tend to influence everything we hear and see around us. But when we are actively listening, we set aside those influences so we can be open to the other person. It is helpful to remember to *not let our own thoughts interfere* with hearing what someone is trying to say.

When we discussed communication in *Session 6*, we also learned about *non-verbal talking, or body language*. In order to be a good listener, we need to pay attention to the body talk of the other person. Paying attention to the posture, facial expressions, tone of voice, personal space, and body movement of the other person can help us to better understand and learn about that person.

Most importantly, when we listen to another person, we should let the person know we *hear and understand* what they are saying. By making eye contact, nodding our head, reflecting back what we hear, and also actively sharing about ourselves, we let the other person know that we are listening to what they have to say.

Activity: Crystal's Listening Skills

Crystal says that her parents never listen to her when she talks to them about what she is thinking and feeling. But as we just discussed, listening works both ways. What can we say about how Crystal listens to her parents when they are talking to her? What evidence do we have that Crystal might be open to what her parents tell her?

The Gift Of Gab

Now that we know the two basic elements to a conversation, *active sharing* and *active listening*, it's time to practice starting a conversation. Interacting with other people can be difficult, especially if we *don't feel comfortable* or *haven't developed the skill* to start talking with another person. Often we use alcohol or drugs to loosen ourselves up so that we feel more comfortable with other people, but by using the substances we are really keeping ourselves away from other people. In order to feel comfortable talking with another person, we first have to learn the art of conversation.

Conversations do not have to be long or just about "important" topics. Sometimes just talking about the weather can be interesting to both people. When starting a conversation, it can be helpful to keep these things in mind.

· It's OK to talk about yourself.
· Listening to the other person is just as important as talking.
· Observe your situation and see if the people around you are interested in similar things.
· Use open-ended questions: questions that can be answered with a "yes" or "no" do not lead into talking.
· Communication and talking can be powerful, and it helps us to feel more connected to the world around us.

Activity: The Art Of Conversation

For this activity, you will need to separate into groups of three or more but no more than five people. Using the **conversation skills** we discussed above, ask each other **questions** about your life, families, hobbies, etc. Be sure to not use "yes" or "no" questions. As you listen to each   person talking, write down things that the whole group has in common. For example, a person may ask another about what they did today before coming to the program. While the person is answering, they may say something about a member of their family. If everyone in the group has a brother or sister, write it down. After a short while, get back into the larger group and share what your group found it had in common. The group with the most in-common things written down by the end of the activity wins.

Deeper Sharing: When Good Communication Skills Make A World Of Difference

Recall the *Johari Window* (*Figure 13*) that we learned about in *Chapter 5—Making a Commitment to Change*. We will now see how the communication skills that we have been learning and practicing are vital when we want to share important parts of our lives.

Activity: Sharing A Deeper Part Of Yourself

Move into a circle where you can see everyone. Your counselor will have a beanbag or a ball, and she/he will say one **honest and deep thing** about themselves, such as being concerned about a child's welfare or being scared about a parent dying. They will pass the bag to another person, any person within the circle. The next person will **give feedback** to the counselor, such as "I hear that you are afraid, and it's causing you to not do what you want to do." After giving feedback to the previous person, they will **then share** something important or meaningful about themselves. The bag will be passed again, and the next person will give feedback and then share. This will be repeated until **everyone in the group** has given feedback, shared, and gotten feedback.

Complimenting And Strengthening Others And Being Open To Hearing Praise

We have all been working hard in this group to develop the skills for *self-discovery and change*. Let's use the remainder of our time in this session to show our appreciation of all the good work we have been doing as individuals and as a team. *Giving and receiving compliments* are important parts of sharing and communication. It also helps us to see the positive things about ourselves. Here are a few tips for giving and receiving compliments:

· Be very specific about what you are complimenting a person for. For example, instead of saying, "Good job" you might offer, "I am impressed at how you have been helping the group to move in such positive directions through your upbeat attitude and helpful comments."
· Take time to listen to the praise.
· Do not deny the praise.
· Though you may not agree, tell how the compliment makes you feel good.

Just as receiving compliments is important in sharing ourselves, *giving compliments* is important in listening and sharing with other people. Everyone likes to hear something positive. Giving compliments is like giving feedback, except that we focus on the *positive aspects* about the other person. The most effective way to give a compliment is to know the person through listening to what they have to say.

Activity: It Takes One To Know One

By now we should know each other pretty well, so stand up and move around the room. Go up to each and every person in the group and **give them one compliment**. Make the compliment honest and sincere, and something specific that you truly think about the other person. Then allow the other person to compliment you. Remember and use what we just talked about in giving and receiving compliments. Listen to the compliment, do not deny it, and let the person know how it makes you feel. Make sure that you give at least one compliment to every person in the group—and be specific about what you are praising the person for.

Putting It Together

· Crystal gets into fights with her parents often. What are some of the problems that Crystal has with her *sharing* and *listening skills*, especially with her parents? How might she better communicate with her parents? Think of some specific examples or situations that will help Crystal be a better communicator.

· Think of some past conversations you have had. Were they good conversations? How did you start them? What did you learn from them?

· How can conversation help you change and develop?

· How did the deeper sharing and giving and receiving compliments bring you closer to some members of the group?

· When we each gave everyone compliments, what did you discover about what people appreciate about you?

SESSION 12: ASSERTIVE SKILLS DEVELOPMENT

Objectives

- Review *Session 11: Give and Take With Others*
- Discuss the four ways people deal with conflict
- Learn and practice the skills of being assertive

Crystal's Story

I couldn't believe it. My friend just took some expensive make-up and put it in her purse. I had a really bad feeling about it, and I said we shouldn't do it. But she just looked at me and asked if I was scared. I said no, I just didn't want to get caught or get anyone hurt. She said that no one gets hurt from shoplifting. The store absorbs the cost and we get what we want. So I stole, and we got caught.

When my mom came to pick me up, she was furious. She didn't say a thing to me until my father came home. And then everything snapped. I tried talking to them, but they got mad at me and called me a spoiled brat and grounded me. I went to my room and slammed the door. When they called me down to dinner, I ignored them. In the morning when it was time to go to school, I ran out the door without even talking to either of them. They deserve to be punished. They got the silent treatment for a long time after that.

Reviewing the art of conversation

Last session we discussed the basics of talking with another person. There are two people involved in a conversation: the *active sharer* and the *active listener*. Although conversations can happen in a group setting, the two roles will always be played by someone. We showed how by using *open questions* and *observing* what is going on around you, starting a conversation can be done without much effort. After looking closely at the characteristics of effective communication, we discussed how *active sharing* and *active listening* are especially important when talking about very personal experiences, even some that you hardly ever share with anyone.

Activity: Practicing Talking Skills

Break into pairs, and try to pair up with a person you haven't had much conversation with up to this point. Take some time to get to know each other and have a good conversation. Remember to ask each other **open-ended questions** and practice **active listening** when the other person is speaking. Also keep in mind the **"I" message** and being **open to feedback**. Try to have as in-depth conversation as you can in the time allotted. Then, after returning to the larger group, share what you learned about the other person during your conversation. What **did you learn** that you didn't know about the other person? What **did you share** about yourself?

MANAGING CONFLICT

Unfortunately, conversations cannot always be positive or easily done. Sometimes talking can be used as means to *try to convince us to* do something that is not good for us, or that we don't necessarily want to do. Sometimes people around us become overly aggressive; they may do or say things that don't seem right. An example is feeling pressured to get in a car with a drunk driver; or being pressured to have sex with someone; or if someone in your family is yelling or playing loud music when you are trying to study. In all of these situations, assertiveness is a skill that can protect us from harm or making bad situations worse. Most importantly, by being assertive, we maintain our self-respect and are confident that we are doing our best when it comes to managing conflict or disagreements with other people.

Before getting into what assertiveness means and how it can be helpful, we will first go over *three common ways* that people deal with problems or conflict which don't usually work. In fact, sometimes these ways can get us into more trouble than before.

Ineffective Styles For Dealing With Conflict

FLIGHT: Avoid the problem or be passive, usually giving in to what someone else wants at the expense of giving up our own rights.

For example, let's say you don't like people smoking in your car. By being *passive*, you would let another person smoke in your car anyway, just to avoid the disagreement or conflict. But by allowing the other person to smoke, you are *giving up your rights* to decide the rules of your car, and your car smells like smoke all over and the smoke gets into your clothes, which you don't like, and into your lungs which disgusts you even more.

FIGHT: We may strike out by attacking others verbally or even by using physical aggression. The *aggressive person* protects their rights, but gets what they want at the *expense* of another person. Others pay at the will of the aggressive person.

In the example above, the *aggressive person* is the one who insists on smoking in the car. All they care about is smoking, *despite the wishes, rights, and desires* of the owner of the car or the other passengers. If challenged, the *aggressive* smoker may strike out by shouting: "It is my right to smoke when and where I want and people who don't want me to smoke have no business offering to take me anywhere. In fact they should just stay away from me. Let me out!"

FAKE: This style is called "passive-aggressive". The person does not necessarily avoid all the problems, but they are indirect about getting what they want. Because the passive-aggressive person does not express his or her needs in a way that other people can respond to, nobody is completely satisfied in resolving the conflict.

Using the example above, the passive-aggressive smoker who is denied permission to smoke in the car might demand frequent emergency stops to the toilet (while everyone has to wait) so they can satisfy their smoking habit. Meanwhile, everyone including the smoker is held up an extra half hour because of the frequent stops… and everyone is upset when the ride is finally over. Another scenario might be that the passive-aggressive person agrees not to smoke in the car but says, "It wouldn't matter if I did because the car stinks anyway."

Activity: A Method Of Dealing

As a group take a look at Crystal's story. What method of **dealing with conflict** did she use with her friend? What method of dealing did she use with her parents? Were the methods different?

Which one worked out well for Crystal, if any of them? Why did Crystal use those methods? What **method do you use** in dealing with conflicts or problems? Give examples of how you might have used each style: **Flight, Fight or Fake** in dealing with conflict.

None of these ways get a positive result or meet the needs of the person in a healthy manner. In fact, these ways of dealing with conflict tend to drive others away. Because they feel *isolated or distanced* from others, some people lean on substance use and criminal actions in order to *satisfy unmet needs* for closeness, dealing with conflict or stress or even to gratify needs for power and control.

Activity: FLIGHT, FIGHT, FAKE

Break into groups of four. For this activity, you will need to **create a skit** that involves the three options described above for managing conflict, **flight, fight or fake**. Have one person **offer the situation**, such as setting fire to an abandoned building. The first person represents the **flight** method of dealing, which would be to quietly go along or leave without anyone knowing. The second person will be the **fight** method, which for our example would be to destroy the lighter/matches or attack the person suggesting the situation. The third person will be the **fake** method, who says that they would do it but the other people are so stupid that they would be sure to get caught. Perform your skit for the rest of the group and allow them to guess which response each person is playing.

Choosing The Healthy Option

FAIR: How do people deal with conflict in a positive manner? By learning how to be assertive or being **fair**. The assertive person stands up for their rights, but does not get something at the expense of another person. A lot of our problems come from the struggle of getting our needs met. Learning to be assertive can get your needs met but not by making other people suffer for it.

Assertiveness is something that doesn't have to be hard or complicated. Here are ten key ways to being assertive.

1) Recognize *your rights* in a situation without trespassing on the rights of others.

2) Know how to *clearly state your opinion* and what you want.

3) Consider the *needs of others* as you get your needs met.

4) *Be flexible and give*, yet still make your situation known.

5) *Avoid blaming*, or using "you."

6) State how *you think and feel* by using the "I" message.

7) Know *what you want*.

8) Become part of the *solution*.

9) Once you've made a decision, *stick with it*. Don't continually ask "what might have been."

10) Attack the *problem* and not the other person.

SESSION 12: ASSERTIVE SKILLS DEVELOPMENT

An assertive driver would insist on not smoking in their car, and calmly *state their reasons*. The person who is being assertive might suggest pulling over once during the hourlong trip or stopping somewhere so the smoker could have a break if they wanted to. Assertive people find solutions that *meet as many people's needs* as possible.

Activity: The Fair Response

As a group, discuss and decide on several different situations in which you might have to use one of the four responses. Then decide on a couple different assertive, or fair, responses to the situations at hand. For example the situation is **whether or not to get into the car** of someone who has been **drinking**. One possible assertive response might be "No thank you, I think I'll walk, because I don't want to be in danger of being involved in an alcohol related accident." Another assertive possibility might be "I don't think it's safe for you to be driving; I don't feel like visiting a hospital tonight; let's take a cab." Be careful that the responses you think of are assertive are not aggressive.

Suppose you are on probation and you go to your friend's house. In front of four other friends, s/he offers you a bag of weed so you can have some smoke and get some easy money. Discuss the different options of **Flight, Fight, Fake, Fair** in this situation.

Using *Worksheet 16, Pathways of Learning and Change* take an event that you recently experienced in which you used one of the three **ineffective** options for managing conflict. Then describe how the situation would improve if you were to use an **assertive** (fair) response.

Putting It Together

· Crystal uses more than one method in dealing with her conflicts. Which methods does she use? How does she use those methods in resolving her conflicts?

· Which of the ways to deal with conflict do you most often use? Give examples.

· Try to remember some past conflict you had. How could it have been resolved if you had been assertive?

· When looking at your thinking report, what happens when you use one of the three methods of dealing other than assertiveness?

· Take a look at your *Plan for Change*. Are there areas that you might need to work on as far as assertiveness is concerned?

· Review your *Self-Portrait* and *Plan for Change*. What will you work on this week? Share this with the group.

· Do you want to add to your *Plan for Change*?

PATHWAYS OF LEARNING & CHANGE

GOOD OUTCOME

BAD OUTCOME

POSITIVE BEHAVIOR

CHOICE

NEGATIVE BEHAVIOR

EMOTIONS

THOUGHTS

BELIEFS

EVENT

CRYSTAL'S STORY

Life is not fair. I'm always getting into trouble for things I didn't even want to do, and when I try to explain myself…forget it. No one listens to me anyway.

So this one time my friend and I were walking through the mall. She was looking for a specific shirt that she wanted to buy, so we were just browsing through the stores. We went into a Walgreens to get some candy when we decided to look at the make-up. My parents don't really like me wearing make-up because they think I am too young for it, but it's sometimes nice to just look and see what the new trends are. So my friend started pulling some expensive make-up off the shelves, and with one glance around, she put it in her purse.

This really kind of scared me. I told her maybe we shouldn't be doing that, and she looked at me and asked if I was scared. I said no I wasn't, even though I kind of was, and I said that I don't want to hurt anyone or get caught. She called me a chicken and said that if I didn't steal the make-up, I would never get to wear any. Besides, according to her, no one gets hurt in shoplifting. The company absorbs the cost and we get what we want.

I didn't really want to, but I ended up taking some lip-gloss and foundation and putting them in my purse. I had a really bad feeling about it, but I figured she was probably right. She's so much more mature than I am. We were walking out the door, and I thought we would actually get away with it, when the security guard stopped us and asked us to open our purses. Suddenly my heart dropped into my stomach and I thought I was going to get sick.

Needless to say, he pulled us into the security office and then began to call our parents. While we were waiting, my friend began to freak out and cry. She started saying it was all my fault, that if I hadn't slowed her down she wouldn't have gotten caught. Ha, some maturity. I reminded her that if it hadn't been for her stupid idea to shoplift we would have never done something that we could have gotten caught for.

Her dad and my mom came to pick us up from the mall. The guard didn't call the cops since he released us to our parents, but we aren't allowed back into that Walgreens forever. I've never been 86'd from a store before; it felt like some judge just descended a sentence of life on my head. And my mom was furious. She didn't talk to me the whole way home. When we got home, she sent me to my room to wait until my dad got home. And then the shit hit the fan.

When I walked into the room, there was an eerie and dead silence. The kind that reminds you of walking into an abandoned house that's supposed to be haunted and that flutters at the base of your heart like butterflies. Before one word was spoken, I was shaking in my shoes and getting goosebumps.

Calmly, almost too calmly for my tastes, my dad asked me why I took that make-up without paying for it. It was like something snapped in me, and immediately I said that they didn't let me wear make-up and the only chance I would have to wear it would be to take it from a store and keep it in my locker. My mom got a dead look on her face and said that it is not their fault I stole and that me not wearing make-up had nothing to do with this. By that time, though, I was in a whirlwind of emotion and tears. Suddenly I yelled that they never spend time with me and that I want so many things that I never get and that it wasn't fair that everyone else got to wear make-up and wear expensive clothes and get to drive their parent's car at fourteen and do whatever they wanted and I was stuck in a cage and treated like a child.

My father snapped. He started yelling that they fed me, clothed me, made sure a roof was over my head, and the thanks they get is a little girl yelling at them and blaming them for a stupid mistake she made of her own free will. I told them they didn't understand, they would never understand what I go through, and they never even try. I told them it's like they don't even love me. My mom stood up, and with a look that could kill a serviceman, called me an ungrateful brat and that I was grounded. I stomped up to my room and slammed the door.

And that was that. When I was called down to dinner, I ignored them. Slowly, I began to go around them, but not very often. And when I did, I didn't talk to them. I can't believe my mom called me a spoiled brat, and they deserved to be punished for yelling at me. I guess eventually things got back to normal. Actually, I don't even know what normal is, was, or if it will ever be that again. I just know that for some reason I get into situations where I get into trouble when I don't even want to be there. **And my parents, they never understand and they will never understand.**

NOTES

Chapter Seven:
Avoiding Trouble and Playing Fair

GOALS OF THIS CHAPTER
- Learn to recognize cravings and urges
- Discuss ways to control our desires
- Understand negotiation and compromise
- Learn skills to avoid and get out of high-risk situations

ANTHONY'S STORY

Living on my block is dangerous. And if you don't belong to a group, you're dead before you are old enough to move away. I was jumped in when I turned twelve, about two years ago. It was what you did and that is exactly what my best friend and I did.

And at that time, it was worth it. Because when we were done, we had a crew at our back. I started running stuff for the crew. And as I got older I began to feel the power of fear. Money and power and all the things I wouldn't have without a membership.

My best friend and I had a good life for once. About a month ago, my bro and I were walking down the street, minding our own business. I think we were gonna get ice cream or something, when suddenly there were screeching tires behind us and gunshots. Suddenly there was a tearing, fiery feeling in my leg and I fell. I heard my friend go down too, but it was different. I could hear a wheezing, breathless sound. I heard he died before he even left the ambulance.

So I'm about to leave the hospital now. I keep thinking I'll see my friend, and it never happens. Not many of the crew have been by. There was this gang counselor that kept coming to see me. But how do I say no? If I turn my back, I am all alone. And damn I want the power and money. The chance to be more than a nobody. Then I think about my friends. My mom's gotten a second job to move us, and maybe the counselor is right. If I have to make a life the hard way, it will be worth it knowing it was for him.

Objectives

- Review *Chapter 6: Basic Communication Skills*
- Learn how to avoid high-risk situations and things that are dangerous to you
- Develop how to deal with cravings and urges when you can't avoid trigger situations

Anthony's Story

I ended up in the hospital with a bullet in my leg. But I guess that isn't all that bad, because my best friend ended up dead. We were members of a gang that controlled our neighborhood, and at first it was great. All the money and cars. And more than that, the power and fear we had over people. It was incredible. This was the dream life coming from the place I did.

While sitting in my hospital bed, I used to think about all the fun I was missing out on. Breaking things, buying and stealing things, and knowing that everyone was afraid but me. But my best friend was dead. There was a gang counselor who always came in to talk to me about my involvement. He said that if there was a time to get out, it was now. And I guess he's right, my friend's memory deserves more than for me to end up dead, too. But sometimes I think of the life and the partying, and I want it so bad I can feel it in my chest. I just know it's time to get out, and talking to the counselor helps me a lot.

Looking back at assertiveness

In the last session, we discussed *assertiveness* and other ways to deal with conflict. Although there are *four ways* to deal with problems that arise in our lives, *being assertive* is the only way we can insure our needs are being met without interfering with someone else's needs.

In order to be assertive, we sometimes need to say no to the people we like and care about. That doesn't mean attack them or be mean to them, merely telling them no and why we feel the way we do.

Activity: Remembering As A Group

As a group **draw a chart** on the flip chart paper. You will have three high-risk situations down the left side, and the four methods along the top. For each situation, **fill out each top method**.

For example, being **offered marijuana** is the first situation. The first method is to be **passive**, then **aggressive**, then **passive-aggressive** and finally **assertive**.

Create **your own situations** and with your counselor fill in how to respond passively and then what the results are. Fill in for each method: **passive, aggressive, passive-aggressive, and assertive**. After filling the chart out, take a moment to look at the results. Which method seems to deal with each situation the best?

SITUATION	PASSIVE	AGGRESSIVE	PASSIVE AGGRESSIVE	ASSERTIVE
1. OFFERED WEED	"I really shouldn't but what the hell?"	"You've got some f---k'n nerve, I'm gonna flush it in the toilet, a--hole."	"I'd smoke it but your stuff always stinks anyway."	"I'm not interested and just being near this can put me in jail. So don't put me in this situation ever again. See you later."
RESULTS	*Caught with **dirty UA.***	*Fight breaks out.*	*Bad feelings all around*	*Feel good about self. Don't overreact. Keep friendship.*
2.				
3.				

Sometimes saying no is not the most difficult part. There are *high-risk situations* like being offered marijuana as in the example above that can pose real problems in relapse and recidivism. Situations are not the only difficulty we face in changing, though. Often *our thoughts* can cause us the most severe problems, and our thoughts are what cause *high-risk feelings* which we refer to as *cravings and urges*.

What Are Cravings And Urges?

A *craving* is the desire to *take a substance* or *participate in criminal activity*, and it is something that will be a part of your life. Although cravings are uncomfortable, they don't last all that long, and they are something that you can overcome.

But cravings don't usually stop at the desire. They begin to move into what we call *urges*. While *cravings are the mental desire* for something, *urges are the actual physical symptom*, like tension or stress, and sometimes even moving towards the thing desired. Let's say you want to smoke a joint because you are hanging out with old friends you used to smoke with. The event triggers the craving for the weed. The urge is when you can feel in your body the desire and you may even begin searching for someone who can supply you with a joint.

Activity: Anthony's Urges

Take a moment to look at Anthony's story. Do you think he has a **craving** for his previous life, or do you think it has moved into an **urge**? What is some of the **evidence** in the story that points to one or the other? Can you think of any cravings or urges you have had recently?

Cravings may be *triggered by events* around you, such as hanging out with old friends or a stressful situation, and then they trigger the physical urge. The urge then may trigger memories and psychological symptoms, such as feeling good, enjoying something you want, and having fun when you are high. Urges happen pretty quickly and then drop off, but the best way to prevent an urge is to **stop the craving**.

Activity: Everyday Urges

As a group, go around and discuss a **craving or urge** you have had in the past week. What was the situation or the thoughts that caused you to crave something? Did the craving become an urge? Were you able to stop it, and how? If you weren't, why not? How would you better deal with it next time?

Things That Can Trigger Cravings And Urges

There are certain common, *high-risk situations* that often *trigger or cause cravings*, which may lead to *urges and relapse*. Below is a list of some common triggers for *relapse to drugs* and returning to *criminal activities*.
· Being around substances.
· Feeling like your life situation is changed, such as getting out of a correctional placement.
· Seeing other people using and being invited to join in.
· Being with people who use or are involved with crime.
· Certain emotions, including tiredness, stress, anger, frustration, and excitement (like when we want to celebrate).

Activity: Anthony's Triggers And Support

As a group, go around and discuss a craving or urge you have had in the past week. What was the situation or the thoughts that caused you to crave something? Did the craving become an urge? Were you able to stop it, and how? If you weren't, why not? How would you better deal with it next time?

WAYS TO DEAL

Although the situations above are something that can happen every day, there are four primary ways to stop the cravings and avoid the situation.

1) ***Sharing with*** family, friends, or someone you trust about the craving, and asking for their support.

2) ***"Toughing it out"*** and getting control of the craving by bearing with the discomfort. It will go away, trust us. Here's how you can tough it out.

- *Notice* how you experience the craving. What are your *thoughts and feelings* about the craving? *Where* does it occur in your body?
- Is it still a *craving* or has it become an *urge*? Remember, urges are when your *physical body* begins to feel it and you take actions to fulfill the craving, such as searching out a friend who can smoke you up.

3) **Talk yourself down.** When the craving becomes an urge, *focus on your body* where you feel the urge. *Talk to yourself*, and *take control* of your actions figuring out alternative ways to feel comfortable.

4) Practice **"urge surfacing"** -- ride out the wave and you can relax at the shore.

5) **Find another activity** that will distract you from the craving or urge.

> ***Control over thoughts leads to freedom and strength.***

Activity: What Triggers Us?

As a group, think of several different **real life situations** or events that will trigger you to have a craving or an urge. Share these **triggers** with each other. Are the triggers the same or different for different people? Now think of different ways that you might **avoid the events** or situations that can cause a craving or an urge. If it is not always possible to avoid these situations, what are some of the **positive things** that you can do to cope with urges and cravings?

Complete *Worksheet 17, Dealing With Cravings*. This is an important task. The plan you make for this exercise will help you to deal with cravings and urges for a long time to come.

Mind Over Matter

Remember at the beginning of the program, when we talked about how substance use and getting into trouble are usually done on impulse? Well, the same idea works with cravings and urges. Usually the *craving occurs* and we are already *on the move* to *fulfill the urge* before we realize what we are doing. Through *self-talk*, we can begin to *control our impulses*.

When trying to talk yourself out of an urge, it is helpful to *remind yourself* of the *bad things* that have happened because of using or committing crimes. Then start *thinking of the good things* that come out of *being clean*, like being able to do what you want or go where you want. The most important part of dealing with cravings and urges is to remember to *stop and think* about *what you have to lose* by using *substances* or committing *crimes*. Keep your *positive goals* in front of you as your guide.

DEALING WITH CRAVINGS

Make up a plan to deal with an episode of craving. Pick two or three of the strategies in class and detail how you would use them when you feel tempted to lapse.

1. List your craving to urge.

_____

_____

_____

_____

2. What activities would you choose to distract you?

_____

_____

_____

_____

3. Who might you call for help?

_____

_____

_____

_____

3. What mental skills did you use? THOUGHT STOPPING? SHIFTING THE VIEW?

_____

_____

_____

_____

Activity: The Role Of Mind

Break into smaller groups of about three people. Create a **skit** in which one person has a **craving and an urge**. The others either try to **convince or stop** (without any physical contact) the person from fulfilling the urge or craving. The first person has to either **decide to participate** in the negative behavior or **refuse**, depending on the strength of the arguments.

Returning to the story of Anthony. How **might he control** his cravings to return to his life as a gang member? What would Anthony have to lose by returning to the gang? Now fill out *Worksheet 18, Loss of Joys and Pleasures* and think through what it would mean to you if you gave in to some of your cravings and urges.

Putting It Together

- While in the hospital, Anthony has *cravings and urges* to be back in the gang. What are his cravings, and what are his urges? What is the difference between cravings and urges?

- How does Anthony *deal* with his urges?

- Think of one specific situation in which you had a *craving that became an urge*. How did that situation affect you? What was the outcome? How could have the outcome been different?

- When you aren't able to avoid the situations, *how can you deal* with the urges? Which of the four ways works best for you?

- Take a moment to look at your *autobiography*. How have *cravings and urges* influenced you in the past? Do you think you can control them?

- Use *Worksheet 19, Pathways to Learning and Change*, to describe how you would use "thought stopping" and "self-talk" skills to prevent a high-risk event from leading to a craving and urge for drugs and crime.

Worksheet 18

LOSS OF JOYS AND PLEASURES

What are your joys and pleasures and would you lose them if you committed another crime or relapse back into full AOD use?

List ten pleasures and joys that you have in your life. Make these your top pleasures and joys.	Would you lose them if you reoffended or relapsed?	
	yes	no

PATHWAYS OF LEARNING & CHANGE

Complete this picture. Take an event that you recently experienced. Then note your automatic thoughts that came from that event. Then note your feelings and beliefs. What was your behavior? Fill in the rest of the squares. What might happen if you decide to change your thoughts and beliefs?

GOOD OUTCOME

BAD OUTCOME

POSITIVE BEHAVIOR

CHOICE

NEGATIVE BEHAVIOR

EMOTIONS

THOUGHTS

BELIEFS

EVENT

SESSION 14: HOW TO BARGAIN & WHEN TO SAY "NO"

Objectives

- Review *Session 13: Managing Cravings and Urges*
- Learn the process of negotiation for a fair deal
- Review important information from *Chapter 4* on *Relapse And Recidivism Prevention*
- Learn and practice *Refusal Skills* to deal with high-risk situations

Anthony's Story

I realize now that I don't really want to be in the gang anymore. I guess having expensive clothes and power isn't really worth my life. I know it wasn't worth my friend's life. But it's so hard to remember that. I think about having to get a job, or not being able to afford any new things for a while, and I start thinking maybe I could be part of the gang but not be involved in the violence. Then again, how can I be part of something that is violent without being part of the violence itself?

My mom has gotten a second job to move us out of the neighborhood. I guess that is probably a good idea. I'm not sure how I'll be able to say no to the crew when all I really want is to be part of the power. I want to be the one feared, not the one who is afraid. But I want my best friend's death to mean something, even if it's just getting me out of the situation. It's going to be a hard struggle, but I guess in the end it will be worth it.

Up to this point: cravings and urges

Last session we spent some time discussing *cravings and urges*. While cravings are the *mental event*, usually because we are in certain situations, *the urge* is the physical symptom, like tension, and the *movement towards the negative action*, such as drug use or committing a crime.

After going over certain events that may begin the chain of fulfilling cravings and urges, we went over several different methods that may help us to avoid the relapse or return to criminal conduct: 1) *sharing with family or friends*; 2) *toughing it out*; 3) *talking yourself down*; 4) *find another activity*. Which of the four do you think is most effective for you? Why? Often, all four methods are useful.

Activity: The Right To Avoid

As a group, think of a **situation** that is really **hard to avoid**. Spend some time thinking of a situation that you are likely to find yourself in that might create a craving or urge. After a review of the **four different** ways to avoid relapse/recidivism, decide **which one(s) are best** for the situation that the group decided on and why. What makes that way better than the others? How effective would the others be for the same situation? Spend some time talking and debating about how to **avoid relapse and re-offending**. Notice that not everyone will agree on the same method, each person is different with their own ways of dealing with things.

Now that we know about how to manage *cravings and urges*, it is time for us to push forward into the actual skills that will help you *avoid the situations* that may trigger these thoughts and feelings.

First we will go over another *lifeline to freedom* and strength, **"negotiation skills,"** because although not all situations are high-risk, most situations can become high-risk when we begin to *have a conflict* with others and *fail to settle our differences* in a fair and honest manner.

We know that *not all situations are negotiable*, however, and that is why after reviewing the skills that we learned to *prevent relapse and recidivism* we will also be learning another powerful tool known as **"refusal skills."** These are specifically designed for situations where there simply is *no room for bargaining*. Actually, even entering into a discussion about how you might come over to the *side of temptation* might only weaken your resolve and increase the likelihood of relapse or re-offending.

DEALING WITH CONFLICT

Ever get into an argument with a parent or teacher because they are *asking you to do something you don't want*, or they *aren't giving you something that you want*? Conflict between people is unavoidable. Everybody sees the world differently (*Principle 2 of Session 3*), and often everyone has their own agenda built around their opinions. As we have discussed earlier, opinions are neither right nor wrong, so how do we work with people in a way that everyone is satisfied? This is called *negotiation*. It's when a deal is struck between people so that we are confident that the solution is fair and everyone's needs are being met. We call this a **win-win** situation. One person doesn't have to be "right" and the other "wrong" -- both come out feeling good.

But negotiation is a difficult goal to reach. Sometimes people don't want to negotiate, there is too much involved, or they view the situation as non-negotiable. In order to know when it is okay to negotiate, and how to negotiate without stepping on someone's toes or moving into their personal space, we need to learn the *negotiation skills*.

Negotiation—A Win-Win Solution To Conflict

Negotiation, which is the *ability to discuss and compromise* in order for the people involved to get what they want, is a way for all of us to *resolve conflict* and be happier in our lives. In order to do that, we first need to learn the different skills involved in negotiation.

Let's say we want our parents to help us buy a car. There are some steps to follow in order to negotiate successfully:
· **Ask**--the first step is to ask if they would be willing to help buy a car.
· **Find out why**--if the answer is "no," then the next step is to ask why they won't. Make sure to listen and hear the reasons the other person is offering for not giving you what you want.
· **Repeat the reason**--"So the reason you don't want to help me buy the car is…" Let the other person know that you have heard them and can see where they are coming from.
· **Compromise**--it is this step that makes negotiation possible. Offer the other person something they may want, or suggest a middle ground. For example, we offer to pay half of the car, and work off the part the parents are putting up. In a **win-win** situation, everybody wins.

Activity: A Skit Of Success

Break into pairs or groups of three. For this activity, you will need to come up with a situation in which **compromise and negotiation** are the main theme. After you have written and practiced the situation, perform for the larger group. Did your negotiations seem realistic? **What steps** did you use? Do you think the situation was resolved to the **benefit of everyone**, or do you think that something wasn't fulfilled in the negotiations?

Dealing With Money

Most of us are interested in *having money* to get some things that we want. Sometimes we *rely on our parents or friends* to help us out, especially if we are not working or are earning too little when the need arises. We all know that "people get funny about money."

Negotiation to get what we want is only possible if the *other person is sure that we will do our part* as well. This is where some difficulty can come in. What happens if we offer to pay back the money put up, but *our word is no good* for the other person because of past mistakes? Here are three skills that will make compromise a little more realistic.

· **Pay your debts**--If our parent has a problem lending us money because of past debts, then we might say "how about I set up a payment plan with you?" If you *pay off your previous debts*, it is easier for people to compromise.

· **Use collateral**--Offer to set up a situation that *benefits the other person* and gives them a reason to trust you. An example is "if I don't make my payments to you, then you can take away the car."

· **Give references**--Offer people who will *back up your word* and give their reputation for your sake. If our mom doesn't believe we will pay back the money, we may want to use our father as a reference. It is important to *not use* someone as a reference without consent.

Activity: A List Of Negotiations

Take a moment to write down a list of **things you want**. Write between 2-3 things you would like to have, but things that you must negotiate with another person for. Next to the items on your list, write down **who would be able to give it** to you. For example, one item that you feel you should be able to negotiate for is a new pair of shoes. The person to negotiate with is your parent. Take some time and think of **ways to negotiate** with that person for the item you want. Share with the group a few things on your list. Are you able to negotiate for everything you want? How does **compromise** play into your negotiations? Will you have to use a reference or collateral in your negotiations? Can you realistically negotiate for everything you want?

Life does not always make it easy to sit down with someone in order to negotiate. Most of us do not own corporations or have boardrooms in order to isolate and focus on the negotiation. So what do we do if the person we are trying to negotiate with is upset, busy, or too distracted to hold a discussion?

· **Offer to help.** If we offer to *help a person in a difficult situation*, the other person will likely be more open to helping us in our situation.
· **Ask to talk later.** Sometimes the time is not right to ask for certain things. *By asking to talk later*, we are able to set up a meeting time in which both people will be more able to focus.

- **Wait for a better time.** Instead of trying to set up a meeting, sometimes it is *better to just wait*. If your mom is busy with the baby, it is better to just wait until the baby is put down for a nap and your mom has time to relax.
- **Ask someone else.** Most of our problems and needs can be met by more than just one person. If the person you are trying to negotiate with is too upset or distracted, it may be better to *ask another person*.

Activity: Distracted Compromise

As a group, make a list of situations that may make it **difficult to compromise**. Write at least three situations, and then go back through the list and **offer suggestions** for how the compromise and negotiation may be **successfully** completed. Make sure to have an open discussion and try to come up with as **many solutions** to the difficulties as possible. The outcome we want is that both sides are winners.

Informed Negotiation

Negotiating for what we want is often like a debate. There is a lot of back and forth before both people reach a compromise that will satisfy both. One of the *worst things* that can happen when in negotiation is *to not be informed*. Learn and know about what you want and how you intend to get it before putting it on the table. Going back to our example, if we didn't have any idea of where we would get the money or how we would pay back our parents, the likelihood of them compromising with us is unlikely. But, if we approach them with what we want, how much it will cost, and what we are willing to do for it, in realistic terms, than compromise is more likely.

Of course, information flows both ways. If the other *person is vague* about what they want from the situation or why they don't want to compromise, *ask them for more* information. It's not a good idea to get demanding or angry, but ask them if they can help you understand *their point of view* and why they don't want to agree. Remember our communication skills. When you are trying to get more information, use the "*active listening*" skills (p. 44) and *really listen* to what they have to say before offering feedback. Active listening leads to **win-win** outcomes.

Of course, some areas are *non-negotiable*, especially areas where another person's rights are being infringed upon. The best thing for you to *know is when to quit*. Some things are not meant to be, and then there are always other things you can negotiate for.

Activity: A Bag Of Negotiation Skills

Form a large circle with your group. Your counselor will have a bean bag or ball that will be passed between the group. Your counselor will toss the ball to a person in the circle, and that person will begin by **saying something they want**. The group will then ask the person who they will **negotiate with** in order to get that. After every answer, the group will ask **more questions** or offer difficulties that may arise in the negotiations.

For example, we want a new car. We will negotiate with our mom. What if she is too busy to talk with us? We can **offer to help** her while we try to talk with her, or we can ask her if she will **talk with us later**. What if she says no? Offer some **collateral** or a **compromise** that will help her as well as get us the car, like we will drive our younger sibling to and from school. What if she asks how much it's going to cost? We will have done some research first, and we will offer her how much it will cost and a plan on how to pay for it. After the person with the ball has **successfully avoided** all problems the group can think of for the negotiations, the ball will be passed to **someone else** in the group and the new person will tell the group of something they want and who they will negotiate with. Continue doing this until everyone in the group has practiced the negotiation skills.

One area that is *completely non-negotiable is any situation that brings you into contact with criminal activities or substance use.* It is important and beneficial for us to know how to negotiate with other people in order to smoothly move through most conflicts, but when in a high-risk situation where you are being tempted or urged to do something you know you shouldn't, negotiation is not applicable. That is when refusal skills come into play.

REVIEW OF RELAPSE AND RECIDIVISM PREVENTION

In *Chapter 4, Sessions 8-9*, we learned about *high-risk situations* and how to spot when relapse or recidivism may occur. Here are some important terms to remember from those sessions.

High-risk situations are the situations that have *led to substance use or criminal behavior* in the past. When in these situations we may think or feel that we need the substance or be involved in negative behavior.

High-risk thinking has to do with the *thought habits* (remember, the automatic thoughts) that lead to using substances or criminal activity. This also includes the thoughts that may put us in high-risk situations for use and trouble.

Relapse starts happening when you engage in *high-risk thinking* or situations that have led to use in the past. It doesn't start with the actual action, but with the thought habits leading up to the action.

Recidivism starts when you involve yourself in the thinking or *thought habits that lead to criminal* behavior. It also happens when you take part in actions or put yourself in high-risk situations.

Activity: Anthony's Slide

Anthony discusses in his story the struggle he has with the thought of not being part of the gang anymore. Do you think he is participating in any of the above? Is he able to avoid any of the above? How? How might he successfully change, despite his thinking and urges?

Remember that relapse and recidivism do not start with the action, but *begin way before* that in the thoughts of our mind.

> *When we control our thoughts, we control our feelings and actions and vastly reduce our chances of relapse or recidivism.*

WHEN AND HOW TO SAY "NO"

We know that not all situations are avoidable. Things happen *outside of our control*, but we are the ones who have control over our own actions and decisions. As with everything we want and like to do, *being able to refuse* taking part of substances and criminal behavior *begins with practice*. This also requires you to be aware of the high-risk thinking and situations you can become involved in.

Here are some keys to using refusal skills.

- **Saying "NO"** without hesitation and in a firm, clear voice.
- **Looking at the person directly** and not avoiding their eyes; this lets them know that you do not want to participate.
- **DO NOT feel guilty** for refusing. You won't hurt anyone's feelings by refusing but you will hurt yourself by accepting.
- **Choose to take part in something different:** take a ride; go to a movie, etc.
- Ask the person to stop asking or putting pressure on you. A friend will understand and give you room.
- **Let the person know** what you have to lose by accepting.
- **Don't debate** with the person. After saying "no" change the subject. If you debate the subject, it means you are persuadable and debating with yourself.
- **Don't make excuses.** Excuses mean you won't now, but you might later.

Activity: Anthony's Refusal

It seems like Anthony **doesn't really want to** change. Why does he want to get out of the gang, and why doesn't he? Could any of the above **refusal skills** help him if his friends ever confront him? Why or why not? How might Anthony be successful in refusing?

Activity: The Role Of Refusal

In groups of three or four, create two skits in which a person has to **refuse their friend's offer** of **something that is bad** for them, for example: two people want to take some acid and go watch a movie. The third person has to refuse the offer of acid without rejecting their friends. In order to do that, the third person may say, "No, I'm still on probation and if I get caught I will have to go to jail. We can all go to the movies straight, though."

In the first skit, the refusal person **will not use the refusal skills** above and end up doing what they were trying to say no to. In the second skit, have the refusal person use the skills above to **successfully refuse** without being aggressive or angering the friends.

Knowing The Situation

Learning the skills of refusal also means that *you know when to use* the refusal skills. In order to do that, we have to understand in what situations our weakness lies, and then figure out how to control our own actions.

Activity: My Own Difficult Situation

Take some time to fill out *Worksheet 20, List of High-Risk - Difficult Refusal Situations* to **identify the situations** you think may cause you **problems with refusing**. Then mark whether the situation fits in **refusing substances** or **criminal behavior**. Then get into groups of two or three to discuss ways that you **can refuse** in the situations that will be hardest for you. Put some effort into it, because the more comfortable you are with them here means the more comfortable you will be with them in a real situation.

Putting It Together

- After reviewing the *negotiation skills*, do you think you negotiate well? How do you compromise with people like your parents and friends? Can you work for **win-win** outcomes?

- Anthony had a hard time deciding if he wanted to change. What *signs of recidivism* did Anthony exhibit? How might Anthony *avoid returning* to the gang and his life of crime?

- In order to use the refusal skills, we first must know that we are in a high-risk situation. How might you become aware that it is a high-risk situation?

- What refusal skills might work best for you?

- Think about how hard it may be for you to *say no* to a friend. Think about how you might do that without hurting them or yourself?

- Review *Figure 12, Relapse/Recidivism Model*. How can it be helpful to you to avoid relapsing or re-offending?

- Review your *Self-Portrait* and *Plan for Change*. What will you work on this week?

- Do you want to add something to your *Plan for Change*.

LIST OF HIGH-RISK -- DIFFICULT REFUSAL SITUATIONS

List all situations. Then check if they apply to AOD use, criminal conduct or both. These situations are both high-risk to relapsing into AOD use or going back to criminal conduct. They are also difficult situations to say "NO" in.

HIGH-RISK -- DIFFICULT TO REFUSE SITUATION	FITS AOD USE AND ABUSE	FITS CRIMINAL CONDUCT

ANTHONY'S STORY

Living on my block is dangerous. And if you don't belong to a group, you are dead before you are old enough to move away. Of course, if you do belong, you are dead before you can legally drink.

I was jumped in when I turned twelve, about two years ago. There was no debate, or any pro and con talk in my head about joining. It was what you did, and that is exactly what my best friend and I did. But you have to understand; it seems like the best life to live coming from where we come from. Man, we saw those guys growing up, and they always had money and clothes and Gee'd-up cars. It's true we would hear about kids dying and gunshots and shit, but what does that matter when those guys had brand new clothes all the time and we were wearing hand-me-downs that would be rejected from the Salvation Army.

So when we were twelve, we got jumped into the gang that ran our block. I hear different stories about different gangs doin' different things to get a person in. I even hear about girls having sex with all the members. It was nothing like that, we just had to take on a couple of guys and get bloodied up. And at the time it was worth it. Because when we were done, we had a crew at our back. No matter what went down, we knew they would be there.

I started off running stuff for the crew. Just deliveries and breakin' shit every once in awhile. But as I got older and proved my loyalty, I started getting more jobs and more inside knowledge. I guess we had this big thing with a neighboring gang. Territory wars and shit. All I know is that sometimes things would get heavy. But I never worried, I had a couple hundred people who would step up for me because I was part of a crew. I never worried about no cops, or any rival gang doing nothing, cause we were a force to be reckoned with. I could walk by the school and throw rocks and break all the windows, and nothing would get done about it cause people were afraid. And as I got older I began to feel the power of fear. I was never afraid, but everyone was afraid of my friends, so that meant I had power and they didn't. Money and power and all the things I wouldn't have without a membership.

My best friend and I had a good life for once. And just because we were part of a crew didn't mean we weren't a pair no more. I knew this kid from way back before I could remember. We wore pampers together. We knew where we were from and where we were, and that's all that matters. Although the gang had us doing different shit. He wasn't much for chaos and destruction, he had smarts. So they had him training for some business shit. I don't know, I was the one who broke stuff.

About a month or so ago, my bro and I were walking down the street, minding our own business. I think we was gonna get some ice cream or something, when suddenly there were screeching tires behind us and gunshots. Suddenly there was a tearing, fiery feeling in my leg and I fell. I couldn't stand, I couldn't move, I had never felt so much pain in my life. I heard my friend go down too, but it was different. I could hear a wheezing, breathless sound. I crawled over to him, he was face down, and I tried to turn him over. They had shot him in the back a couple of times, and I think one got his lung, cause it sounded like he was breathing through his back. I tried to stop the blood as a bunch of people swarmed around us. I couldn't talk or look at any of 'em; I only saw my friend and so much blood. When the ambulance got there, they separated us cause they were gonna take him flight for life to some better hospital than the General. I heard he died before he even left the ambulance.

So I'm about to leave the hospital now. They kept me here for so long cause I guess the bullet pierced some major vein in my leg. They were worried it would hemorrhage if I moved too early. I've also had some depression. I keep thinking I'll see my friend, and it never happens. I dream about him a lot. Not many of the crew have been by. They are weird about any cop involvement, so I've been alone most of the time. There was this gang counselor that kept coming to see me. In fact, he was here just this morning. Kept talking about how he knew where I was coming from, about how he had been there, and about how it was time to get out. But how do I say no? All that money, all those clothes and women. And more than that, the power and protection. If I turn my back, I am alone. If I want to break a window, the cops will be all over me. And damn I want the power and money. The chance to be more than a nobody. I want it so bad I can feel it in my chest and bones. The memories of the parties and the life are more real to me than the bullet in my leg.

Then I think about my friend. And all the friends that have been lost along the way for some higher purpose of one person that most of us don't even know. My mom's gotten a second job to move us, and maybe the counselor is right. If now is not the time to get out, then I will die in. And I think my friend's memory deserves more than for me to go back into what killed him. **If I have to make a life the hard way, it will be worth it knowing it was for him.**

NOTES

Chapter Eight:
Responsibility to Others and the Community

GOALS OF THIS CHAPTER
- Define value, moral, and community norms
- Understand your own set of values and morals
- Discuss moral dilemmas and how they help us change
- Learn about empathy and its role in interaction with people

HUNTER'S STORY

People are too weak. And if you let them, they will feed off of you. Pretty soon here I will be old enough to drive, and that is going to suck. People I don't even know are gonna start mooching off me, bumming around so I can be their little servant. Nothing but a bunch of bums. And bums are the scum of society. Why can't they get a job? My mom used to give the bums downtown money. She wouldn't buy me candy, but she always gave them money. My dad used to get mad at her. My dad says they are like alley cats. But my mom's gone now, left after crying. Said she couldn't live with my father anymore. Whatever, we're better off without her.

So one day a friend and I were walking around downtown. Friends are just moochers, so we became space fillers to each other. I was thinking about throwing some rocks at the stupid musician bums when I ran into this girl.

I was going to say something rude when I looked at her. But then I couldn't. There was something so soft and weird about her eyes. So I said hi. She said hi back. So I sat down with her on the steps of some building. She said she was looking for a job and some money. Then she told me about how her dad got cancer. And then he lost his job and now they live in their car. I couldn't believe it. She was a bum. I really didn't know what to do. I know I'm not supposed to feed them. That just keeps them from getting a real job. But this was different....I couldn't stand the thought of her hungry. So I bought her a couple of hot dogs. I really didn't feel like talking to her after that. She is still a bum. Why did I feed her?

Objectives

- Review *Chapter 7: Avoiding Trouble and Playing Fair*
- Learn pro-social values
- Understand your own set of values and morals, including your ideas of morality
- Discuss what you see as the morals and rules of the society around you

Hunter's Story

People are weak, and if you let them, they will feed off of you. Like parasites. And bums are the absolute scum of society. Dirty, filthy, mooching little parasitic mites that beg for my hard-earned cash. I can't even drive yet, but I have a job. Why can't they get a job?

My mom used to give the bums downtown her change. She wouldn't buy me a piece of candy, but she would give them change with tears in her eyes. My dad would get mad at her. Said she was encouraging them and keeping them from getting off their lazy asses and becoming a part of decent society. Dad says they're like alley cats. You feed one of them and the next day there are twenty at your doorstep.

How to bargain

In *Session 14*, we discussed and learned about negotiation skills and refusal skills. Conflict often comes up when we are dealing with other people, especially when wants and needs are involved. Since everyone has a different opinion, and opinions are neither right nor wrong, sometimes it is difficult to get what we want from the people around us. That is when negotiation comes into play. Once we have learned to negotiate and compromise, it is easier to work with people towards a common goal.

Activity: Means Of Negotiation

Take a moment to review the **negotiation skills** for **win-win** outcomes that we covered in *Session 14, How to Bargain and When to Say No*. Go through a **thinking report** (*situation, thoughts and beliefs, feelings and actions*) and see if there were any cases where you negotiated, or if there were any situations that negotiation would have worked for. Break into pairs or groups of three and share with your group members the situations in your thinking report that would have either, **1)** been more successful with negotiation, **2)** successfully used negotiation, or **3)** did not successfully use negotiation. Then discuss with each other how each situation could have been more successfully resolved, to arrive at a **win-win** solution.

There are, however, situations in which *negotiation skills* are not useful or would actually do more harm. High-risk situations, or situations that put us at risk for recidivism or relapse, are situations where we should not use negotiation. Rather, refusal and avoidance are better suited for dealing with these situations in order to keep us from doing something we don't want to do.

Activity: Steps Of Refusal

As a large group, make a list of the **refusal skills** covered in the last session. Think of situations in the last month that required refusal skills. Which of the refusal skills did you use, and how successful were you at avoiding relapse/recidivism? If the skill was not successful, what possible options do you have for next time? Review your *Self-Portrait* score on **Criminal Conduct**. If it was high, this session is very important to you.

MAKING PERSONAL CHOICES ABOUT RIGHT OR WRONG

Our personal choices about what is worth bargaining for, what is worth living (or dying) for and what should unquestionably be rejected or refused, depend on our personal values or goals, what we think is right or wrong, and if we think certain actions can get us in trouble with those in authority. Before we move into this session on *taking personal responsibility for our actions*, we are going to define certain ideas and words that we will be using.

· *Values:* These are things that we see as *worthwhile*, or that mean a lot to us. These become *guiding principles* of our life. An example of this may be *loyalty* to friends and family. Another might be to have a *comfortable life*.

· *Personal Morals:* This is what we see as *right or wrong* in relation to human behavior or action. An example of a moral is whether or not harming or killing another human is right or wrong.

· *Community Norms or Standard of Conduct:* These are *rules or guidelines* that we live by. This is about the right or wrong of our conduct in relation to the *community and society* that we live in. Robbery or vandalism falls within these lines. In other words, common norms refer to the actions that are *valued* by our community such as safe driving as well as those that will be *punished*, such as driving under the influence of drugs or alcohol.

· *Pro-social:* Thinking and acting in such a way that we take part in and build positive family, community, and social relationships.

Activity: Hunter's Values

Break into smaller groups and take a look at Hunter's story. What **values** do you think Hunter is exhibiting? What sort of **morals** does Hunter have, and how do they agree with pro-social thinking, if at all? What are some of the values you share with Hunter?

Activity: My Own Values

Take a moment to look at *Worksheet 21*. In the first column, from the list of values shown below, write-in **five of your values**, ordering them from most to least important. Be sure to include some of the things that are most important to you and some that are least important. They could be love, friendship, family, or any number of things that you place high, medium or low values as to their importance in your life.

Sometimes you might live up to your values, and sometimes you might not. Just place a check in **"no," "sometimes,"** or **"yes"** according to whether you think you are living up to your values or

Worksheet 21

VALUES, MORALS AND NORMS

List of Your 5 Most Important Values	Do You Follow These Values?		
	No	Sometimes	Always

List of Your 5 Most Important Morals	Do You Follow These Values?		
	No	Sometimes	Always

List of Your 5 Most Important Community & Society Standards	Do You Follow These Values?		
	No	Sometimes	Always

not. Then, as a group, make a list of some **common values** that are held by the majority of the group. What values are common in the group? Which values do the group follow, and which values do the majority of the group not follow?

THINGS THAT PEOPLE VALUE

Comfortable life	Equality	Exciting life
Family security	Freedom	Happiness
Inner harmony	Mature love	National security
Pleasure	Salvation	Self-Respect
Sense of accomplishment	Social recognition	True friendship
Wisdom	World of beauty	World of peace

THE VALUES OF THE PROGRAM

In the beginning we started this program with the idea that thoughts cause and interact with feelings and actions. We also discussed that the very basis of our thoughts begins with our beliefs and attitudes. During the process of this program we have not necessarily tried to teach you any particular morals or values. Yet, throughout our program we have been trying to give you some very important ideas that have something to do with values and morals.

· *Change:* We have talked about and taught you the value of change. The skills you have been learning are meant to help you value and understand change.

· *Freedom and control:* A lot of the skills we have been trying to teach you have the end goal of gaining freedom and control over your life.

· *Building positive relationships with others and your community.* We have mentioned this once or twice before, but this essentially means being pro-social (which is the opposite of being criminal or antisocial).

· *Concern for Others.* Although left unstated, this is a clear goal of this program.

Activity: Hunter's Values

Take a look at the last two values of the program (positive relationships and concern for others), and then compare that with Hunter's story. How does Hunter show the last two values, or does he? Would it be possible for Hunter to learn to accept the last two values, and why or why not?

Activity: My Morals

Take some time to fill out the part of *Worksheet 20* that covers *Looking at Your Moral Beliefs*. List **five morals** that are important to you and that you feel you would like to live by, e.g., *do not harm others, respect people's property, be faithful, no sex before marriage, keep your word*. Then check whether you live up to each of those morals using no, sometimes, and yes. If you have any questions about what a moral is, look at the definition above or ask your counselor. Which morals do you follow, and which morals do you tend not pay to attention to?

Activity: Standards Of Conduct

Use *Worksheet 21* to list **five basic norms or standards of conduct** that your society lives by, e.g., *don't steal, no drugs or alcohol*. For this activity, you can get into small groups if you would like. Then check whether you don't, sometimes, or do live by those societal norms. Which societal norms do you agree with, and which societal norms do you think are pointless? Why?

The Dilemma Of Values

Sometimes a conflict can occur between our values and our morals. This can happen when what we value goes against what our personal morals are or even the societal norms of the community. An example of this may be that one of your values is loyalty, which means you are very loyal to your friends. But what if your friend wants you to break into a house. The value of loyalty to your friend is now coming into conflict with your moral against breaking and entering or even the community moral of upholding the law. Can you be loyal to your friends and at the same time, be a responsible citizen? Can you achieve a **win-win** situation?

It doesn't have to be that complicated, though. It could be a value of expensive clothing or cars, or wanting a lot of money, in conflict with the moral of not stealing. For some people, our values can compete and come into conflict with our morals on a regular basis.

Activity: Competing Minds

Take a moment to look at *Worksheet 21*. Do any of the values you listed go against or conflict with the morals or the basic societal norms you listed? If a value conflicts with a moral or norm (community standard of conduct), then put the number of the value next to the norm it conflicted with listed on your worksheets. Then as a group get together and discuss some of the values that conflict with the morals and norms. Write these down and then discuss why they conflict, and how you can possibly deal with each so they don't conflict or there aren't any problems arising from the conflict.

Where Do Values And Morals Come From?

So now that we have talked about values, morals, and standards of conduct (which are the rules and expectations of society), we are going to take a moment to look at how our values and morals develop.

Although television and other forms of media have some influence on how we develop, the values we usually get from those media are related to the standard of conduct for the society around us. It is important for us to remember that what we see on television is meant to entertain, they are not to be rules of living.

So where do we get our *values and morals*? Usually the *people closest to us*, such as our parents or family members, are the ones who teach us our values and morals. We may even get them from our neighbors, friends, and the people we see every day, but more often than not they come from the people closest to us and that are around us all the time.

But our values are not always positive or healthy. Because of the influence of others on our values and morals, negative things can develop within our belief system. Sometimes our beliefs and values can cause harm to other people and ourselves. In order to avoid harming those around you and your community, thinking about and becoming aware of your values and morals can help you to be more aware of what some of your core beliefs are; and then you—and only you—can decide if they should change.

Activity: The Growth Of A Value

Break into groups and begin discussing Hunter's story. Who do you think **Hunter got his values from**? Why do you think that? Are Hunter's values a positive influence in his life, or do you think his values will cause him problems? Why? Would it be possible for Hunter to change his values in his current environment? Are his values helping him to become a responsible citizen?

Activity: The Belief Of Me

Get into pairs and review *Worksheet 1*. Use a **real situation** and fill in the blanks about the **positive and negative results** of choices. How could the results affect the choice you will make next time? Spend some time discussing how you would change your **thinking** to arrive at a more positive outcome.

For this activity, the room will be separated into two parts, with one side representing agree and the other side representing disagree. The far side of each part will be the strongest you can feel, and the closer to the middle, the less absolute your belief is. The counselor will then begin to read off beliefs, and you will go to each side of the room that represents how you feel about the issue. For example, the phrase is that the color black means depression or death and shouldn't be worn. Depending on how you believe about the issue, you will move to the area of the room you think represents your stance. Then one at a time you will say one to two sentences on why you take a certain stance on a value.

AGREE			**DISAGREE**		
Strongly Agree	Middle Zone	Slightly Agree	Slightly Disagree	Middle Zone	Strongly Disagree

Do our values and morals help us to reach win-win outcomes? Does the community gain from our values and morals?

Putting It Together

- Hunter shows some really strong values, but are his values positive or negative? What do you think Hunter's morals are?

- Our morals and values are taught to us by the people closest to us. Where did Hunter get his values? Where do you think Hunter should have gotten his values? Why?

- Values and morals are the basis of our belief systems. What values do you hold about the world around you? What morals do you have?

- Take a moment to look at your worksheets. Who do you share your values with? What values and morals do you have in common with your parents or people closest to you?

- What values and morals do you have that are different than the people closest to you?

- Do any of your values and morals show up in your autobiography, and which ones are they? How do they affect your choices?

- Review *Self-Portrait* and *Plan for Change*. What did you work on last week? What will you work on this week?

SESSION 16: UNDERSTANDING & PRACTICING EMPATHY

Objectives

- Review *Session 15: Understanding Values and Moral Development*
- Continue looking at morality and values
- Understand the difference between sympathy and empathy
- Learn to consider the position of other people—learn empathy

Hunter's Story

One day when my space filler and I (that's what I call this guy I hang out with because neither of us want friends—friends only want things) were walking around downtown when I ran into this girl. My "friend" told her to watch out, and I was just about to say something rude to her when I looked into her eyes. There was something soft and weird about her eyes. It gives me the willies thinking about how her eyes made me feel. So I asked her if she wanted to walk with us. She said no she wanted to sit, so I sat on some steps of a building with her. I could see that she was poor, but I didn't know how poor.

She began telling me that she lived in a car with her family. I guess her father had gotten cancer and they didn't have the insurance to cover the medical bills when he got better. And then he got fired for missing so many days when he was sick. She was looking for a job or for money, but she kept talking about how hungry she was. I felt bad for her, I really did. But I also know that feeding bums encourages them, and she was a bum, no matter how good-looking she was. But I bought her a couple hot dogs, enough to feed her family too. I can't let anyone I know go hungry. But then I left, I didn't want to be around her anymore. I won't feed bums anymore, and I can't believe I did it that once. I'm kinda confused.

Our last session

Last session we began to define and discuss values, morals, and standards of conduct. **Values**, which are a little like opinions but stronger, are our guidelines to life and the ideas that we hold close. An example of this may be loyalty to a friend. **Personal morals** are rules we give ourselves concerning the right or wrong of human action. One moral may be the feeling that it is wrong to let another person starve. Both morals and values are things that we personally hold close and follow in our belief systems. Often our values and morals are developed and run along similar lines as family members, parents, or people who are close to us.

Activity: Accepting Other People's Values

As a group, think of a **value** or **moral** that is common in everyday life. Then separate into two groups according to those who **agree** with the value and those who **disagree** with the value. Sit with the two groups in a line facing each other. One-by-one, those who agree **will share** why they think that. The person across from them will then say they why they disagree.

An example of a value for this activity would be placing great importance on doing what it takes to get a **really expensive, fancy car**. One person who agrees might say, "You need it to get respect." A person who disagrees might say, "It doesn't make you cool." Continue going back and forth until everyone has spoken once. Listen to the other people and their reasons for agreeing or disagreeing. Can you see their point of view?

Standards of conduct, also known as **community norms**, are the things that the society and group of people around us believe and collectively follow as right or wrong behavior. Similar to values and morals, our parents and family do have a role in passing to us the community norms, but the law also impresses community norms upon us.

Common Values

Values and community norms, or standards of conduct, differ across countries, cultures, and ethnic groups. Yet all laws in all nations have one value and norm in common: *the safety and welfare of people and the concern for people*. This concern for others, what we call **empathy**, is basic to most communities and cultures. Empathy is one of the most important values we can learn in order to change our actions and behaviors because once we begin considering other people's attitudes, feelings, and views of the world, it becomes easier to make positive choices about how to think, feel and act. Empathy is the basis for **win-win** outcomes.

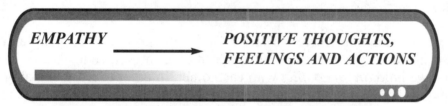

EMPATHY → *POSITIVE THOUGHTS, FEELINGS AND ACTIONS*

Difference In Sympathy And Empathy

We often hear *sympathy* used in common language. Sympathy, however, is not what we are talking about in this session because sympathy and empathy are different. When we have sympathy for another person, we may:
· Feel sorry for that person, or pity them
· Have compassion or caring for another person
· Sense another person's hurt or pain

But empathy takes one more step past sympathy in our caring for others. While sympathy *cares*, or *feels sorry for* another person, empathy means *actually being able to understand and to see from that person's point of view*. Empathy is a deeper experience and a deeper emotion than sympathy because we are putting ourselves in the other person's situation. When we have empathy for another person, we can:

· Take the other person's position
· Relate to or know another person's feelings, motives, ideals, or situation
· Feel concern for another person
· Feel another person's pain and suffering, because we are able to put ourselves in the place of the other person—meaning we can "walk in their shoes."
· "I understand your pain in my heart and head."

Activity: Hunter's Feelings

As a group, take a look at Hunter's story, and then discuss whether you think Hunter felt **sympathy or empathy** for the girl. What is the difference between the two? Use some examples from the story to back up your opinion on whether it was sympathy or empathy. Can members of a group feel sympathy or empathy for Hunter? What are some differences between feeling sympathy or empathy for Hunter?

Activity: A Walk In Someone Else's Shoes

Worksheet 22, Practicing Empathy has four stories telling about something that happened to another person. Carefully read each story and then **put yourself in the place of that person**. Close your eyes if you need to, and really try to think and feel what the other person in the story is going through in their situation. Then write in the second column what your feelings and thoughts were after you put yourself in that person's place. Then get together as a group and discuss the thoughts and feelings that each of you had. Were you able to visualize and feel what was going on?

A Moral Dilemma

A *moral dilemma* is a situation where our *ideas clash* with those of other people, when a value or moral we hold is in *conflict with a rule* that is placed on us by someone else, or when two or more *beliefs* that we hold *are in conflict* with each other. In order to learn empathy, we must change our thinking. But in order to change our thinking, we often have to come in contact with a moral dilemma. So how do we recognize a moral dilemma?

Activity: A Dilemma For Hunter

When Hunter meets the girl and begins to speak with her, he begins to face a **moral dilemma**. What was Hunter's moral dilemma? How did he resolve his dilemma? How did Hunter change from the dilemma, if at all? What do you think could have been done differently on Hunter's part in order to change?

Activity: The Search For A Dilemma

Break into groups of three to four people while your counselor hands out pages of newspaper. With your group, try to find at least one moral dilemma in the newspaper. Then fill out *Worksheet 23,* about the situation or article your group found. After you have filled out your worksheet, join the rest of the larger group. Elect a person to speak for the group, and then one at a time, share and discuss the moral dilemma your group has found. Discuss why you think it is a **moral dilemma**, and then go around the group sharing what you would feel in that dilemma and what you would do if you were in that situation.

Putting It Together

· Hunter feels sorry for the girl he meets downtown, but is he exhibiting *sympathy or empathy*? Why?

· How does Hunter's *moral dilemma* change him, if at all? How would you have dealt with the situation, and what would you have done differently?

- Take a moment to look at your autobiography. Were there any moments in your life that fit as a moral dilemma? What did you do in those circumstances?

- When looking at some of the conflicts you have had recently, how would have empathy helped solve the conflict to the advantage of both people?

- Often in negotiation, empathy helps us to see where the other person is coming from. Think of a situation in which you have negotiated, and think about how empathy might have helped in arriving at a fair solution.

- How does empathy help us reach a win-win outcome?

- Review your *Self-Portrait* and *Plan for Change*. Do you need to change your ratings on your *Self-Portrait*? Do you need to add to your *Plan for Change*?

Worksheet 22

PRACTICING FEELING EMPATHY FOR ANOTHER PERSON

Carefully read each brief story. Then close your eyes and put yourself in the place of the person in the story. How does the person feel? What is the person thinking? Then write the thoughts and feelings that you had when you put yourself in the place of the other person.

Below are four stories. Each story is about a particular individual who has experienced something of great importance in his or her life. Read each story carefully.	Put yourself in the place of the person in the story. Then write down what you think the other person was thinking and feeling.
John is 9 years old. He was hit by a drunk driver and was in the hospital for two months. He lost his right leg in the accident. He loved baseball, was a very good player, and was feeling a great deal of sadness because he knew he would never play baseball again.	
Marie, who is 35 years old, struggled all of her life to make a living and support her family of four children. Her husband was killed just after the youngest was born. She works as a cook at a high school. Her oldest son is very smart and will be finishing high school this year. He wants to be a doctor, but Marie knows she does not and never will have the money to send him to college. The other day, her son came home and told her that he received a full four-year scholarship to attend college.	
Hank, age 22, a construction worker, was leaving work when a robber hit him on the head and stole his car. The robber then drove over Hank when getting away. Hank has been in the hospital for two months. He has severe spinal injuries and will have to be in rehab for many months, and he may never walk again.	
Pete, who is 17, has been alcohol and drug-free for the past year. He was out with some friends and they bet him $20 that he couldn't do six shots of tequila in 10 minutes. He did it, then got in his car, started to drive to his girlfriend's, and critically injured 3 children. The judge gave him 5 years for his third D.W.I..	

Worksheet 23

MORAL DILEMMA

Find a newspaper article that presents a moral dilemma to the people involved.

1. Describe the situation.

_____

_____

_____

_____

2. Who was the central character in the event?

_____

_____

_____

_____

3. Why do you believe this is a moral dilemma?

_____

_____

_____

_____

3. What should have been done in the situation?

_____

_____

_____

_____

People are too weak. And if you let them they will feed off of you. Like parasites. Most people do not even deserve to live, if you ask me.

Pretty soon I will be old enough to drive, and that is going to suck. I mean, I'll be able to go where I want without needing anyone else to get me there. Not that I ever ask my dad for a ride anywhere, he always says that's what legs are for. But I wouldn't want to ask him even if he did give me rides, cause I can do everything on my own and when I can't then I don't do it. But being able to drive is going to suck because everyone is going to come around and ask me for rides. People I don't even know are gonna start mooching off me, bumming around so I can be their little servant.

Nothing but a bunch of bums. And bums are the absolute scum of society. dirty, filthy, mooching little parasitical mites that hang around and beg for my hard-earned cash. I can't even drive yet but I have a job. Why can't they get a job?

My mom used to give the bums downtown money. She would look at them with tears in her eyes and a sickening look on her face and she would give them money. She wouldn't buy me a piece of candy, but she would always give them money. My dad used to get mad at her. He said she was encouraging them and keeping them from getting off their lazy asses and becoming a part of decent society. My dad says they are all like alley cats. You feed on of them and the next day you have twenty on your doorstep. But my mom's gone now, left after crying and telling me she had no other choice. Said something like she couldn't live with my father anymore. Whatever, we're better of without her.

So one day a friend and I were walking around downtown. I guess you can't even call us friends. We are, um, space fillers to each other. Friends are just moochers, and neither of us wanted friends, so we became space fillers to each other. Ya know, whenever I'm bored I'll go downtown and eventually I'll run into him and we'll walk around. Usually kicking or spitting at the bums or making fun of the suits. Just wasting time. After all, that's what like is...just moments to waste and time to spend while waiting for the ultimate, and happily satisfying day of death. That's what my dad always said when my mom asked him how his day was. What a stupid question, "how was your day, dear?" People are idiots.

Anyway, back to downtown. I was thinking about throwing some rocks at the stupid musician bums, which are a little cleaner than the average bum but still nasty insects, when I ran into this girl. She said sorry, and my space filler said "well you should be," and I was going to say something rude when I looked at her. But then I couldn't. There was something so soft and weird about her eyes. I get the willies just thinking about how I felt when I looked at her.

So I said hi. She said hi back. I asked her if she wanted to walk with us. She said no she would rather sit down. So I sat down with her on one of the steps of some building. My "friend" said he was gonna keep walking and he'd catch up with me later. I could tell by looking at her she was really poor. But I didn't know how poor.

I asked her what she was doing downtown. She said she was looking for a job or some money. The she told me about how her dad got cancer, and how they didn't have insurance so they weren't able to pay the hospital bills when he got better. And then he lost his job cause he missed so many days from being sick, and now they all live in their car. I couldn't believe it. She was a bum. A good-looking and clean bum, but still a bum.

That's not to say I didn't feel bad for her. I really did feel sorry for her. It would suck to lose everything, all you toys and Play Station and CDs, cause you had to pawn them for food. I really didn't know what to do. I liked her, and she was nice, and I know that it's hard when your dad nearly dies from cancer, but what was I supposed to do? I know I'm not supposed to feed them. That just keeps them from getting a real job. But I don't even let my space filler of a friend go hungry. We both work and usually get something to eat from the vendors as we're kicking and spitting together. Sometimes I pay, sometimes he does. But this was different. I didn't want to encourage bumming, but I couldn't stand the thought of her hungry.

So I bought her a couple of hot dogs. And then I went home. I didn't really feel like talking to her after that. After all, she is still a bum, no matter how it happens that she ended up there. But I also fed her. Why did I feed her? And gave her enough for her family, even. As long as I don't have to see her again, everything will be fine. I definitely won't make it a habit of feeding bums, even the clean, young ones. **It's survival of the fittest, and bums are just parasites that need to be taken out of society in order for society to be the strongest and most evolved form it can be.**

Chapter Nine:
Zeroing in on Negative Thinking

GOALS OF THIS CHAPTER
- Learn what negative thought patterns are and how they can control our actions
- Discuss how to change and control our negative thoughts
- Understand about the "entitlement trap"
- Learn how to control our thoughts and actions

GAVIN'S STORY

I hate school. I hate it so much. I've always had a hard time at school. I can't focus. I can't listen to the teacher. More often than not I just sit and stare out the window. All adults hate me. So I got suspended this one time over nothing. I knew it was trouble as soon as I walked into school. The advisor, he came up to me with this look on his face. I was just talking with my friends. And he told me I better watch it. Lunch was coming up, and then I could go to the one class I like. Art.

It was really cool feeling the paint and the canvas and trying to create something. My mom got mad that I had paint all over my clothes. That wasn't fun. I'm always in trouble. At lunch I got in a fight. I was messing around and stole this kid's chips. I never have money cause we're poor, so why shouldn't I have his? Don't I deserve chips too? But then this big kid got all up in my face. I told him to mind his own business. He told me I was nothing but a stupid punk. So I punched him in the face. He's just a stupid jerk.

Class had just gotten started when the advisor came in. I knew he was there for me. That man hunts me down sometimes, like some hunter who stalks an innocent deer. I almost got in a fight just waiting for my mom. So I was suspended. Which didn't matter, cause that meant I didn't have to go to school for a couple of days. My mom was mad, but it doesn't matter because she is always mad. And I go sit in my room, watching TV, or reading comic books. Yeah, school sucks.

SESSION 17: RECOGNIZING & CHANGING NEGATIVE THOUGHTS

Objectives

- Review *Chapter 8: Responsibility to Others and the Community*
- Recognize negative thought patterns
- Realize how negative thought patterns contribute to problem behaviors
- Learn to control negative thought patterns and replace them with positive thoughts

Gavin's Story

I knew I was going to be in trouble as soon as I walked into school. All adults hate me, but the advisor really hates me. He's always got it out for me. As soon as I saw him walking towards me, I knew he was going to say I was in trouble for something. But I was just talking to my friends, which isn't against any law or anything, so I asked him what the hell he wanted. He wasn't very nice.

I hate going to school. Not just because all adults hate me, especially the advisor. I just can't focus. Really, I'm stupid. So I let my mind wander and then the teacher calls on me and I don't know the answer. She's so mean when she does that cause she knows I'm stupid. It makes me really angry, so I talk back and she sends me to the advisor. Not that it matters, cause he usually hunts me down for something anyway. Yeah, school sucks.

How are values and morals formed?

In *Chapter 8* we began to discuss the ideas of *values and morals* and their importance in our dealings with the world. Included in the idea of how we deal with the world is the idea of *empathy*. While *sympathy* means pitying or understand another person's feelings and situations, *empathy* takes the idea one step further so we actually can *think and feel like the person*, to "walk in their shoes."

Up to this point we have talked about how attitudes and thoughts affect our feelings and actions, but in the last chapter *(Chapter 8: Responsibility to Others)* we began to touch upon an even deeper part of our personality, our ideas or beliefs about *what we think is important in life* (**values**) and our personal *sense of right and wrong* (**morals**). They influence our thoughts and attitudes, and in turn, largely influence our feelings and actions. We looked at how our values and morals can lead to **win-win** outcomes for ourselves and our community,

Activity: All My Neighbors

Arrange the chairs of the group in a circle, but **leave one out** so there is one too few for the entire group to sit down. A volunteer or the counselor will stand in the middle and make a statement, such as "All my neighbors who like cartoons." Everyone who likes cartoons will stand up and move to another chair, but not the one right next to them. While they are moving, the person in the middle is trying to get into a chair, leaving a different person without a chair to sit in. That person will then make a statement, the group will rearrange, and then a new person will be in the middle.

Notice how, although the values are different for different people, there are often a number of people who have the same value in common. At the end of this exercise discuss how our values are formed.

Our values and morals are usually formed as a result of the *situations* we find ourselves in, and the *people* we meet, when we are children. Sometimes the values and morals that we learned when we were younger are simply not in our best interest and may even have led us to hurt others. Can you think of a value or moral that you would like to change so that you can have better outcomes?

An important way we *change a value or moral*, is by being presented with a *dilemma* (an internal conflict), which puts the value or moral to the test: "Do I want to hold onto this idea of what is right or important?" It is usually *empathy for another person* that brings about the dilemmas in our morals and values. An example might be holding the belief that it's o.k. to steal if you can get away with it and then realizing that someone just stole your mom's brand new CD player.

When we see something from another person's point of view, we understand things from a different (less self-centered) perspective—outside of the narrow space of our personal values and morals. The fuller view of the world can allow us to become aware of what our values really are, or if we want to change some of them, and whether they are positive or negative.

THE IMPACT OF NEGATIVE THINKING

Negative thinking can influence us to *betray our own values and morals*. For example, if someone thinks "life sucks," then trying to gain *self-respect* or finding *mature love* or even living by the moral principle of being honest, doesn't hold much meaning. Sometimes negative thinking is so deeply a part of us that it forms the basis of our values, morals and beliefs about the world. For example, a negative belief like "life is about being hurt or hurting others," could easily result in having such distorted views as "it's good to take advantage of people" and "it is not wrong to take whatever you can get."

In either case, *negative views affect our immediate thoughts* in most situations. Negative thinking often becomes a roadblock to changing our actions for the better, and the difficult thing with negative thinking is we often don't see it. Similar to our values and morals, negative thinking can become so ingrained in us that we don't see it until we are aware and in control.

> ### *NEGATIVE THINKING BETRAYS OUR VALUES AND MORALS AND CAUSES NEGATIVE OUTCOMES*

How to Recognize Negative Thoughts

The way we think controls how we feel and act, but we have power over the way we think. We can control our thoughts and influence ourselves to make the right decisions. But first we have to learn how to be aware when we are having negative thoughts.

Distortions in what we think about and how we see the world around us represent negative thinking. Here are five types of negative thoughts that can adversely affect us:

1) **Expecting the worst**
   This is when we *expect something negative* from everything around us, or sometimes we always count on bad results. "I know it won't work out, it never does."

2) **Self put-downs**
   This is when we think the *problem is within us*, and we constantly remind ourselves that. "I am no good."

3) **Jumping to conclusions**
   We automatically assume that *bad things will happen* when we don't have proof that they will. "I know he's going to hate me."

4) **Self-blame**
   Assuming that everything that happens is *our fault*. "I deserve it."

5) **Negative View of the world**
   When we assume that the world is just a *horrible* place. "The world sucks."

Activity: Gavin's Thoughts

Let's look at Gavin's story for a minute. **What thoughts does Gavin have that are negative?** How do they fit into the categories above? Does his story have elements of all the errors in thinking or just a few? Why do you think Gavin has those errors in thinking? What errors in thinking do you think you participate in the most?

Activity: Seeing Our Thoughts

Take some time to individually fill out *Worksheet 24, Negative Thoughts and Thinking Errors*, using **Column 1** to list **negative thoughts** that you have regularly and **Column 2** to label these thoughts according to the **list of errors** above or the list of errors in *Session 5* of *Chapter 2* (*Worksheet 3, Errors in Thinking Checklist*). After you have completed your worksheet, compare your results with those of one of your neighbors. How are they similar? How are they different? Do you share some of the same errors with Gavin?

Cycle Of Negativity

Let's take a moment to return all the way back to the beginning of the program. In *Session 2* we talked about how our attitudes, thoughts, and beliefs affect our actions. We then took a step further to show how our thoughts and feelings affect the actions that we choose. But we also talked about how our actions can affect our thoughts and feelings. We mention this again because it's an important part of *negative thinking* and how it affects our decisions.

Take an event or situation, such as an adult yelling at us. This event triggers a negative thought in our head, such as "the world sucks" or "I'm getting screwed," and that in turn affects our feelings and behavior. We may get angry and strike out against the adult. Each situation or event that occurs goes through our thoughts before we feel or act out anything about the situation.

Worksheet 24

NEGATIVE THOUGHTS & THINKING ERRORS

LIST OF NEGATIVE THOUGHTS	WHAT KIND OF ERRORS IN THINKING

Activity: Gavin's Actions

Take another look at Gavin's story. How are his actions, thoughts, and feelings interacting with each other? How do his thoughts affect his feelings and then the actions Gavin chooses? How do his feelings affect his thoughts about other people?

You are in Control

By recognizing this cycle of negativity, we have a chance to take control and have freedom over the events and situations that occur to us. Since our thoughts are in our mind, we have the ability to control or change them when they occur. As we discussed in earlier sessions, we have the freedom and the choice in every decision we make, including what we think and say to ourselves.

Activity: The Choice Of Negative Thought

Use **Worksheet 25, Negative Thoughts That Lead to AOD Abuse and Criminal Conduct**, to list the negative thoughts that you may have had that led to abusing substances or participating in criminal activities. Is there a pattern in your negative thoughts? Do you use the same thoughts more often then others?

But as we said before, you are in control of your thoughts. There are three ways you can control and change your negative thinking:

1) **Thought stopping:**
   Allow yourself to think a negative thought. Then **STOP** the thought right away. Be aware of the thought, but *tell yourself to stop the thought*. At first, just choose one negative thought ("The world sucks."). Every time that thought happens, *be aware that you are thinking it and then stop it.*

2) **Positive thought planting:**
   Instead of just stopping the thought every time a negative one occurs, try *replacing it with a positive thought*. Every time you are thinking "the world sucks," replace the thought with something positive about the world, such as "I can choose the way I live my life from now on."

3) **Self-talk:**
   When you become aware of a negative thought, or start thinking negative thoughts, talk to yourself about why you are having the thought, and *what you can do to change that thought.*

The idea behind *thought planting* is to stop the process in the thought, and change where it is going to end. When an event occurs, be *aware* of the negative thought that is going through your mind and *replace it* with something more positive. That in turn will change how you feel and the action you will take.

Arsenal Of Thoughts

Although it may be possible to think of positive thoughts on the spur of the moment, it is helpful to arm yourself with some *positive thoughts ready* for when a negative thought occurs. This way we don't have to struggle as much trying to replace our thoughts. Here are some suggestions:

Worksheet 25

NEGATIVE THOUGHTS THAT LEAD TO AOD USE & CRIMINAL CONDUCT

NEGATIVE THOUGHTS THAT LEAD TO AOD USE	NEGATIVE THOUGHTS THAT LEAD TO CRIMINAL CONDUCT

· **Remembering good things:** What are the good things in life, *the things you do well, and the people you care about* are *always* helpful thoughts.

· **Statements of hope:** Instead of self-blaming or put-downs, *use positive thoughts about yourself*. "I am strong enough to do this."

· **Self-rewards:** When you have done something well, tell yourself that. *Reward yourself for your decision-making and positive thinking.* "It was hard, but I did a really good job at coping."

The important point we are trying to make is to *talk positively to yourself*. Self-talk, or hearing our voice in our head can be very helpful in being aware of our negative thoughts and being able to *change or replace* them with more positive ones.

> ***POSITIVE SELF-TALK HELPS US TO MANAGE
> OUR FEELINGS AND ACTIONS***

Activity: Arsenal For Control

Your counselor will have some flip-chart paper up on the wall. Separate the paper into three columns, with the **first column for negative thoughts**, the **second for replacement thoughts**, and **third for the results**. As a group think of several different negative thoughts that occur throughout the day. Try to make these thoughts as close to your real thoughts as you feel comfortable. After you have listed the negative thoughts, try to think of some replacement thoughts and list them in the second column. These thoughts should be realistic as well. Then discuss how the replacement thoughts may influence decisions and actions taken from that point. Write that down in the results section. How might **thought replacement be helpful for you**?

Putting It Together

· Gavin shows some errors in his thinking and some negative thoughts. What do you think are his negative belief systems? Why do you think those belief systems are negative? Which one does he use most often, and how can you tell (use evidence from the story)?

· How do Gavin's thoughts and feelings affect how he acts?

· How do negative thoughts lead to negative outcomes?

· Do a Thinking Report (event, thought, feeling, action) when your negative thinking is involved. How can this be changed?

· Of the five categories of negative thoughts, which do you think you use most often?

· Which of the three ways to stop or target negative thoughts do you think will be most effective for you? Why?

· Review your *Plan for Change*. Would you like to add *"Changing Negative Thoughts"*?

Objectives

- Review *Session 17: Recognizing and Changing Negative Thoughts*
- Understand how negative thought habits can cause negative action choices and stop us from change
- Learn to recognize distorted thinking patterns and how to change them
- Understand and change the "entitlement trap"

Gavin's Story

Like I told my mom, it wasn't my fault I got into trouble. The man hates me, and no matter what I did I was still going to get suspended. Just like I can't help that I'm stupid. The more I try to pay attention, the harder it is for me to focus. And the teacher should know that.

Of course, my mom asked me about my fight. The one where I took some kid's chips and his big ol' ape of a friend came after me. But I was right in that fight. It was none of the jerk's business, and besides I never get chips. We're poor so I can never buy those things at lunch, but don't I deserve to have snacks too? The kid's parents are rich; they can afford to get him more. The f--ker had no business calling me a punk, and he deserved to get punched in the nose.

Review of negative thoughts

In *Session 17, Recognizing and Changing Negative Thought*, we spent some time talking about negative thoughts and how they can make us feel bad or choose negative actions. These thoughts can happen automatically, and it is *only when we are aware* that we are having a negative thought that we can take control.

We covered several different ways that we can stop and control our negative thoughts. Although we are not able to always avoid situations or events in our life, we can be aware of the thoughts that occur. By controlling our thoughts, we can help ourselves make better decisions and feel better about our life. We also discussed errors in thinking, which we also covered earlier in *Phase I*, which can cause negative thoughts.

Activity: How I Control Negative Thinking

Break into pairs or groups of three and think of situations that have happened in the past week that involved **negative thoughts**. Be honest and share with each other what these situations were. Did you use any of the methods (**thought stopping, thought replacement, or self-talk**) when a negative thought occurred? If you did, how did the method helped you to change the negative thought and the situation? If you didn't, how might have one of the methods changed the outcome of the situation?

But errors in thinking do not just cause negative thoughts. They can also be roadblocks in our desire to change. By falling into these errors in thinking, we cause ourselves to stop the change and fall back into old habits. Now, review how you rated yourself on *Criminal Thinking* in your *Self-Portrait*; on *Thinking and Feeling Patterns*. Rate yourself on these. Did the ratings change?

ERRORS IN THINKING:
THOUGHT HABITS THAT PREVENT US FROM DOING WELL

Thought habits, the *automatic thoughts* that happen in a situation, can *often have errors* in them that stop us from changing and allow us to participate in negative behavior. Here are some automatic thoughts that can block change:

· **"I had no choice:"** Spending time writing and reviewing our thinking reports should have shown us that this is rarely true, but it is one of the most commonly used excuses.

· **"Everyone thinks the way I do:"** Remember *Principle 2* in *Session 3*? ***Everyone sees the world differently***, and because of that no one really agrees on everything. It's easy to steal something if you think that everyone would do it if they weren't afraid, but that is *rarely* the case.

· **"I'm right and my thoughts don't need to change:"** Sometimes being right or wrong has nothing to do with the situation, but being stubborn in your thinking is an easy way to get in trouble. Every issue has two sides, and being stubborn can stop you from having freedom.

Activity: A Choice For Gavin

When looking at Gavin's story, **which of the above** do you think applies to his automatic thoughts? Does he participate in more than one error? How do Gavin's automatic thoughts affect the decisions he makes? How might Gavin change his automatic thoughts?

Errors In Thinking Get Us In Trouble

Errors in thinking tend to become habit for us. They *become so automatic* that we accept them no matter what the evidence against them is. But these errors are really distortions of the real situation. It's like putting on green sunglasses. Things are still what they were, but the colors are different and some shapes stick out more than others.

Activity: Labeling The Errors

Go back to *Worksheet 3* in *Session 5, Errors in Thinking Checklist* in which you checked how those errors in thinking applied to you. Now use the list in *Table 2,* to **label and name the errors in thinking** that you participate in. Try to use some **self-talk** in reviewing this, and try to replace some of the thoughts that you have had. For example, the label **SCREWED** may apply for feeling like the world is against you at all times. Instead of thinking that, **replace your thought** with something like "there are some people who I can actually trust" or "that's not true, there are some people that have been real good to me."

By *recognizing* the thought habits and thinking errors that we take part in, we can take control of our thoughts and change them. Just as we can change our negative thoughts by being aware of them, we can also change and correct our errors in thinking by becoming aware of the ones we use most often.

TABLE 2

COMMON THINKING DISTORTIONS OR ERRORS IN THINKING

LIST OF ERRORS IN THINKING:

1) POWER THRUST -- Put people down; dominate over others
2) CLOSED CHANNEL -- Seeing things only your way
3) VICTIM STANCE -- Blaming others
4) PRIDE -- Feeling superior to others
5) DON'T CARE -- Lack of concern as to how others are affected
6) CAN'T TRUST -- Can't trust anybody
7) WON'T MEET OBLIGATIONS -- Refuse something you don't want to do
8) WANT IT NOW -- Want what you want now and won't settle for less
9) STEALING -- Take what you want from others
10) DON'T NEED ANYBODY -- Refuse to lean on anyone
11) PROCRASTINATE -- Put off things until tomorrow
12) DON'T HAVE TO -- I don't have to do that
13) STUBBORN -- Won't change your ideas
14) RIGID THINKING -- Think in black or white terms; has to be one way or the other
15) CASTASTROPHIZING -- Mountains out of molehills; blowing things out of proportion
16) FEEL PICKED ON -- Feel singled out and picked on
17) THEY DESERVE IT -- People have it coming; people deserve to get ripped off
18) SCREWED -- Feeling that you are being screwed over; mistreated
19) SELECTIVE HEARING -- Tune out what you hear people say if it doesn't fit your thinking
20) WON'T GIVE -- Demand from others but won't give
21) CRIMINAL THINKING -- Think about criminal things; doing crimes
22) LYING -- Lying is almost automatic for you

ADDITIONAL LIST OF ERRORS AND THEIR NAMES:

1) ANGER -- Rage that makes you illogical and irrational
2) LONER -- Feeling separated, isolated and different from others
3) REFUSAL -- Feeling that you don't have to do that
4) FAIR DESERTS -- I deserve more than what I'm getting; I've been cheated
5) THEY DESERVE IT -- People have it coming
6) NO EMPATHY -- Can't put yourself in another person's position
7) FAILURE TO CONSIDER HARM TO OTHERS -- lack of concern about how others are affected
8) SEE SELF AS GOOD -- In spite of having harmed others
9) NO EFFORT -- Won't exert energy to achieve a goal; do what comes easy
10) CONCRETE THOUGHTS -- Won't change your ideas
11) FICKLE -- Change your mind or goals all the time
12) SEXUAL POWER -- using sex as a way to increase your self image
13) ZERO STATE -- Feeling of no value; worthy of nothing

Activity: Most Often Used Thought Distortions

Take some time to fill out *Worksheet 26, Thinking Distortions,* with the two distortions you participate in the most often. Use *Table 2* and *Worksheet 3* to help you with this. After everyone has filled out their worksheets, get into a group and **discuss the two distortions you think you use the most**. Then as a group discuss the ways you might **change or alter** the errors in thinking in order to have a more positive outcome. Make sure everyone gets plenty of feedback about their distortions, but do not blame or accuse anyone.

THE "ENTITLEMENT TRAP"

People who use substances or get into trouble with the law often use the *"Entitlement Trap"* as an excuse to explain away their behavior. This trap is when, because of past problems or hurt, you feel like you were the victim. If we think we are punished, deprived, or badly treated, we often feel like we are *"entitled"* to things because we have it coming to us.

Activity: Gavin's Error

In looking at Gavin's story, do you think he is using an "entitlement trap" as an excuse for any of his actions? Which of his actions do you think uses the trap? **How does he use the trap as an excuse?** Do you think Gavin is right in using that excuse? What entitlement traps have you used or fallen into recently?

Just like errors in thinking, the "entitlement trap" is *an excuse to get in trouble* or use substances and is not right. In fact, this trap can cause us more problems and can stop change.

Activity: Escaping From the Trap

Remember a thought that you have had recently that falls into the excuse of "entitlement." Now spend some time **arguing why that thought is not good** and is harmful for you. Share with the class the thought and then how you argued with it. Be sure to share how it felt to argue with the thought and how you felt when you were done. Then take some time to fill out *Worksheet 27, The Entitlement Trap..* Be honest with yourself, and fill out the worksheet as completely as possible.

Just as we can use the *three skills* we learned in *Session 17* to change a negative thought, we can also use the three skills to escape the *"Entitlement Trap."* Here's a reminder of what those skills are.

· **Thought stopping**

· **Replacing it with a positive thought (these are thoughts that you thought up for your arsenal)**

· **Strong countering (self-talking)**

Worksheet 26

Pick two thinking distortions from "Common Thinking Distortions" that you use a lot of the time. Or, pick any other thinking distortions that you use a lot that are not listed. Put the number from "Common Thinking Distortions" in the blank spaces. Describe how you use each error. Did it get you in trouble? How?

1. DISTORTION NO.   :

    Describe the situation.

_____

_____

    How did you use it?

_____

_____

    Did it get you in trouble? How?

_____

_____

_____

2. DISTORTION NO.   :

    Describe the situation.

_____

_____

    How did you use it?

_____

_____

    Did it get you in trouble? How?

_____

_____

_____

Worksheet 27

THE ENTITLEMENT TRAP

Describe a situation in which you did something wrong because you felt like you had the right to do it. Then answer these questions:

1. How did you justify the act?

_____

_____

_____

_____

_____

2. Did you get away with it or were you caught?

_____

_____

_____

_____

_____

3. Knowing what you know now, would you do it again? Why or why not?

_____

_____

_____

_____

_____

_____

_____

Activity: Entitled To Be Free

Throughout the whole program we have been talking about how your thoughts, feelings, and actions interact to create your response to situations. But you are the one who has control over your thoughts. Break into groups of four and **create a skit** in which there is a **situation and a problem**. Give each person an **entitlement thought**, and try to show what can happen in a situation when the entitlement traps are in play.

An example might be a car wreck in which all the people involved think they are the victim. The situation gets out of control because everyone is blaming the other people. Make sure to let the audience know what entitlement trap is in play in your performance. One person might feel that they were entitled to turn right because they had a nicer car, even though it was the other person's right of way.

Then create a skit in which the **entitlement thoughts are stopped** and the situation is resolved. How can thoughts of entitlement lead to criminal conduct and substance abuse?

Putting It Together

- Gavin's thoughts often allow him to choose actions that get him into trouble. What are some of Gavin's *errors in thinking*? Could he have changed the outcome of the situation?

- One excuse Gavin uses falls into the "*entitlement trap.*" Use the story to give an example of how Gavin uses the entitlement trap. How does it make Gavin feel about his negative actions? What would happen if Gavin didn't use the trap?

- The way we think about a situation often affects what we do in a situation. Recall some of the situations where your *thoughts of entitlement* had negative effects on your actions. Were there errors in the thought? Could you have made the situation end differently?

- Think about situations where *you did change your thought*. Did you feel more in control of the situation? How can you empower yourself more?

- Update and add to your *Plan for Change*. Choose a problem to work on this week.

I hate school. I hate it so much. The only reason they make me go is because they like to torture me.

I've always had a hard time at school. I can't focus. I can't listen to the teacher. I'm stupid. So I sit there, minding my own business. Sometimes I draw. Sometimes I talk to the person next to me. More often than not I just sit and stare out the window.

But then the teacher calls on me. And I haven't been listening. And I don't know what she's talking about. Or what she's asking me. So I get angry. Why does she have to put me on the spot like that? She knows I'm stupid. I talk back. I get loud. She sends me to the advisor's office. And he hates me. All adults hate me.

So I got suspended this one time over nothing. I knew it was trouble as soon as I walked into school. The advisor, he came up to me with a look on his face. I knew I was gonna get in trouble, even though I hadn't done anything yet. I was just talking with my friends. And some of my friends like to talk. But I don't mind cause I like to talk too. But the advisor, he hates me so he's always looking for a way to get me in trouble. So before he even said something I asked him what the hell he wanted. And he told me I better watch it. I walked off. What does he know anyway?

I went to class. I was a couple of minutes late because I took the long way. Sometimes I like to wander the halls, check out the tiles on the floor. Sometimes I get to see some stuff written on somebody's locker before the janitor can clean it off. You can learn a lot by wandering the halls. But as soon as I walked in the teacher started nagging, asking me why I was late and stuff. I told her it was none of her business, cause it's not. She's not my mom. I told her so too. She said I better sit down. I asked her why, it's not like I learn anything in her class anyway. School sucks and it's a waste of my time. She told me to go to the advisor's office. I took off, but not to his office.

First I wandered the halls some more. But then I thought that wasn't smart, I could get caught. So I went to the park to hang out and wait for my friends. Lunch was coming up, and then I could go to the one class I like. Art.

This one time in art class we were learning how to paint with oils. My teacher said we should get a feel for the um…what's that called? Oh yea, the medium we are using to portray our feelings. So I stuck my hands in the paint. It was kinda cool, all slippery and gooey. It was really cool feeling the paint and the canvas and trying to create something. My mom got mad that I had paint all over my clothes. That wasn't fun. Not that I get to have fun at school very often. I'm always in trouble.

At lunch I got in a fight. I was messing around and stole this kid's chips. I never have money cause we're poor, so why shouldn't I have his? Don't I deserve chips too? But then this big kid got all up in my face. I told him to mind his own business. He told me I was nothing but a stupid punk. I punched him in the face. Before it got too much further, all the kids separated us. He's just a stupid jerk.

By then it was time to go to art. I was happy. I was excited. It's the only thing that I can focus on. I think we were learning charcoals that day, which is only black and white but I've seen some crazy stuff done with charcoals. But class had just gotten started when the advisor came in. I knew he was there for me. That man hunts me down sometimes, like some hunter who stalks an innocent deer. So he ended up taking me out of my favorite class to go sit down in his office. And sit and sit and watch kids and teachers walk in and out of the office. And they all stare and make snide comments. I almost got in a fight just waiting for my mom.

So I was suspended. He said something like defiance and disorderly conduct and whatever. Which didn't matter, cause that meant I didn't have to go to school for a couple of days. My mom was mad, but it doesn't matter because she is always mad. And I got to sit in my room, watching TV or reading comic books and wait at the park for my friends to get out of school. **Yeah, school sucks.**

NOTES

Chapter Ten:
Handling Anger, Guilt and Depression

GOALS OF THIS CHAPTER
- Recognize negative feelings
- Discuss how negative feelings can lead to negative behavior
- Learn steps on how to deal with negative feelings
- Learn how to avoid violence and aggression

TRISTAN'S STORY

I'm going to beat on her, I swear I'm going to really hurt her. But what am I going to do without her? We met two years ago, at the town fair. I think I fell in love with Audrey within the first week. Everything was great for about a year. Then some friends and I started experimenting with some harder drugs than pot. But Audrey had a hard time dealing with my drug use. Then one night my friends and I ran into her hanging out with a couple of her friends. Some guy from her class was talking to her. And I freaked out.

Before I realized what I had done I saw him with blood running down his nose like lava leaving an erupted volcano and Audrey staring at me with tears in her eyes. She helped him stop the blood and my friends pushed me into our car before the cops got called. The next morning I felt like crap. I couldn't believe what I had done. Boy did I apologize. We set a date for the next night, and everything was fine. I had a little voice in my head asking me why Audrey helped that guy when I was her boyfriend.

Everything was good for a while. Until I found out he was going to be her lab partner. I ended up drinking most of my dad's beer one night before Audrey and I were supposed to go out. As soon as I walked into her house, she started in on me being drunk for our date and how I knew she didn't like it when I was like that. I accused her of cheating. I turned around and backhanded her. I went home angry and trashed my room. She broke up with me. It's all my fault, and I'm so angry about that. I hear she is dating that guy now. I'm so hurt and angry I want to kill her. I pray I never run into them together. Who knows what I'd do.

Objectives

- Review *Chapter 9: Zeroing in on negative thinking*
- Recognize angry thoughts and feelings
- Discuss how angry feelings can lead to trouble
- Think about how anger is related to and works with guilt and depression
- Learn some steps for handling anger, guilt, and depression.

Tristan's Story

Everything was fine, and Audrey and I were in love. I started doing more drugs, which she didn't like, but they made me feel good for a little bit. But then one night I saw Audrey talking to a guy, and I got so angry that I punched him.

The next morning I felt so bad about hitting him that I couldn't even leave my room. Not to mention I was sure I had lost Audrey. I trusted her but then I just up and hit a guy talking to her. I couldn't understand it, and I didn't think Audrey would either. I just felt so damn guilty and sad. But that didn't stop the voices in my head, whispering that she was cheating or that he was making a move on Audrey.

Review of negative thinking

Up to this point in the program we have been focusing on the thoughts that can cause us to act out negatively or take drugs. In *Session 17, Recognizing and Changing Negative Thoughts*, we discussed how to recognize negative thoughts, and how negative thoughts are automatic and affect the choices and decisions we make. *Session 18, Errors in Thinking*, began with the *distorted thinking* that we often fall into, leading us to substance abuse and criminal behavior.

Activity: Thinking Of Errors

Take a moment to review your sessions from last week. Did you recognize any **patterns of negative thoughts** or thinking errors, and if so, what were they? What did you do to change them, if anything? Then share with the group the negative thoughts and errors you had the last week, and if you were successful in using your skills to stop and change them. Go around the room until everyone has had a chance to share.

In *Session 2* we talked about how our thoughts, feelings, and actions all work together in a cycle to help us make our decisions. Up until the last session, we have been discussing how *thoughts affect our feelings and actions*, and possible ways to stop or correct our negative or distorted thoughts. Now we are going to spend some time on *feelings*: how they affect our decisions and possible ways we can control them. Review your Self-Portrait ratings for anger, depression and anxiety. This chapter will be especially helpful for those who had high ratings.

DEALING WITH ANGER

All of us get angry sometimes. After all, anger is a normal human emotion. But not being aware of our anger, or ignoring our anger, can often have some very negative effects on our lives and us. Although we don't like to think so, anger has been the basis of a lot of substance use and criminal actions. Often we are hurting others and ourselves by participating in these actions. Unless the harm is clearly by accident, *hurting anyone* is an act of anger.

This is not to say that anger is isolated from the rest of our mind, like some caged beast ready to spring out at any moment. There are some well-known automatic thoughts that predictably result in the very powerful and often dangerous emotion of anger.

THOUGHTS THAT LEAD TO ANGER

- Thinking of being "shortchanged"
- Thoughts of not being treated fairly
- Thinking that you are the victim
- Thinking that your space has been violated

Notice that a lot of these thoughts that lead up to anger can fall under the category of the *"entitlement trap"* that we discussed in the last session. For example, " If I am not being treated fairly, then I have the right to strike out with anger and violence." By becoming aware of the thoughts you are having in the moment of anger, you can begin to take control over your anger.

Activity: Tristan's Anger

Review Tristan's story about his anger. What do you think were the **thoughts that made him angry**? There may be more than one right answer, so discuss in the group which thought you think it is and why. Use examples from the story to back up your opinion. How do you think Tristan could have controlled his anger?

The Big Three

The largest difficulty in dealing with anger, though, is that *anger is not isolated* from our other feelings. In fact, anger is usually pretty closely tied to our feelings of *guilt and depression*. When we get angry, we often feel guilty or depressed. We will take a look at this cycle a little later, but it is important to know that these three emotions play heavily in returning to earlier patterns of drug abuse (*relapse*) and re-offending (*recidivism*).

Often when we are trying to recover or change our habits, we feel guilt, anger and depression. The reason we are going to go over some of the steps to dealing and managing these emotions is because they are *high-risk emotions*, similar to high-risk situations and thinking, that can lead to both *relapse and recidivism*, which in turn leads to more of the three emotions. It becomes a vicious cycle, a downward spiral with us at the bottom of it.

The ties between guilt, anger and depression

Emotions are something felt by all people, including the negative emotions of guilt, anger, and depression. The fact that, in your case, these emotions have led to substance use and criminal behavior -- is different. In order to keep your freedom of choice you must be able to control these emotions.

As kids we were often *not allowed to feel* negative emotions. Anger gets a response of "cool it," guilt often brings out "it's okay, don't feel bad," and depression often gets returned with a fake smile and a "cheer up, it's not that bad." Because of this, we never really learned how to deal with our negative emotions. Instead, we may have used drugs and alcohol to forget or strike out with anger and violence in order release the tension. But these methods do not control the emotions; rather, they lead us into *the guilt-anger cycle.*

The *"guilt-anger cycle"* is something that occurs over and over again within our minds. Because we did not learn healthy ways to deal with our negative emotions, we built them up inside. When there was *too much pressure, we got high, got angry and irrational, and hurt others emotionally or physically.* But after the act was done, the decision made, and the substance out of our system, we often have strong thoughts and *feelings of guilt.* We don't know how to deal with the guilt so we become *depressed,* and the whole time our anger never gets dealt with. So the feelings build up again and then the cycle starts all over. Take a look at *Figure 14, The Guilt - Anger Cycle,* which shows how the cycle starts and continues. We use the term "significant other" (SO) to describe any important person in your life who plays a role in your feelings of guilt, anger or depression. In Tristan's case, Audrey is his SO.

Activity: Tristan's Downward Spiral

Discuss in a group Tristan's story and his **cycle of anger, guilt and depression**. Tristan's negative actions began with the feeling of anger. How did he feel the next morning? Do you think he ever dealt with his anger? Why or why not? What was the cycle of Tristan's actions?

Activity: A Spiral Of My Own

For this activity, use **Worksheet 28,** and **Figure 14, The Guilt -Anger Cycle**, to begin drawing a spiral of your own. Think of a situation in which you lost your temper, and then try to think and become aware of how the situation fits into the cycle. How do your feelings fit within the cycle? How and where can you change the cycle so it doesn't end with the feelings of anger being repeated?

Ways To Deal With Stressful Emotional States
Adapted from: "Pull the Plug on Stress", Harvard Business Review, July 2003

There are proven techniques for managing stressful emotions that have been of enormous help to the people from all walks of life, throughout the world. We use the word **BRAIN** to help us remember *5 essential skills* to handle stressful situations.

Figure 14

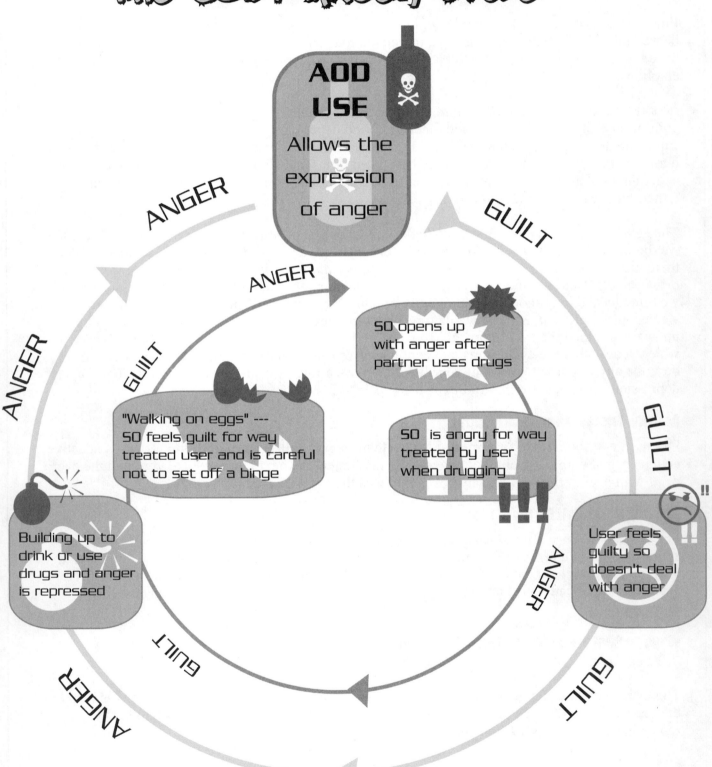

Worksheet 28

THE GUILT-ANGER CYCLE

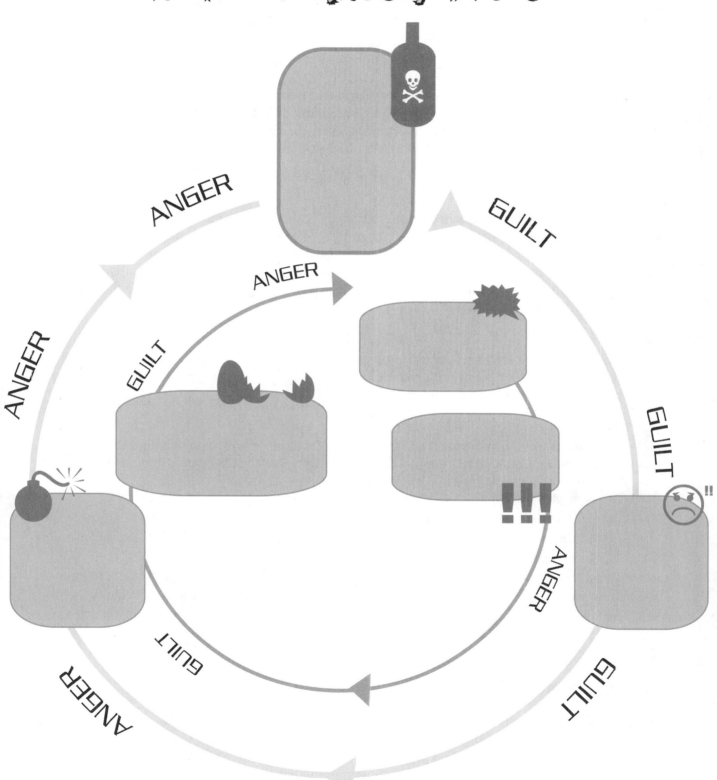

B - **Breathing:** Concentrate on focusing your attention on the area of your body near your heart. Inhale deeply for about 5 seconds, imagining the breath flowing in through your heart. Then exhale for about 5 seconds, visualizing the breath flowing out from your solar plexus (the area in the center of your body just below the middle of your rib cage).

R - **Recognize and disengage:** Notice your mood and the physical signs of distress (e.g., knot in the stomach, raising the level of your voice, tenseness of muscles, flushing of face, etc. Make a decision to "freeze the frame" of this discomfort, almost like pressing pause on your VCR and then moving on to a different experience. A bit like skipping over an E-mail that holds no interest to you.

A - **Ask yourself, "Is there a better alternative?** Is there a different way of managing the situation without getting angry, depressed or guilty? What other thoughts might we use to replace the thoughts that are leading to uncomfortable emotions? In *Chapter 9, Zeroing-In On Negative Thinking*, we discussed ways of changing your negative thoughts. Use self-talk skills: "Why am I angry? What can I do about it positively?" Discover what thoughts are causing the feelings, and then replace them with some of your positive thoughts.

I - **Input a positive feeling:** Focus on images that make you feel good. An example might be a walk in the woods; or laughing with some childhood friends in the playground; or being on top of your game in some sport that you have enjoyed

N - **Note the change in perspective:** In a very quiet manner notice any change in your mood, physical sensations or negative thoughts. Maintain these positive changes as long as you can.

Activity: The Role Of Anger

Break into groups of three. Together with your group, think of a situation in which all the people involved are **likely to get angry or upset**. An example might be, the teacher or counselor orders a lock-down and nobody is allowed to have any time for recreation or going out of their room. Develop a skit that **deals with the angry situation** and uses the above **BRAIN** skills to keep the anger from exploding in a negative way. Perform your skit for the larger group. When watching a skit, keep in mind these questions. Is the skit believable? Is the way the anger is dealt with done in a positive manner? Did it utilize the **BRAIN** technique? Do you think it is realistic to use these skills in a real situation?

As Always, Be Aware Of Your Thoughts

We keep going over it, but it is important to remember that your *thoughts, beliefs and feelings* are all in a meeting in your head. Every thought you have affects your feelings and actions. Every action you participate in will affect your thoughts and feelings. In order to learn to control and deal with your emotions, try to be aware of the thought habits, or automatic thoughts, that lead up to the emotion. Here are some examples.

- *Magnifying* - Blowing negative events out of proportion. "This is the worst thing ever."
- *Jumping to conclusions* - "She didn't smile at me, she hates me."
- *Over-generalizing* - "I fail at everything."
- *Self-blame* - "I am no good."

Activity: The anger in me

Form into a circle, and one at a time discuss a **situation** in the last week that **made you angry**. Try to share the **thoughts and feelings** that lead up to the anger, and tell the group what was the result or **action** you chose. Then, as a group, try to decide which of the four thought habits the situation fell into. Offer a way that you might have changed the situation, and listen to the feedback of the group. Go around the circle until everyone has discussed at least one situation in the past week where they either dealt with or didn't deal with anger, guilt, and depression.

A Simple and Effective Way to Deal with Anger

Perhaps the simplest way to diffuse an angry situation is to follow the **ABC** method below.

A - Acknowledge that you are angry

B - Back Off

C - Consider your alternatives

Believe it or not, this simple technique has actually saved lives.

Putting It Together

- Tristan became angry when he saw his girlfriend talking to another guy. What do you think his *automatic thoughts* were? How could he have changed his thoughts in order to choose a different action? How could he have used the BRAIN or ABC methods to deal with his anger?

- *Anger, guilt, and depression* often *create a cycle* in which the feelings keep getting stronger and nothing gets resolved. Review *Worksheet 28, The Guilt-Anger Cycle* and see if the cycle plays a part in your life. How might you change this?

- Of the four thinking errors above, which ones do you think you use the most often? Why?

- Take some time before the next session to write up a thinking report for a situation you encountered in which you became angry. How were you able to use the **BRAIN** and **ABC** methods for dealing with anger?

- Update your *Plan for Change*. Do you have a new problem to add to your list? What will you work on this week?

SESSION 20: PREVENTING AGGRESSION

Objectives

- Review *Session 19: Dealing with Feelings*
- Understand the different types of aggression and violence
- Learn and practice self-control skills

Tristan's Story

Before I knew what happened I had pulled the guy away from her, asked her what she was doing, and punched him, all in like a minute. The next thing I know is that he is staring at me with blood running down his face, and Audrey is looking at me with tears in her eyes.

We talked the next morning, and I thought everything was fine. But the voices in my head wouldn't leave me alone. Why did she help him? Does she like him? Is she cheating on me? One night I couldn't handle it and drank most of my dad's beer before I went to pick her up for a date. She got angry with me and in my face, and I ended up backhanding her. She slammed the door in my face and broke up with me the next day. And now I'm alone.

The big three emotions

Last session we spent some time discussing the three negative emotions that can affect our actions the most. They are *anger, guilt, and depression*. All of these emotions interact with each other in a cycle, making it hard for us to move forward and heal. By being aware of the thoughts that lead up to these emotions, we are able to control and deal with them in a healthy manner.

Activity: Thinking About Emotions

Share with the group one situation in which the **cycle of anger, guilt, and depression** played a part. How did you handle the situation? How might you have handled it differently? Share and offer to others ways that each person can better deal with the thinking errors and the cycle in order to better deal with their emotions.

Unfortunately, anger does not stop with the emotion or the use of a substance. Often it can be *verbally or physically* taken out on another person or an object, like in the case of vandalizing. This session is about *controlling your angry* actions so you can continue making positive choices and enjoying more freedom in your life.

What's The Difference Between Aggression And Violence?

While *anger* is an emotion we feel and not necessarily wrong, aggression and violence are actions we participate in when we are *not able to control* our anger.

AGGRESSION is non-physical behavior that *abuses, hurts, or injures* another person emotionally or psychologically. It can be controlled or uncontrolled. It can be calculated or happen on the spur of the moment. Consider some of the damage aggression can do to another person.

- It can lower their self-esteem.
- It can damage their sense of dignity and self-respect.
- It can damage a person emotionally, creating fear, depression, anger and stress.
- It can cause a person to withdraw and feel threatened.

VIOLENCE occurs when *aggression becomes physical*. Violence is everything that aggression is, but *causes physical harm* and damage to things and people. It can be directed towards objects, such as smashing and breaking things, but usually relates to a person you know or who made you angry. Violence is often directed to specific people and centers around *three primary positions* in the relationship between perpetrator and victim.

Position of strength or power: The victim of violence has power to *get in the way of* the violent person's needs or goals.

Position of weakness: The victim is *weak* and the violent person has to maintain a *position of strength*.

Position of sex: The victim is a target of the violent person's *distorted sexual needs and drives*.

Activity: Violence Or Aggression?

As a group go over Tristan's story. Could Tristan's actions be considered **aggression or violence**? Use evidence from the story to support why. If you consider it aggression, think of what the damage did to Audrey. If you consider it violence, decide and think which of the three above positions it would fit under. There may be more than one right answer so **use evidence from the story** to back up your opinion.

If aggression is *not dealt with*, it often *becomes violence*. That is why it is important to deal with aggression in a positive manner. The important thing to keep in mind is that *events do not cause anger*. The *thoughts we have about the event* lead to anger, and are usually caused by some problem. *High-charged* situations, similar to *high-risk situations*, are situations that usually will cause some anger or problems in our minds. Whenever possible, these situations should be avoided in order to prevent the build-up of angry thoughts and feelings.

Violence associated with gangs or drugs
What *about group violence* such as *gang activities; or violence and aggression around the manufacture and sale of drugs*? How do the above stated positions (*power, weakness, sex*) help to understand these types of violent activities?

Activity: My Own Violence

Take a moment to fill out *Worksheet 29, Managing High-Charged Situations*. Write in some **emotionally charged situations** that could lead to the **expression of anger**. Then check whether or not the situation could lead to **violence**. Break into groups of three or four and share your situations. Help each other figure out how to avoid violence in each situation.

Be aware and in control
Here are some of the signs that we can be aware of that will let us know when we are getting angry.

Worksheet 29

MANAGING HIGH-CHARGED SITUATIONS

List high-charged situations that can lead you to anger or aggression. Then check if these can lead to violence.

LIST HIGH-CHARGED SITUATIONS THAT CAN LEAD TO ANGER, ANGRY THOUGHTS, AND FEELINGS OR TO AGGRESSIVE BEHAVIOR:	CHECK IF COULD LEAD TO VIOLENCE

- Feeling irritable, agitated, and tense
- Losing your temper
- Feeling impatient; feeling like things are not going your way; feeling not in control
- Being provoked or pushed by someone
- Thinking and feeling you are not being treated fairly

SKILLS TO AVOID AGGRESSION AND VIOLENCE

When the clues begin to tip us off that we are getting angry, there are skills and steps we can take to avoid striking out aggressively or violently.

- Use **Relaxation**.

- Use **Self-talk** to calm yourself down. Be aware of the angry thought and use **Thought Stopping** (Session 17).

- Use **Thought Replacement:** Replace the angry thoughts with *positive thoughts*. Use the list you created in *Session 17*.

- **Share** your angry thoughts with someone without becoming aggresive.

- Use **Problem Solving:** When you begin to feel angry, try to *solve the problem*. Problem solving is something we will cover in *Session 24*.

- Keep in mind that the **other person may be angry** too. Since they may not be reasoning well, you may be at risk.

- Use the **BRAIN** and **ABC** techniques covered in the last session.

- After you successfully **manage** your anger, be proud, reward yourself.

Activity: Irritation Log *(adapted from ART)*

Take a moment and individually fill out **Worksheet 30, The Irritation Log,** for a specific situation that you have encountered within the last few weeks. Describe the **situation and your reactions**. After everyone has finished the worksheet, go around the group and share about your situation. Discuss what you think triggered the anger, and whether you think you dealt with it well or not. Keep in mind these questions:
- Did you handle the situation well?
- How could you deal with the situation differently?
- What are your triggers to anger?

Commitment For Self-Control

Sometimes making a *promise to practice anger-management* provides an excellent framework for keeping your commitment to remain in control. The form below may serve as an important tool for keeping your anger in check.

Worksheet 30

THE IRRITABILITY LOG

Where were you?

❑ Classroom
❑ Bathroom
❑ Outside
❑ Bedroom
❑ Counselor's office

❑ Halls
❑ Recreation Room
❑ Dining Room
❑ At work
❑ Other:_____

What happened?

❑ Somebody teased me
❑ Somebody stole from me
❑ I was told to do something
❑ I didn't like what someone was doing

❑ I broke a rule
❑ Someone started a fight with me
❑ Other: _____

Who was the other person?

❑ Student
❑ Counselor
❑ Teacher
❑ Correctional officer
❑ Adult
❑ Resident

❑ Family member
❑ Gang member
❑ Other:_____

What was your response?

❑ Hit first
❑ Hit back
❑ Told a friend
❑ Ran away
❑ Ignored it
❑ Yelled
❑ Cried
❑ Broke something

❑ Was restrained
❑ Told counselor
❑ Walked away
❑ Talked it out
❑ Used skills to control anger.
If so describe skills: _____
_____

How do you think you dealt with it?

❑ Poorly
❑ Not so well

❑ Okay
❑ Good

❑ Great

How angry were you?

❑ Red hot
❑ Really angry

❑ Moderately angry
❑ Mildly angry

❑ Not angry at all

ONE DAY PLEDGE TO REMAIN CALM

Adapted from the Anger Control Workbook

I, _____, promise to remain calm and not to lose my temper between

_____(day/time) and _____(day/time). I will not become aggressive

or violent no matter what stress or provocation may occur.

_____(your signature)

_____(witness)

Activity: A Moment Of Self-Control

Sit in a circle and for a moment imagine a scene that causes you to feel angry. Take some time to imagine and begin to feel the anger the scene causes. Now begin to practice these relaxation skills.

- Take slow and deep breaths.
- Inhale slowly, in five-second intervals, and then slowly release your breath, also in 5-second intervals.
- Repeat the breathing several times.
- Now clear your mind of all thoughts, and if a thought does occur, tell yourself "I am relaxed." Repeat this as long as needed.

After everyone has had a chance to relax completely using the skills, imagine another scene that makes you angry. This time use **self-talk** to confront and control the anger. Use your **thought stopping** and **thought replacement** skills in order to do this. Also, practice using the **ABC** and **BRAIN** techniques for managing anger. Go around the circle and one at a time say out loud the techniques that you are using. What ways seem more effective than others?

Putting It Together

- After drinking and taking drugs, Tristan became very angry, aggressive, and violent. What were some of the clues that Tristan was going to be violent? What *thoughts and anger management skills* might Tristan have used to calm himself down?

- Unresolved anger can lead to aggression, and aggression can lead to violence. Think about *when* you may have been *aggressive or violent*. Did you feel in control when you were acting out on your anger? What could you have done to stop your anger and deal with it?

- Is violence *more likely to occur* when you are with your *friends or a gang*? If so what are some of the skills that you could use to change the pattern.

- Think about the *different ways to control anger* in order to avoid violence and aggression. Which way would work best for you?

- What problem area from your *Plan for Change* will you work on this week?

- Re-rate yourself on strengths in your *Self-Portrait*. Are the ratings higher?

TRISTAN'S STORY

I'm going to beat on her. I swear I'm going to really hurt her. But what am I going to do without her?

We met two years ago at the town fair, sometime around the fourth of July I think. She was beautiful, with long honey hair, and bright green eyes with a bit of blue around the center. Always laughing and joking around, I think I fell in love with Audrey within the first week we started hanging out. We were pretty much inseparable, going everywhere together and always making our plans around the other person's schedule.

Audrey had just moved to our town that summer, and in the fall she was going to be a freshman at the school I was currently attending. Although I was older than her, it didn't matter when we were together. I think her parents had some problems with the fact that I was already sixteen, but they didn't stop us from dating. My dad didn't really give a rat's ass, just as long as I stayed out of his way. Everything was great for about a year.

Then some friends and I started experimenting with some harder drugs than pot. Nothing serious, and it wasn't like I was even close to being an addict, it just made me feel better for a little while. But Audrey had a hard time dealing with my drug use. She said it made me act weird and do weird things, although I never understood what she was talking about. I was merely trying to expand my mind and spend as much time away from my violent drunk of a father as possible.

Then one night my friends and I ran into her hanging out with a couple of her friends. When we walked up, some guy from her class was talking to her. And I freaked out. It all happened so fast, but I grabbed the guy's shirt, pushed him away from her, asked her what the hell she was doing, and then turned around and punched the guy, all in like a minute. Before I realized what I had done I saw him with blood running down his nose like lava leaving an erupted volcano and Audrey staring at me with tears in her eyes. She helped him stop the blood and my friends pushed me into our car before the cops got called.

The next morning I felt like crap. I couldn't believe what I had done, and I definitely didn't know why. All I knew was I felt guilty as hell for doing that to the guy, after all he talks to her every day and it wasn't like I didn't trust her. All I could do was sit in the dark void of my room, not eating or anything because I was sure I had lost Audrey.

Finally my prick of a father knocked on my door and told me Audrey was on the phone. I felt so guilty I couldn't even talk to her. But I did, and boy did I apologize. I told her I knew she wasn't doing anything, and she said that was why she didn't like me doing drugs. We set a date for the next night, and everything was fine.

But it wasn't. I had a little voice in my head asking me why Audrey helped that guy when I was her boyfriend. Why couldn't she understand it from my point of view? Did she like him or something?

Everything was good for us for awhile. Until I found out that he was going to be her lab partner. I thought I handled it, but soon I couldn't handle the voices in my head anymore, and I ended up drinking most of my dad's beer one night before Audrey and I were supposed to go out. He came in while I was drinking, but he didn't say anything. Just smiled and walked out. As soon as I walked in her house, she started in on me being drunk for our date and how I knew she didn't like it when I was like that. Immediately the little voices in my head jumped up and accused her of cheating. For a second she just stared at me and then she got in my face yelling at me about how dare I accuse her of being like that and to get out of her house. I wouldn't leave so she pushed me, and I turned around and backhanded her. She shoved me out the door and slammed it in my face. I was so angry I went home and trashed my room.

She broke up with me. It's my fault, and I am so angry about that. I hear that she is dating that guy now. I am so hurt and angry I want to kill her. Instead, I just sit and drink, while thinking about what I once had and praying I never run into them together. **Who knows what I'd do.**

PHASE III NOW!

Ownership of Change
and
Calling the Shots

Chapter Eleven:
Overcoming Prejudice

GOALS OF THIS CHAPTER
- Develop an appreciation for ethnicity, culture, and diversity
- Understand the basis for prejudice and stereotyping
- Review values and morals
- Learn about gender roles and issues

CONNOR'S STORY

Most people are so loud and inconsiderate it makes me ill. Especially those kind of people. You know the ones I'm talking about. The other night I was trying to do my homework when the neighbors were being loud and obnoxious. My dad says that's just how they are, those kind of people. My dad grew up in this neighborhood. He said there didn't used to be all these different ethnicities and cultures and PC crap. No one told him that some other guy would swoop down and steal your promotion right out from under you. Who cares, except for my dad, ya know, because he's the one who's getting his job stolen and his job ruined.

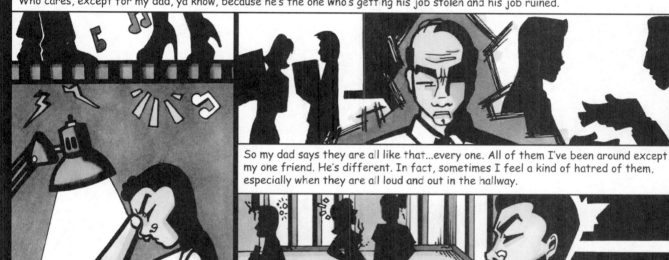

So my dad says they are all like that...every one. All of them I've been around except my one friend. He's different. In fact, sometimes I feel a kind of hatred of them, especially when they are all loud and out in the hallway.

My mom always tells me that we should practice tolerance. And what does she know anyways? I guess she did try to go to night school once. But then we didn't get dinner half the time. My dad put his foot down. He said it's either the family or her uppity education. So she cried a lot, and then finally decided to stay home.

Women don't know nothing about the world. I can't even get a break at school. The teacher always thinks this person is smarter because they are this race, or the coach picks this person because they are that race.

But my dad says it's because the PC crap has ruined the world. My dad's got a point. I have a right to be here, and most of them don't. And if my mom tries to tell me different, I'll hit her like my dad does.

SESSION 21: RESPECTING OTHERS

Objectives

- Review *Chapter 10: Handling Anger, Guilt and Depression*
- Learn the meanings of ethnicity, culture, and diversity
- Understand the basis for prejudice and stereotyping
- Understand and respect the rights of others

Connor's Story

They are all loud, obnoxious, and lazy, and they make me ill. You know the people I'm talking about. My dad grew up in this neighborhood, and he said it never used to be like this, all different ethnicities and cultures and PC crap. He said everyone used to be the same, and that's how it's supposed to be. Of course, he lost his promotion cause some other guy got hired. Probably because the boss liked his race better or because he would work for cheaper. Dad doesn't like uppity people either. He says they have no business thinking they are better than us.

I can't even get a break at school. The teacher always thinks this kid is smarter because he's of this race, and the coach picks that kid for the team instead of me because he's of that race, and she gets to talk with her friends because she's more responsible and gets her homework done. My dad says that it's because I'm male and not the right race. The teachers and coaches say I can do anything I want if I tried, but my dad says that's just an excuse they use to make it my fault.

Review of how we deal with our feelings

In our last two sessions, *Dealing With Feelings and Preventing Aggression,* we discussed how improperly managed anger can cause a cycle of depression and guilt, which causes us to be even angrier. We learned how *automatic thoughts* and *deep-seated beliefs* can move us to *highly charged feeling states* involving guilt, anger and depression. We become angry as the result of our immediate interpretations of a situation, usually around thoughts of unfairness, violation of territory or rights, or the thought that we are being disrespected in some fashion. Our immediate thoughts are usually guided by some deeply ingrained attitudes and beliefs about what is good or bad, right or wrong, fair or unfair. Because anger, guilt and depression are such painful feeling states, we are easily swayed—sometimes by our families and closest role models—*to take the easy way out,* that is to *push these emotions aside* and avoid dealing with the originating circumstances, thoughts and beliefs. As young children, we are often told to "cheer up;" or that "guilt is pointless because it isn't your fault." Unfortunately, because these emotions are shoved aside, with repeated attempts to bury them out of view, *they have a tendency to break out* when least wanted.

As a matter of fact, we don't have any "bad" emotions. But how we *deal with our emotions* can cause problems in our life. If we don't deal with our anger, guilt or depression, they will likely build-up in our minds until we explode. Have you ever shaken up a bottle of soda really hard, and then tried to open it? Once the bottle is only slightly opened, the whole thing explodes because of built up pressure. That is how our emotions are. If our anger is bottled up under pressure, once we get slightly mad we are likely to *erupt in aggression or violence.* It is very important to learn how to deal with negative emotions as they arise. Do not bottle them up, or they are likely to explode.

In order to cope with uncomfortable feelings, we must first become aware of the thoughts and beliefs that underlie our discomfort. When we notice ourselves feeling anger, guilt or depression, practice the skills that we learned through the ABC and BRAIN models for dealing with feelings. Remember to take some time to stop and think about why you are feeling badly, and what you can do positively, in order to take care of that emotion. Of course, emotions can have a lot of influence over us when we are trying to deal with our relationships with people.

Activity: A Moment To Think

Take a moment to look at *Worksheets 29, Managing High-Charged Situations* and *Worksheet 30, The Irritation Log* for *Session 20*. Then break into groups of three and share the **thoughts** that surround a recent situation in which *you became angry*. What **thinking errors** do you recognize in each other's examples? How might the person change their thinking errors? Which of the methods of dealing with anger, guilt or depression works best for you?

PREJUDICE: FALSE BELIEFS THAT LEAD TO INFLICTING HARM ON OTHERS

What is ethnicity?

Ethnicity is a term that gets thrown around a lot in politics and the media. But what specifically is ethnicity? What does it mean to be ethnic? A dictionary would provide a definition such as "belonging to a social group on the basis of shared traits." In common terms, ethnic is usually meant to refer to a racial group living amongst a larger group who share different racial characteristics. The smaller group becomes known as a "minority." Actually, *we are all part of an ethnic group*. Religion, language, and family history are a part of ethnicity, not just our physical appearance.

What is culture?

While a person's ethnicity is the background traits (i.e., physical appearance, religion, family history, country of origin), a *person's culture* is their social behavior, or how they act according to what they learned from society. An example might be music culture. Let's say a person listens to rap music. This person may wear clothes and speak in a manner that exhibits the *cultural lifestyle* that society and media have labeled "hip-hop," "rap" or any number of other labels.

Because people are allowed to immigrate to this country in order to have a better life, the U.S. has a large *number of different cultures* in small regions and areas of the country. Consider all the ethnic groups who live or work on the small island of Manhattan or in the city of Los Angeles. This can cause some difficulties and problems. But culture can also be expanded to consider all social influence, meaning there is a *United States culture*, no matter how many different ethnicities reside in the USA.

Activity: Diversity Profile

According to your own beliefs and opinions take some time to fill out the questions on *Worksheet 31, My Diversity Profile*. Each statement is to be filled out according to your specific values and beliefs, which come from many different places, including our teachers, families, friends, neighborhood, the region we grew up in, and our religious and spiritual backgrounds.

Generalities And Stereotypes

As human beings, we like to group things in order for us to understand and feel comfortable with them. Let's say, just for an example, that while walking one day we see a person who has *dark hair and is wearing a purple shirt*. We may note it, but we won't think about it until we see a few more dark-haired people. On seeing several people with the same color shirt and hair, we may say to ourselves "All people wearing purple shirts have dark hair" or "All people with dark hair wear purple shirts." We have just *set a generality* about people wearing purple shirts or people with dark hair. In some way, this will make us *feel comfortable*, the expectation of dark-haired people wearing purple shirts will give us some sense of understanding and comfort about the world around us.

One step further is a *stereotype*. A stereotype is when we begin to classify all people that look the same or belong to a certain group, and we *begin to treat them all the same*. A stereotype, similar to a generality, gets applied to a group that may have some of the *same attributes or features*. When we form *negative stereotypes*, we are quick to judge people that have some characteristics of a known group (e.g., language, or race) as being "bad," … "inferior,"…or "undesirable." So again, errors in our way of thinking can negatively influence how we think and how we act towards a whole group of people.

Using our previous example, let's say that we tried to talk with one person who wore a purple shirt and had dark hair. That person was rude to us. We may think it's just that person, but what if another person with a purple shirt and dark hair was rude to us? And another? Then we might begin to believe that *all people* with purple shirts and dark hair are rude. It may even become more spread out than that, like all people with purple shirts, no matter the hair color, are rude or all dark-haired people are rude. This does not mean our belief is true or accurate, it is just what we've learned to expect from our surrounding environment. When we reject or inflict harm on someone because of a negative stereotype, we are acting out of prejudice.

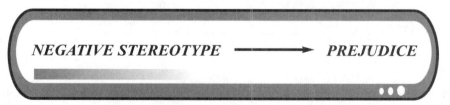

NEGATIVE STEREOTYPE ⟶ PREJUDICE

Activity: Connor's Stereotyping

Break into smaller groups and take a look at Connor's story. What stereotypes, generalities or prejudices do you think Connor uses? What do you think causes Connor to stereotype the way he does? Do you think any of Connor's stereotypes are correct, and why or why not?

Worksheet 31

MY DIVERSITY PROFILE

How we look at the world is made up of our beliefs and values. Although sometimes given to us by the media, our beliefs and values are based on what we hear from our parents, family, and friends, or may be based on our religion or spirituality, from the region we live in. This profile will help you see your view of the world and where your beliefs and values came from.

Please complete the following:

GENDER

A woman is characterized by: _____

A man is characterized by: _____

SEXUAL ORIENTATION

A family consists of: _____

A relationship is: _____

FAMILY

Our family traditions are: _____

AGE

In my generation, we like: _____

REGION

Where I live, we value: _____

ETHNICITY

One of the ethnic groups that I belong to is _____ and what makes us

different is: _____

What I like about my ethnic group is: _____

What I don't like about my ethnic group is: _____

Activity: The Surrounding Stereotypes

Take a moment to look over some of the items you have listed in *Worksheet 31, My Diversity Profile*, and think of things you do not like about your family or ethnic group. Do these fit into a stereotype or generality? Where do you think you got these stereotypes and generalities? As a large group, list the stereotypes on a piece of paper. Then write down reasons to disagree with the stereotype. What exceptions do you make to certain stereotypes, if any? An example of an exception would be that you think dark-haired people are rude, except your one friend, who happens to have dark hair, but who isn't rude. When do stereotypes become a form of prejudice?

HOW IS PREJUDICE FORMED?

As we've said before, a stereotype most often begins in a generality, such as that all people have certain features or that certain people with a certain look will act a certain way. Generalities come from our experience and our drive to understand the world. But stereotypes take generalities one step further. While there are exceptions to generalities and they can often be proven wrong, *stereotypes tend to go unchecked and unquestioned*. Remember, the most damaging part of forming a negative stereotype is the harm that we inflict on others through prejudice.

Need for Superiority

When people feel threatened or scared, they often strike out against that which is making them uncomfortable. By insisting that *we are better than* a group or a person, we can pretend that the group does not threaten us. For an example, let's say we have lived in a neighborhood our whole lives and we know almost everyone there. And let's say that *we all wear orange shirts and black shoes*. Suddenly a family wearing *purple shirts and white shoes* moves in next door. We are still in the majority, and we may make a point of letting the new family know they are alone. As time goes by, however, *more* people with purple shirts and white shoes move into the neighborhood. Suddenly we are the minority. So we act out against what is being threatened. We may feel they are taking our jobs, or ruining our schools, or changing our culture. So we begin to hate them as a group. It may even be that a purple shirt/white shoes got promoted over us, or has a bigger house. We begin to hate all purple shirt/white shoes because of our supposed degradation. Can you think of any real-life examples of how this may occur?

Failure to Discriminate -- to recognize differences

It may seem crazy, but when we do not see differences between people within a group, we become prejudiced. If we think all people from New York City are the same, we form a stereotype that would lead to prejudice.

Lack of Information

Sometimes we dislike or hate another group because of the *information that is given to us*, by our parents, by our friends, by the media. Remember, some of our *core beliefs* are taught to us from a very early age, and sometimes they can become part of us without us ever really knowing it. Instead of getting to know a person as an individual, we allow ourselves to *stereotype them* according to *what we have learned*. Our father may have lost his job, or a promotion might have been given to someone different than him, let's say a *black shirt/purple shoes*. Because of his feelings of rejection and anger, he may lash out against black shirt/purple shoes by saying, "they are lazy," or "they don't belong here," or "they only get work because they do the jobs no one else wants."

Whether we want to or not, we hear what our dad says about the other group, and it becomes a *core belief*. When we are out on the street, we will likely run into a few of the people that appear to be the way our father (or some other role model) says they are, supporting his stereotype and our generality. The more we hear our father, the more we look for the people who fit his definition, and the more our generality becomes a stereotype. At some point we may act *out of prejudice and inflict harm* on someone from the black shirt / purple shoes group.

Activity: The Need To Stereotype

Once again break into groups and take a look at Connor's story. Where do you think Connor gets his stereotypes? To which of the above categories (**superiority, information, failure to discriminate**) do most of Connor's stereotypes fit, or does he seem to fit in both of the categories? Why or why not, and use examples from the story. How could Connor get over his stereotypes? When does Conner show signs of prejudice? Discuss how discrimination or sorting out differences can make us less prejudiced.

Stereotyping can be problematic because it doesn't give people a chance to be good at what they do, or be an individual and different than other people that may seem similar to the person. The fact is most of us belong to someone else's stereotype, like addict, delinquent, or gang member. And more often than not, being stereotyped works against us. Stereotypes lead into prejudice and hatred for people because of religious differences, appearance differences, history differences, or even a difference in fashion.

Activity: The Difference In Me

For this activity, break into groups according to the color of shirt you are wearing. If everyone is wearing the same shirt, break into groups according to whether you like to play sports, or prefer listening to music. Give each group a name according to the means of separation, such as the "tee-shirts" or possibly the "sneakers." Spend some time in your group sharing and writing down all the **differences** there are **between you and your other group members**. Try to list as many as possible. When the larger group gets back together, each person will say which other group they don't like according to an appearance (tee shirt, sneakers, blond hair, blue eyes, etc.). Then that group will read the list of differences between members of their own group to the rest of the group.

Notice that when separated according to appearance, people in the small groups looked similar to each other, but when they began reading their differences, there *were more differences* than the similarity of appearance. In other words, when we *use a stereotype* to describe a person, we *omit all of the characteristics* that make them *unique or different*.

Appreciation Of Differences

For a minute, let's try to imagine a world where everyone is the same. One morning we wake up and suddenly everyone is wearing exactly what we are wearing. They have the same color hair, and they even look just like us. We go to the movies with our friends, all of whom look just like us and say the exact same thing as us at the same time. Imagine how you would feel if that were in this situation when you woke up? Do you feel comfortable with the idea of everyone being just like you? That is the *joy in differences*. Because we all feel and think differently (*Principle 2, Session 3, Everyone Sees the World Differently*), there is change and excitement to our world. Trends change, thoughts change, and what we appreciate changes as well. Because there are so many different ethnicities, and even cultures, we can appreciate and experience things that would otherwise not exist. Different foods, sights, and experiences allow us to try out experiences that make life exciting and interesting.

Activity: Differences Within A Group

Break into smaller groups according to **ethnic or racial affiliation** (Hispanic, African-American, Caucasian, etc.), and then answer these questions in your group.
· Why did you affiliate yourself with this group?
· What are some of the similarities you have with the group, outside of skin color or racial identification?
· What are some of the differences you have from the group?
· Do you have more **differences** or more **similarities** as a group?

Unfortunately, many of our *stereotypes and prejudice* tend to be set into our minds as *"core beliefs."* Our *values* and *morals* are *types of core beliefs* about *what is important in life* (like the value of being a good friend) and what is *right or wrong*. Since our values are our way of looking at the world, it is really hard to think about a value not being positive or in our best interest. But sometimes our values can get in the way of changing for the better and living a happier life. Remember *Chapter 8, Responsibility to Others*, when we talked about *moral dilemmas*? It takes a moral dilemma in order for us to change our thought and value system for the better. Think of a *moral* that you have, such as "slavery is wrong." But if you have a *core belief* that some people are better than others, doesn't that conflict with your moral?

We are not saying that everyone has to change their beliefs or values, we are just saying that sometimes these may conflict with our morals, and our thinking needs to change in order to take control over our thoughts and have freedom in our lives. Are you open to changing some belief, value or standard of right and wrong that you may have held on to for a very long time?

Activity: Difference In Diversity

Take a moment to look at **Worksheet 31, My Diversity Profile** that you filled out earlier in this session. What are some of the beliefs represented in your profile? What are some of the stereotypes and generalities? Go down the list, and try to think of why you think that way about certain issues? Then as a larger group, discuss each topic and belief from the different points of view. Remember to respect and value each other's opinion. Are there certain things the group can agree on? Are there certain things that everyone disagrees on? Take some time to go back and think about your answers and where they came from. What are some alternative answers?

Putting It Together

· This story about Connor shows *several different stereotypes* and generalities. What are some of the stereotypes? Why does Connor believe in those stereotypes?

- Stereotypes often begin in generalities. What are some of the generalities or stereotypes that *you believe in*? Why do you believe in them?

- What are some of the stereotypes that have been *used against you*?

- Have you ever *encountered* prejudice? What was the situation and how did you react?

- Make a list of all the things your friends and you have in common. What are some of the differences? Would you be friends without those differences?

- Update your *Self-Portrait*. Do you want to decrease or increase any of the scales?

- Now update your *Plan for Change*. What about your errors in thinking?

SESSION 22: GENDER ISSUES

Objectives

- Review *Session 21: Respecting Others*
- Increase awareness of gender roles and stereotypes
- Understand the external pressures that influence our view of gender and sexuality
- Understand our personal views about men and women

Connor's Story

My mom always tells me that we should practice tolerance and get to know them as individuals, even though she thinks they're lazy and terrible housekeepers. Besides, what does she know anyways? She's not out there working to keep this family sheltered and fed. All she does is cook, clean, and watch her stupid soap operas. What does she know about what's going on out in the world?

I guess she did try to go to night school. But half the time we didn't get dinner and the other half she was talking about stupid stuff. My dad said that it was either the family or her uppity education. She cried, like women do, and she whined, like women do, and then she finally decided to stay home again. She didn't need an education, besides it was that stupid night school that got her talking about tolerance.

A reminder of stereotypes

Last session we discussed and learned about stereotypes and prejudice, where they come from, and why we have them. *Stereotypes begin as generalities*, which are helpful because they help us understand our world and put it into categories for quicker remembering. Unfortunately, when a generality becomes a stereotype, negative things can occur, such as *prejudice and hatred*. They are based on our failure to see differences within a group.

So why do stereotypes occur? There are many reasons for the development of stereotypes and prejudice, but last session we discussed two of them in particular.

- The need for superiority
- Lack of information

Some people feel the *need to be better than others*, and sometimes that comes around because *we are threatened* or our place in the world is threatened. By using negative stereotypes, it allows us to feel better about ourselves and our position in the world. But we shouldn't have to put others down to feel better about ourselves.

Another reason for stereotyping comes about through lack of information. When we discussed values and morals in *Chapter 8, Responsibility to Others*, we went over how our values come from the people around us, more importantly our parents and close friends. Sometimes we are surrounded by stereotypes our whole lives and so we begin to believe and follow them without even thinking about it. Most of us don't question our values, so we don't usually try to find out if the information we are going off of is correct.

Activity: Appreciation Of Differences

Take a moment to think about the people you were with last week. Were there any situations in which you treated someone **based on a stereotype** and not the individual? What were the situations you found yourself in, if any? Break into groups of three or four and discuss the different situations each of you had over the past week. What were the thoughts behind the situation? Help offer each other alternatives or different views of the situation in order to support the appreciation of differences.

Of course, there are some stereotypes that are so ingrained within our society, that most of us don't even think twice when we say or do something. Some of these stereotypes are called *gender roles*, or how we expect men and women to behave and feel in society. In this session, we will discuss gender roles and stereotypes, and find out how we think and feel about certain gender issues.

ARE MEN AND WOMEN MORE ALIKE OR DIFFERENT?

What is gender?

Strictly speaking, *gender* refers to male or female, based on the genitalia assigned when developing in the womb. Gender in the physical sense can become confusing, however. There are people who are termed *hermaphrodites*, which means they are born with both genitalia. There is nothing wrong with hermaphrodites, and most of them have corrective surgery in order to become the sex they feel most a part of.

There is also confusion in the *mental view of gender*. Some people who think they are opposite from their biological sex are considered to be transsexual. Transsexuality occurs in both males and females, and it does not mean they are homosexual. Usually a transsexual will dress and act according to the sex they feel they are *most mentally aligned* with, disregarding the physical genitalia. Some go through *corrective surgery* in order to become the *physical gender* of the mentality they are most comfortable with.

The gender differences bring to light an issue that is prevalent throughout our society. That is the issue of *gender roles*. How are members of the male or female gender expected to think, feel and act?

Activity: Our Gender Stereotypes

Break into groups of three and take a look at the *List of Soap Opera Characters* shown below. For this activity you will be helping to create a soap opera. **Your job is to name**, first and last names, all the characters in the soap opera. You will need to agree on the names as a team. When you have completed the list, return to the larger group. Each smaller group will give a report on what they named the characters. Your counselor will put a mark on each character whether the name was male or female. After all groups have reported their names, tally up the numbers and take a look at whether the majority of the group thinks the characters are probably male or female.

LIST OF SOAP OPERA CHARACTERS

- A doctor who is rude to patients and thinks they are better than everyone else
- A doctor who goes out of their way to help the homeless people of the city
- The administrator in charge of the hospital
- The secretary for the hospital administrator
- The security guard
- The janitor
- The operating room nurse
- The nurse who works in the new baby ward
- A volunteer who helps in the children's ward

How do men and women differ?

Society begins teaching us very early in life whether we are girls or boys, and what is expected from us because we are a certain gender. We learn early what clothing and accessories are appropriate for males and females, and as we grow older the expectations become more complicated and detailed. These expectations (automatic thoughts) become so ingrained that we rarely see them ourselves. They can vary from what we think people should look like (what we wear and how we do our hair), to who does the cooking and cleaning in a household, or who should go to work, or what we are expected to talk about at social gatherings. What do members of the group believe to be differences between men and women?

Activity: Connor's Expectations

Break into groups to discuss Connor's story. What were some of the expectations Connor had for his mom? How did Connor react when his mom tried to do **something different** than housework?

There is a problem with this, however. Similar to stereotypes, these gender roles become *so ingrained* that we act on them without thinking whether we agree with them or not. Similar to our values, we get them from our role models who may be parents, teachers and friends, but even society, media, and television as a whole tend to play up to and strengthen the gender roles. The truth, however, may be far from the specific gender role assignment.

Activity: The Role Of Gender

As a large group, think and write down **all the gender roles** you can think of, for both males and females. You don't have to agree with them, but think of commercials, television, and what your parents have told you to think of the roles. Once all the gender roles you can think of are written down, one by one go through them and pick out **one gender role you know an exception to**. For example, a gender role may be that "women are supposed to be the cooks for the family." If one of you knows that your father, or a male friend, is a better cook than your mother or another female, that is a role you know an exception to. Keep going around until everyone has picked up one exception. If time allows, keep going around until there are multiple exceptions for all the gender roles. Notice that very few people you know actually fit within these gender roles.

There are exceptions to every gender role, but when a person becomes *too different* from an expected gender role, they *become labeled*. A female who is referred to as a *tomboy* is an example, but there are also instances that warrant more attention. A transvestite is a person who prefers to *dress and act* like the opposite sex. While a transsexual has the mentality of the opposite sex, a transvestite usually likes and prefers being the sex they are; they just like dressing in the opposite sex's gender-specific clothes. While a transvestite can be of either sex, the most apparent and well known are males who dress as females, such as drag queens. Keep in mind that a transvestite does not have to be homosexual. Some heterosexual males prefer to dress as females.

Transvestitism brings to light an important criticism for society, however, which is why transvestites, as well as transsexuals and hermaphrodites tend to be stigmatized and looked down upon. Society, and generally the world at large, prefers to see things in black and white in order to avoid confusion and ambiguity. But there are many people out there who *behave differently* from what most people have come to expect as "normal." And being different is not something that is wrong or should be punished. Life is often set along a continuum, instead of just black and white, there is a lot of gray middle ground where the majority of people fall. Like we discussed in the last session, differences should be *enjoyed and experienced*, not shoved down and hated. And besides, as we learned in the section on stereotyping, there are many differences between members of any indentifiable group.

Labeling and stereotyping are certainly not always in reference to something as uncommon as transvestitism. A mother who *chooses to work* and have a family is sometimes stigmatized for trying to have a career. The same with the man who prefers to *stay home with his kids* rather than work at an office. Some people call them nasty names; but that doesn't mean their choices are wrong or that they are inferior in any way. This program teaches tolerance and acceptance for people's choices, as long as they are not injuring themselves or others.

Activity: A Role Apart

Break into groups of three in order to write a skit. Act out your character in the skit according to how you think the other sex would behave. For example, the group is trying to decide where to go to eat. If you were a male, then act out your character according to how you think a female would act and react. If you are female, try to act out your character how you think a male would act and react. When other groups are performing, notice how the characters seem like they are from a really bad sitcom. Most of them are contrived and based on gender roles and stereotypes that we are taught and fed from the media from the time we are born. Then individually write or draw out some things you believe and expect from yourself and your gender. Write down all that you can think of, even some things that you do every day. Then, as a larger group, compare everyone's answers about what they expect from their gender or themselves. What are some things that everyone wrote down? What are some things that are different? What expectations do you think you unknowingly hold about your own gender?

Who cares about gender roles?

The difficulty that arises from *gender roles* is that it is often used as the means of "putting a person in their place" or designating one person as better than the other person. Unfortunately, it gets drawn down the line of male versus female. The truth is that society needs both in order to function. Can you imagine a world without the opposite sex? It would get pretty boring. But by *insisting on conformity to gender roles* and stereotypes, people are not being allowed to explore their own talents or their individuality.

Activity: All About Control

Break into your discussion groups, and take another look at Connor's story. How did Connor and his dad **try to control** Connor's mom through gender roles? Was there any respect between Connor and his mom? Explain your answer. How would Connor's life be different if his mother would have been allowed to continue to go to school?

It comes down to respect

Respect comes in many forms, whether it is the job you work at or how much you are paid, to cultural and social pressures, to how you are treated and how you treat your friends and family. In order to get along, *we need to respect other people*. And in order to do that, we shouldn't force them into stereotypes or occupations or even clothing according to their sexuality. Everyone plays a role in society, and it doesn't have to fall along specific gender lines.

Activity: Gender Respect

Break into groups according to gender (male or female). Pick a person to record the answers and then answer these questions:
· What do you **like** about being male/female?
· What do you **not like** about being male/female?
· What are your **opinions** of the opposite sex?
· How do you **get respect** from women/men?
· What do they need to do to **earn respect** from you?

After you have answered all the questions, get back together as a large group and share your answers. What answers did both males and females answer similarly? What were some of the differences? How will you improve your respect for the opposite sex?

Putting It Together

· Connor shows some pretty specific gender role expectations for his mom. What are his expectations? Where did Connor get his expectations for his mom? What do you think about his expectations?

· Gender roles are stereotypes that tend to be placed in our value systems rather early. What are some of the gender roles you expect from yourself? What are some gender roles you expect from the opposite sex?

· Although seemingly simple, once we take a closer look at gender roles, they can become more confusing. What gender roles do you think are really confusing?

SESSION 22: GENDER ISSUES

- No matter the gender or sexual orientation of a person, respect is something that most people deserve. How do you show the opposite sex or people who have different sexual orientations that you respect them?

- Look at your thinking patterns ratings on your *Self-Portrait*. Do some of these patterns cause you to be prejudiced? Do some cause you to make gender stereotypes?

CONNOR'S STORY

Most people are so loud and inconsiderate it makes me ill. Especially those kind of people. You know the ones I'm talking about.

The other night I was trying to do my homework when the neighbors were being loud and obnoxious. I guess they were having a party. They are always having a party. My dad says that's just how they are, those kind of people. Inconsiderate, loud, obnoxious, and really shouldn't be here.

My dad grew up in this neighborhood. He said there didn't used to be all these different ethnicities and cultures and PC crap. Everyone was the same, and that's how it is supposed to be. He was raised that if you worked hard and did your job, you would be rewarded for it. No one told him that some other guy would swoop down and steal your promotion right out from under you. Just because the boss likes the other race better than yours, or because the other guy will work for cheaper. Who knows? Who cares, except for my dad, ya know, because he's the one who's getting his job stolen and his neighborhood ruined.

So my dad says they are all like that…every one. And I can kinda see his point sometimes. Most of them are like that. All of them I've been around except my one friend. He's different. He's not like them, although I'm not sure how he turned out differently. I guess maybe he's just smarter. All I know is I'm starting to not like any of them. In fact, sometimes I feel a kind of hatred towards them, especially when they are all loud and out in the hallway. They always give me a look like I don't belong here. My dad grew up just down the street, and I don't belong here? So I just give them a nasty look back.

My mom always tells me that we should practice tolerance, and try to get to know them as individuals. Even though she says they are all lazy and poor housekeepers. And what does she know anyways? She's not out there making a living to keep this family sheltered and fed. All she does is cook, clean, and watch her stupid soap operas. What does she know about what it's like out there?

I guess she did try to go to night school once. But then we didn't get dinner half the time, and the other half of the time she was always talking about stupid stuff. My dad put his foot down. He said it's either the family or her uppity education. My dad hates uppity people; they have no right thinking they are better than us. So she cried a lot, like women do, and whined a lot to my dad, like women do, and then finally decided she would stay home. She has no right being out there getting educated anyway. Women don't know nothing about the world. So my dad says. Besides, it's that stupid night school that got her started on the whole tolerance thing.

I can't even get a break at school. The teacher always thinks this person is smarter because they are this race, or the coach picks that person because they are that race, or she gets more chance to talk with her friends because she's more responsible and does her homework. Maybe he is smarter, and he is better at sports than I am, and maybe she is more responsible. But my dad says no it's because I'm male and not of the right race, and the PC crap has ruined the world. The teachers and coaches don't say that, they tell me I can do anything if I try, but my dad says that's just an excuse they use to make it all my fault when it's really their fault.

My dad's got a point. I have a right to be here, and most of them don't. And I have a right to a job when they are lazy and stupid. And I should be the one educated, not her. I have the right to do what I want to do when I want to do it, and they can't say nothing about it. And if my mom tries to tell me different, I'll hit her like my dad does. **She deserves it, she can't even cook right.**

NOTES

Chapter Twelve:
Exploring Individual Intimacy

GOALS OF THIS CHAPTER
- Discuss and understand individuality and personal identity
- Understand how emotional and sexual intimacy are related
- Learn how to decide if sexual intimacy is right for us
- Understand about contraceptives and their uses
- Learn about STDs and prevention

ALYSSA'S STORY

So I kissed a girl. And even though it was a bet, and I feel a bit weird about it, I kind of liked it. So does that mean I'm bisexual? Last night I went to a party with my best friend. I don't usually even drink because it gets in the way of soccer, but she really wanted to go see this guy....some of the guys were really cool. Especially these two guys. They bet my friend and I a beer that we wouldn't kiss each other. So we kissed, and the guys made a lot of noise, and we got some more beer. It was kind of weird this morning, but then we talked about it. It was just a kiss, and she's like my best friend. I'm just a little confused.

I'm like the most guy crazy of all my friends, but I sort of enjoyed the kiss with her. So now I don't know if I'm gay, or straight, or both. And I guess there are some benefits to sleeping with girls. I mean, I don't have to worry about getting pregnant.

But the thing is, I really like guys. Everything about them, even their sloppiness. I mean girls are softer, and cleaner, and a lot more classier, and if I got involved with a girl I could share clothes with her, which would like, increase my wardrobe by like, two times. But there is something about a guy picking you up, and dancing with you, and looking at you with those eyes that guys get, especially when they want sex. But I'm not even sure what it means to be bisexual.

Am I supposed to have a girlfriend and a boyfriend? So the question is, am I gay or not? Or bisexual? It's so confusing. But if I got bet again that I wouldn't kiss a girl, I wonder what I would do.

SESSION 23: IDENTITY AND EMOTIONAL INTIMACY

Objectives

· Review *Chapter 11: Overcoming Prejudice*
· Discuss identity development
· Understand how emotional intimacy develops
· Learn how to develop close relationships

Alyssa's Story

Last night my best friend and I went to a party. I don't usually drink because it gets in the way of soccer, but she really wanted to see this guy who would be there, and I figured why not? It's always good to try something new. So these people were totally not in our group, and at first I felt young and immature. But then everyone started drinking and they all started acting dumb and I felt better about how young I was. Some of the guys were even pretty cool.

Especially these two college freshmen. They dared my friend and me a beer that we wouldn't kiss each other. We looked at each other, and then kissed. I mean, she's like my best friend. We've known each other since kindergarten, and we share all our secrets. Like when my parents got divorced I didn't want to tell anyone, but I told her almost as soon as I found out. We're that tight. So kissing her wasn't a big deal.

A review of stereotypes and gender roles

In the last chapter we began discussing *generalizations, stereotypes, prejudice* and *gender roles*. *Generalizations* help us understand our world, and stereotypes lead us to have closed minds about the differences and positive aspects of people who we see as different than us. Similar to our values and morals, stereotypes are usually so ingrained in us that we are not aware of them unless they are pointed out. We discussed three reasons for developing stereotypes.
· *The need for superiority*
· *Lack of information*
· *Failure to see differences*

Activity: How Does Prejudice Feel?

Individually decide on one feature or **superficial aspect** of people that you will use to illustrate stereotyping and prejudice, such as brown eyes or blue jeans. Then walk around the room as a group. Show **non-verbal cues** of **discomfort and rejection** for those people who possess the trait that you decided upon. Everyone will have a different feature, but pay attention to who is avoiding whom, and what possible feature the people who were avoided have in common. Often when we stereotype and use prejudice, the victims aren't aware of what we are thinking or feeling about them. How did you feel when certain people of the group avoided you? What were you thinking as you tried to avoid certain people? Was it easy avoiding all the people with the feature you wanted to avoid, or did you start wanting to make exceptions? Explain your answer.

In *Session 22, Gender Issues*, we began talking about the roles that males and females are expected to play in society. Look back at *Worksheet 31, My Diversity Profile* and recall the activity in *Session 22, Our Gender Stereotypes*. Discuss whether you agree or disagree with the gender roles that are defined for your sex.

SESSION 23: IDENTITY AND EMOTIONAL INTIMACY

An important part of forming stereotypes, as well as how our prejudices get fostered and settled, is our *values and morals*. In *Chapter 8, Responsibility to Others*, we went over how *values and morals* develop to give us a specific point of view. Although values and morals are something we pick up from our family and the world we're in every day, they become a major part of who we see ourselves as, in other words our identity.

Values And Identity Development

As teenagers, we often move from group to group in a search of *who we are* and what we can relate to. Although some people remain relatively constant throughout their childhood and adolescence, some *change friends* almost as often as trends change in hairstyles, clothing, and music. A group may not hold the same values we do, or may go against our morals, and so we move to another group trying to *fit in*. "Clique bouncing" is common when we are young as we are trying to search out our boundaries and are looking for people like us. In truth we are searching for what it means to be us, and who we are in comparison to the rest of the world by experimenting with our appearances, our friends, and reactions of others to us. In the language of psychology we are "finding our identity."

Activity: That Clique's Not Mine

As a group, take a look at Alyssa's story. Why did she go to the party with her friend, even though she doesn't like to drink? What did she find when she got to the party, and how did she feel at first? Did her feelings change, and if so what made them change? Was she accepting of the new groups of people, or did she reject them? Do you think she would hang out with them again, why or why not?

Individuality

While our values and beliefs tend to make a large part of our identity, our experiences and interests also become a large part of who we are. Since no one can experience the same things in the same manner, we are all different individuals with different identities and ideas that help shape our sense of personal identity. Although we may belong to a certain culture, or we may even hang out with a closed group of friends, we are as different from other people as they are from us. In searching for an identity, most of us pick and choose from our experiences and surroundings to decide what is right for us, allowing for a unique and individual personality.

Activity: My Individual Identity

Take a moment by yourself to list certain things about you that you think help to make up your identity. Just make a note of what you think makes up who you are. Now think of three ways **your identity** has **developed a role for you** in society. For example, you see yourself as a good athlete, so you are on the football team; or you can manage money well, so you take charge of making the arrangements when something needs to be paid for. What part of your identity has developed around drugs and crime?

Return to the larger group, and one by one **list the things** you think **make up your identity**. Then allow the other group member to say if they think there is something that was forgotten from the list or if there is something they see as part of your identity. How does your identity form **your role** in society? Does the role you assume help define your identity, or is your identity separate? What aspects did you have in common with another person that you may think has a completely different identity? Why do you think you share the aspects but not the identity?

Many people experience *confusion* when they are engaged in discovering their individuality and forming a unique identity. It's not often that a person wakes up one morning and decides they are going to be a certain way. Development of an identity happens slowly over a long time, taking a lot of group *experimentation and rejection* before we have even a beginning idea of who we are. That can cause a lot of problems with our family and the people close to us. In pressing forward in our search for identity, we often push away people who are close or who care about us. Rejection of our parents' ideals and values is sometimes an important part of *declaring independence*.

Rejecting Negativity

In trying to carve out our role in the world around us, we often reject some of the expectations of our families and friends. We may refuse to conform to the roles that society seems to have created for us. After all, not all of us are cut out to be good students, then get a great job, a family and a two-car garage. *Rejection of family and social pressure* can be healthy and normal. Everyone goes through this to some extent, but when the new identity becomes *harmful or dangerous* to our mental or physical well-being, or injures people, we call it a *negative identity*. When we repetitively conduct ourselves in ways that limit our life opportunities or reduce our freedom we may come to the conclusion that we are influenced by a *failure identity*.

While some people like the *recognition* that a *negative or failure identity* can offer, these styles of relating to ourselves and others are not beneficial to living a happy and healthy life. Crime and substance abuse often become a major part of our identity, and often can keep us from forming bonds with other people that can support us and offer us emotional shelter.

As we said above, some people really don't go through much confusion concerning their identity. These people move through childhood and adolescence into adulthood with relatively little confusion. Other people can have a lot of confusion about the role they play and the part they want in society. Sometimes young people suffer because of an *unstable outside environment*, others feel the *need to reject* everything other people offer. Most of us experience some confusion and experimentation about our roles in life, but form a strong identity and sense of self by the time we are ready to move forward into adulthood. An identity search can take years, but most people will in the end find out who they are. The search for identity is so frustrating for some people that they make *sudden and dramatic choices*, like *running with a gang or hanging out with a group of heavy drug users*, even if it doesn't feel that good, in an effort to end the confusion about where they belong.

Emotions And Intimacy

Identity serves a purpose outside of helping us decide what clothes to wear and how we do our hair. Our *identity and sense of self* allows us to be *attracted to and close* with certain people who share our values, beliefs, and sense of the world. All of us have friends, family, and people who we care about. These relationships form a large part of our lives, and affect everything we think and feel about certain situations and life experiences. In order to be genuinely close to another person, though, we need to know who we are and what we expect from the world. Emotional intimacy, or closeness, doesn't always have to be with a boyfriend or girlfriend, or even our parents and family. Often we develop emotional intimacy with our friends who we are often around and with whom we share secret and private parts of our lives.

The most important element in developing emotional closeness is **trust**. This occurs on many levels, and is not the same for everyone. We trust that our friend or loved one *cares about us*. We trust that the other person *would not do anything to harm or hurt us*. And we even trust that we can go *to the other person* when we are having difficulties or just need to talk. That is not to say we trust everyone we are close to in the same way, or even to the same degree. In the last chapter we began discussing the continuum of life, about how there is a lot of gray between the black and white of opposites. Just because we do not necessarily trust a person with some of our secrets does not mean that we think they will try to hurt us or that we don't want to get to know them better.

Activity: An Intimate Friend

Break into small groups and take a look at Alyssa's story. Who do you think Alyssa is emotionally intimate with? Using examples from the story, show why you think that. If we have a continuum of intimacy, where do you think her friendship is and why?

Just as Alyssa explores a continuum of physical intimacy, emotional intimacy can occur along a continuum. We find ourselves caring for some people more than others, yet being intimate with just a few.

> ## INTIMACY = DEEP FEELINGS OF TRUST, CARING AND CLOSENESS

In this program, we have tried to develop a sense of trust between the group members. Although we may get along with some members better than others, there is a level of closeness among the group. For some, the group has become *like family*. For others, the group has *become acquaintances* that we can share some things with. For most of us, the group falls somewhere in the middle. Some of us may feel a *sense of intimacy* with other group members.

Activity: Where Do We Stand?

Break into pairs for this activity, but make sure that the pairs are randomly selected, such as the person across from you. Sit down slightly isolated from the rest of the pairs, and begin talking to each other about **how you think and feel** about the person you are sitting with. Be honest with each other. If you think you don't really know the other person and can't really trust them, say so. If you think you can trust the other person, let them know that you trust them and why. Then discuss how you think the two of you could become closer, if possible. If not possible, discuss why you think you wouldn't be able to become closer.

Where To Start?

We know that there are people in our lives that we care about and who care about us. The question really is how do we keep those close intimate friends and family? There are times when we fight with the people we care about, and disagreeing with other people is a fact of life. But there are some things we can do to help foster and take care of the emotional ties we develop with other people.

Communication: We have discussed communication several times throughout the program. The reason we keep repeating the *importance of communication* is because by having good *verbal* (talking) and *non-verbal* (body language), *active sharing and active listening* communication skills, we can be effective in supporting others and having our own needs met. Imagine trying to share and become friends with a person if you couldn't communicate. You would never know what they were thinking or feeling. Good communication will help you in several important ways.

· Feel closer to another person
· Understand each other better and get to know each other's point of view
· Solve problems and arguments with each other
· Have more positive feelings and less bad feelings towards each other
· Have a network of people who will look out for your well-being and best interests
· Be less likely to use substances or get involved in criminal acts again

Activity: Talking With A Friend

Taking another look at Alyssa's story, what do you think is an example of the **communication** between her and her friend? What problems are they able to solve together? Would you be comfortable talking to one of your friends about something like that, and why or why not?

For a reminder on how to communicate effectively, take a look at *Chapter 3, Talking About Yourself and Listening to What Others Say About You*, and *Chapter 6, Better Communication Skills*. The key ideas are active listening and active sharing. If you can develop and maintain these two skills, then communication will become easier.

Activity: A Circle Of Friends

Form a circle. Your counselor will begin with something that happened to him or her in the past week (**active sharing**). It can be something positive, something confusing, or something negative that your counselor had thoughts and feelings about. The person to the left of the counselor will then use the **feedback skills** to tell the counselor what they heard, and if applicable offer some advice that would help the counselor with the thoughts and feelings the situation created. After the feedback, the person will then **share something** that happened to them in the past week. Go around the circle until everyone has shared at least one thing and given feedback and advice if applicable at least once.

Time to Get a Little Closer

We've decided that good communication will help us to remain close with the people we care about. But how do we become closer to people who we may like, or would like to be more involved with? Here are some ways that we can become closer to people in our lives.

- *Don't expect people to read your mind.* Everybody thinks and feels differently in the same situation, and it's not fair to other people to expect them to automatically know what it is you want, feel, or think.

- *Don't let things build up.* It is easy to ignore or avoid issues that may cause disagreements or uncomfortable moments. But in ignoring them, they are still there but getting stronger. Just like how we talked about anger, depression, and guilt get stronger the longer we ignore them (*Chapter 10, Handling Anger, Guilt and Depression*). The same can happen between people when something bothers one or the other person. Use good communication skills to let the other person know what is bothering you.

- *Express your positive feelings.* It is important in any relationship or friendship to express and let the other person know the good things you like about them. The positive must always outweigh the negative, otherwise things get built up and the relationship turns sour. Remember the compliment skills from *Chapter 6 (Basic Communication Skills)*. Those can come in handy when trying to keep positive feelings between people.

- *Remember **win-win**.* When workng on differences or resolving conflicts, be sure that each of you is better off.

Most importantly, active *sharing and active listening* can play a crucial role in interacting with other people. If we can't share or listen, then there really isn't an emotional intimacy. A balance between *closeness and separateness* is also very important aspect. When being around another person begins to interfere with other activities that we may enjoy by ourselves, then the relationship becomes unhealthy. Being together is important, but having time to ourselves can be just as important.

Activity: My Feelings Apart

Individually fill out *Worksheet 32, Being Close and Apart*. Answer the questions about how you feel about a person close to you. Make sure you are honest about how you think and feel, and how you might be able to resolve any negative things about the relationship.

In the boxes shown in *Worksheet 32*, consider the overlapping circles in the *"Example of a Balanced Relationship"* as an ideal degree of separateness and closeness. In the next box, which indicates *"You and Your Significant Other,"* draw how you see your relationship with a person that is either your significant other or someone you are very close with. Put the circles **far apart** if you are too distant or **very overlapping** if you are too close or into each other's private space. How can your relationship become more balanced?

Worksheet 32

BEING CLOSE AND APART

QUESTION 1:
Who do you think is the person closest to you, and why do you think they are the person you feel the most for?

QUESTION 2:
What are some of the things that bother you about that person? What are the things you become angry or annoyed with about that person?

QUESTION 3:
What are some of the positive things about that person? What do you like about that person, and why do you trust them the most of all the people you know?

QUESTION 4:
What are some of the compliments you could give that person the next time you see them? How do you think they will react when you give them the compliments? Can you sincerely give them compliments?

Example of Balanced Relationship

You and Your Significant Other

Putting It Together

- Alyssa goes to the party because her friend wants to go. How do you think this relates to the formation of Alyssa's identity? Do you think going to the party is a *risk to her identity and role*; why or why not?

- Alyssa is emotionally intimate with her best friend. Where do you think the friendship falls on the continuum?

- What are some of the aspects of *your identity*, and why do you think you developed or accepted those aspects?

- Of your friends, how many do you trust? How many can you communicate with and share things important to you? *How can you develop closer friends?*

- Look at your Strengths and Resiliency ratings on your *Self-Portrait*. How important are these strengths in developing and keeping close and intimate friends?

- Re-rate yourself. Have your strengths increased?

- Update your *Plan for Change*.

SESSION 24: SEXUAL INTIMACY AND ORIENTATION

Objectives

- Review *Session 23: Identity and Emotional Intimacy*
- Discuss sexual intimacy
- Understand sexual orientation
- Learn what our personal view is about sex

Alyssa's Story

So I kissed my best friend. Even though it was a bet, I kind of liked it and now I feel sort of weird about it. So now am I bisexual or gay or something? I mean I really like guys; I'm like the most guy crazy of all my friends. But the kiss was with my best friend. I mean, things were a little weird, but then we talked about it and how we didn't want something more in our friendship and now everything is cool. With a guy I would be wondering if he liked me, or if he wanted to see me again, or if he thought I was a slut or something.

But because we kissed, does that mean I'm bi? I guess it could be worse. At least I'm not a guy, cause once a guy kisses another guy he's gay, right? There is no bisexuality for guys; they are either gay or straight. I'm just so confused.

Sexual Intimacy

While emotional intimacy is about *trust, caring and closeness* with another person, whether it is a family member or an acquaintance, *sexual intimacy* becomes a little more complicated and *a lot more selective*. Almost all of you have been through a health class that talks about reproduction. In the most biological sense, sexual intimacy is about reproduction. But in social circles, sex begins to take on more and different meanings than the physical means of having a baby.

As teenagers walking the halls in school, almost everyone hears and talks about sex. In fact, sex is most often considered part of entering adulthood. To a lot of people, sex becomes a physical means to prove oneself an adult ready to take on adult responsibility. But the truth is more complicated than that. *Sexual intimacy* is the physical act of emotional intimacy, and is part of a relationship with another person. Sex is about sharing a part of oneself with another, uncovered and exposed to another person's view. Sexual intimacy is not just limited to intercourse with another person, however. Sexual intimacy can include kissing, "touching each other's genitals,""outercourse" (dry humping), and mutual masturbation.

The truth and problem is we often get involved in sex with other people before we aren't even sure who we are or what we want from life. This begins to complicate matters since adolescence is confusing enough as it is. In order to be sure about taking part in sexual intimacy with another person, we first have to become aware of what we think and feel about sex ourselves.

Activity: My Values About Sex

Take a moment as a group to **review values and morals**. Then as individuals, begin to fill out *Worksheet 33*. Do not answer according to what your friends or the person you are in a relationship with would say, but think about **what your own answers are**. Write as specifically as possible when answering your questions. Then take a moment to think about and clarify what your **personal values** about sexual intimacy are. What are your **personal goals** concerning involvement in sexual activity?

In *Chapter 4, Backsliding to Drugs and Crime*, we discussed the *Rule Violation Effect*. This occurs when we break a rule we set for ourselves, and often we tend to give up completely instead of reinstating our values. While we discussed this in *Chapter 4* in relation to *relapse and recidivism*, this rule also applies to sexual intimacy. If we become sexually involved after we decided not to, we don't have to completely give up our values. We can reinstate our values and move on from that experience. In other words, if we do something sexually that we are not proud of, we can decide not to repeat the action and *return to conducting ourselves* in a manner that we consider to be *in line with our values and morals*. Could this be an option for Alyssa and her friend?

Trust Between Partners

One very important aspect of becoming involved sexually with another person, similar to emotional intimacy, is the **level of trust**. Trust is the most important thing to have between two people who have decided to share both their physical and emotional selves. But how does the trust develop to the point of being able to be physically intimate with another person? There are several different things that have to be in place before the trust is at a level for sexual intimacy.

· **Always** have each other's consent, that is, their *verbal permission*
· **Never** use pressure to get consent
· Be honest with each other. Communication is a big thing here. Talk about what you like and don't like, and listen to what each other has to say
· Treat each other as equals
· Be attentive to each other's pleasure
· Protect each other against physical and emotional harm
· Be clear and honest about what you want to do and what you don't want to do
· Respect each other's limits
· **Always** accept responsibility for your actions

Activity: The Right To Say NO

Create a skit in which one person is **asking or telling** an imagined person to have sex. Try to take this activity very seriously as it really can **help you to be kind** to someone you care about. Pay attention to the list above, and have the group decide whether the imagined person should **refuse or agree** to have sex according to the above standards for sexual intimacy. Is the first person using pressure? What sort of **communication** is involved? How is the speaker in the skit **showing respect** for the imagined partner, and how are they exhibiting responsibility for any action they take?

Worksheet 33

My Values About Sex

- How do my family members view dating?

- How do members of my ethnic group view sexuality among teenagers?

- Are the rules the same for guys and girls?

- What do members of my ethnic group say about sexual intimacy before marriage?

- Does my religion influence my views of sexuality?

- What do I think is too far for intimacy between adolescents?

- Am I comfortable with how far I have gone sexually?

- What is my personal opinion concerning sexual intimacy?

How Do The Following Fit Into My Ideas And Goals About Healthy Sexuality:

- Kissing on a first date?

- Petting or necking?

- Masturbation?

- Oral sex?

- Intercourse ("going all the way")?

- When am I old enough for different sexual behaviors?

- What sexual activities are healthy for you?

Sexual intimacy is about choices, and only we have the control over our choices. Remember, our thoughts determine our choices. We choose when we are ready and what we are ready for (kissing but no petting, or petting but no intercourse). We choose our partners and we always choose what we want to do and what we don't want to do with our partners.

Sexual orientation and intimacy

In recent years the media and other forms of social information have begun openly discussing sexual orientation. While most people see themselves as heterosexual, there are some who may have different views of their sexual orientation, as shown below. This gives us a better idea of what this continuum looks like.

Continum of Sexual Behavior and Orientation

1	2	3	4	5	6

0 -- Exclusively heterosexual
1 -- Mostly heterosexual with minimal homosexual experience
2 -- Heterosexual with a lot of homosexual experience
3 -- Equal heterosexual and homosexual experience
4 -- Homosexual with a lot of heterosexual experience
5 -- Homosexual with minimal heterosexual experience
6 -- Exclusively homosexual

So let's take a moment to discuss and differentiate between sexual orientation and experimentation. **Orientation** means our *personal tendency* towards something. If we are good at drawing, then we could say we are oriented towards the visual arts. Orientation is something that occurs in our *thoughts and feelings* about a certain situation or action. **Experimentation**, on the other hand, is more the *physical behavior* of testing our boundaries and realizing our identities. So if we become sexually intimate with a friend of the same sex just to see what it's like, that would be considered experimentation. If we find the same sex to be more attractive than the opposite sex, that would be our orientation. Everyone has a sexual orientation, whether it is to the same sex, the opposite sex, or both. Most people are sexually oriented toward the opposite sex, but everyone has a sexual orientation.

Activity: Alyssa's Orientation

Discuss Alyssa's story and what you think her orientation might be. What examples or signs are there that Alyssa is gay? What signs are there that Alyssa is not gay? Do you think Alyssa was just experimenting or do you think she is genuinely attracted to the other sex? Why do you think that, and make sure to use examples from the story.

Sexual experimentation frequently occurs during adolescence. Even if we are not sexually active, most of us have daydreams; some may have "wet" dreams, and many are involved in some sexual actions that may not include intercourse. Just because a person happens to have an episode of experimentation with a person of the same sex, it does not mean that person is automatically of homosexual orientation.

Intimacy Versus Abuse

When someone becomes involved in sexual actions against another person's will, or without their consent, this is sexual assault. When a person has fantasies about forced sex, this is a sign that they may be heading toward sexual misconduct. Remember, thoughts lead to actions. If an adult or peer blackmails us, or uses certain power advantages in order to have a sexual relationship with us, that is considered assault or abuse. Remember the three things that are needed in order for healthy sexual intimacy to take place:

> ## COMMUNICATION, RESPONSIBILITY, AND RESPECT

If any of these, *especially respect*, are missing when confronted with starting a sexual relationship, you have every right to say no. And you have every right to say no at any point before or during any sexual interaction. If, for any reason, you feel uncomfortable or unsure about any sexual actions, talk with your counselor or a trusted adult about your thoughts and feelings. Everyone has rights, and you have the right to say no.

WHAT IS A HEALTHY SEXUAL INTIMACY?

1. Healthy sexual intimacy takes place after two people have developed a healthy social, emotional and spiritual closeness and intimacy. This means there is commitment to the relationship.

2. Any sexual intimacy, whether it is kissing or intercourse, takes place when the two persons involved give consent and mutually agree 100 percent. If one person has doubt about taking part in sexual intimacy, then it is probably not healthy.

3. Healthy intimacy is based on trust and respect for the other person.

4. Physical intimacy is healthy when it is part of the long-term goals of the relationship.

5. Finally, sexual intimacy that occurs **because** one or both are under the influence of alcohol or other drugs is **not healthy sexual intimacy**.

Putting It Together

- Because of the kiss with her friend, Alyssa *thinks she might be bisexual*. What do you think her sexual orientation is and why? What do you think about sexual experimentation?

- What are your *personal values* concerning sexual intimacy? What are your goals?

- Do you think emotional intimacy is important in sexual intimacy, why or why not?

- Update your *Plan for Change*.

SESSION 25: SAFE SEX

Objectives

- Review *Session 23: Identity and Emotional Intimacy;* and
  Session 24: Sexual Intimacy and Orientation
- Discuss and talk about sex
- Understand whether sex is right for us

Alyssa's Story

I guess there is one good thing about being gay or bisexual. At least I can't get pregnant with another girl. That is pretty much impossible. And if I was gay from the beginning I could have still called myself a virgin. Besides, I'm probably too young to get pregnant anyways. There was this girl in our class that got pregnant when she was like fourteen, but that was because she was really developed and a slut.

I can't really do anything about not getting pregnant anyways. I mean, if a guy doesn't have a condom, then what can I do about it? I don't want to have sex with a guy yet, anyways, so it's not like I'm at risk for getting pregnant.

Review of emotional and sexual intimacy

In the last session we began talking about emotional intimacy and sexual intimacy. Emotional intimacy involves *caring for and trusting* certain people around us, including our family, friends, as well as teachers and counselors. Sexual intimacy involves sexual actions towards or with a person we have an emotional intimacy with. Sexual intimacy does not just involve sexual intercourse. There is a *continuum of sexual intimacy*, which includes something as seemingly insignificant as holding hands or kissing, all the way to outercourse or intercourse.

It is important for us to know our own *values and moral standards* when sexual intimacy is concerned. By being aware of what we think and feel about sexual intimacy, we can make better decisions for our lives. That is not to say that once we have gone against a value that we can't reestablish it and move forward with our lives. If we decide we aren't going to have sex until we are older, and we find that *we have violated that commitment*, there is no reason why we can't *reassert our value*. Remember when we discussed *Rule Violation in Chapter 4*? When we break a rule we set for ourselves, often it is easier to keep sliding downwards than to reinstate our value. This, however, is not the best option for us. Instead of *giving in*, or even becoming promiscuous, we can *reassert our values about sex* and learn from our slip.

With sexual intimacy and adolescence come experimentation and our first good idea of our sexual orientation. Last session we spent some time differentiating between *experimentation* and *orientation*. *Experimentation* is the *physical behavior* of pushing our limits and setting our identities. *Orientation*, on the other hand, is more related to our *thoughts and feelings* towards a certain situation or event. Some people have experimented with members of the same sex, but their orientation may be toward the opposite sex.

Activity: Alyssa's Sexual Orientation

Think back to last session and discuss whether the group thinks Alyssa was experimenting or if she is bisexual. Remember the continuum of orientation, and discuss whether you think it is possible for a guy to be bisexual. Then discuss your **individual values** concerning sexual experimentation. Are your values different than the people around you? What can you do if you go against your values?

What Is Sex?

Although we discussed *sexual intimacy* in the last session, we are now ready to discuss the part of human behavior that is responsible for reproduction, sexual intercourse. Intercourse can be broken down into three categories: *vaginal, anal, and oral*. Vaginal sex, usually referring to *heterosexual intercourse*, is when the penis is inserted into the vagina. Lesbian females can also have vaginal sex using alternative methods. Anal sex is when the penis is inserted into the anus, and is often what is thought of when males have sex with each other, although it can also be part of a heterosexual relationship. Oral sex is when one or both partners use their mouth on the genitals of the other partner. It is important to keep in mind that *all three methods* are considered sexual intercourse.

Technically a person loses their virginity the first time they participate in vaginal sex. This technicality can cause some difficulties, however, because homosexual action is still considered sexual intercourse, meaning that they have lost their virginity as well. On the level of biology, a female *loses her virginity* when the hymen, a thin tissue across the vaginal cavity, is punctured. In modern day, however, the hymen often dissolves or is broken by sports or highly physical activities. There are people who have become "born again virgins," which means that although they have participated in sexual activities previously, they have reinstated non-sexual values. For them, being true to their personal values is attainable by holding themselves to a standard of sexual abstinence, even though they may have been sexually active in the past.

Activity: Our Personal Definitions Of Intercourse And Virginity

Break into smaller groups and discuss what you think **virginity means** and what **sexual intercourse** means. Pay attention to the different definitions that everyone can have, and how that affects certain actions they choose. See if your group can decide on one **definition of virginity**, and one definition for **sexual intercourse**. Then regroup with the larger group and discuss. If your group decided on one definition for each term, tell the larger group what the definitions are and how you decided on those definitions. If your group was unable to decide on one definition, tell the larger group about the discussion and why you weren't able to agree.

When A Choice Is Made

Most adults and this program suggest that young people *wait before becoming sexually active*. Adolescence is a time when our bodies become different and our emotions are often up and down. Sexual intimacy, and sexual intercourse specifically, is a *huge decision* when so many other things are up in the air. Ultimately the decision is up to each individual. Just as we have freedom over our thoughts and actions, we must take personal responsibility to decide whether sex is right for us or not.

Worksheet 34

PROS & CONS OF DIFFERENT SEXUAL ACTIVITIES

Activity	Pros	Cons
Kissing		
Petting		
Outercourse		
Masturbation		
Oral Sex		
Intercourse		

SESSION 25: SAFE SEX

There are some things to keep in mind if we decide to become sexually active. As mentioned in the previous section, the biological reason for sex is mostly for *reproductive purposes*. Being a teenager and parent, however, is <u>not</u> a good combination. In order to be responsible about sex (part of building trust in a partner), we have to be aware of the means to prevent an unwanted pregnancy and sexually transmitted disease.

Activity: What Do I Know About Safe Sex?

Individually, fill out *Worksheet 34* on Pros and Cons of Different Sexual Activities. Which activities do you think best fit your values and morals? Why?

The Benefit of Abstinence

Abstinence, or *not participating* in sexual intercourse, is the best and only method that is 100% guaranteed to not end in pregnancy.

Activity: A Choice To Be Made

As a large group, discuss when you think is the **right time** for sexual intimacy, or more specifically sexual intercourse. Talk about when and why you would feel comfortable enough with a person to have sex, and what you expect after you have sex with a person. Be honest about what you think.

If the decision is made to participate in sexual activity, there are some methods that can *reduce the chances* of an unwanted pregnancy and sexually transmitted disease. For more information about birth control and contraceptives, speak with your counselor or doctor, or call the Health Department at 1-877-696-6775 (www.os.dhhs.gov). Keep in mind that this information is provided as a means of *providing safety*, **if** you become sexually active, but should not be thought of as our recommendations for what you should do. This program takes the position that abstinence is the only method of ensuring safety for protection against pregnancy and sexually transmitted disease.

Activity: The Act Of Being Responsible

Discuss your opinions about whether teenagers should have sex or not. What kind of influences and factors are there in choosing to have sex? Discuss what sort of problems can occur from choosing to become sexually active.

Activity: Alyssa's Choice

Alyssa claims there isn't anything she can do to prevent a pregnancy. What do you think? Do you think Alyssa is too young to get pregnent, and why does she think that way?

DRUGS AND SEXUAL INTIMACY

Drugs will prevent a person from making healthy and good decisions about taking part in sexual intimacy. Drugs:

- Lower your ability to make good judgments about sexual intimacy.

- Prevent you from seeing the consequences or outcomes of taking part in sexual intimacy.

- Put you at high risk for contracting sexually transmitted disease and pregnancy.

- Prevent you from seeing how sexual intimacy fits in with the big picture of relationship intimacy.

DRUGS AND SEXUAL CONDUCT ARE DANGEROUS COMBINATIONS

Putting It Together

- Alyssa claims that she is too young to become pregnant. Do you agree or disagree with this and why?

- Along with claiming she can't become pregnant, Alyssa states that if the guy *doesn't have a condom* there is *nothing* she can do about it. Is she being smart by not using a contraceptive, and what do you think about her choice?

- If you are sexually active, how might you get information on sexual health and pregnancy prevention?

- Do you think teenagers should be having sex? What are some of your reasons?

- Update your *Plan for Change.*

- What is healthy sexual intimacy?

Objectives

- Review *Session 25: Safe Sex,* and basic information from all sessions in this chapter
- Discuss the importance of preventing pregnancy and sexually transmitted disease
- Discuss the occurrence of sexually transmitted diseases (STDs) and infections
- Learn what the specific symptoms and names are
- Understand how to protect yourself

Alyssa's Story

Another good thing about being bisexual or gay is that I can't catch a STD or anything like that. I mean everyone knows you can't spread diseases between females, and then I wouldn't have to worry about a condom or anything.

But I would miss being with guys, and I really like guys, a lot. The way they can pick me up, and dance with me, and when they look at me, especially when they want to have sex. I guess I don't have to worry too much, cause I'm not with like dirty guys. All the guys I'm with are clean and I would be able to tell if they had something. Besides, I think STDs are a grown-up thing.

Review of emotional and sexual intimacy

Throughout this chapter, (*Session 23, Identity and Emotional Intimacy; Session 24, Sexual Intimacy and Orientation; and Session 25, Safe Sex*), we began to discuss the importance of *communication and trust* in close or intimate relationships. Many young people decide to wait until they are older—when they are truly ready to accept the *commitment, responsibility, and consequences* of being intimate with another person—*before engaging* in any form of intimate sexual contact, including intercourse. If, however, a person decides to participate in sexual activities, clear thinking about the issues of *emotional and physical safety*, for both your partner and yourself, are *some of the most important considerations* in life. Of most importance, are the *prevention of pregnancy* and *sexually transmitted diseases*.

Pregnancy and the possibility of being responsible for the *care and support* of another human being is not the only risk of intercourse. Sexually transmitted diseases and infections can cause serious health problems that can have *lifetime effects*, even resulting in *severe illness* and *premature death*. In this lesson, we will first discuss sexual activity and pregnancy and then focus on the prevention of sexually transmitted disease.

Preventing Pregnancy

If you are sexually active, there are certain methods to prevent pregnancy, which can be discussed with your counselor or doctor.

SESSION 26: STDS AND HIV PREVENTION

Activity: Safe Sex and Pregnancy

In the past two sessions we have been discussing emotional and sexually intimacy. As a group talk about what you consider sexual activity to mean, including your personal definition of sexual intercourse. Notice how everyone's definitions are still different from each other. Are there any sexual activities that you consider safe? When do you consider losing of one's virginity? How does someone get pregnant and how might they prevent pregnancy? What are your options for information resources about birth control and contraceptives? What is the only method 100% guaranteed to prevent pregnancy and disease?

PREVENTION OF SEXUALLY TRANSMITTED DISEASE

Upon making the decision to become sexually active, pregnancy—*a major life-changing event*—is not the only thing to be concerned about. It is estimated that *one in five* people in the U.S. has a *sexually transmitted infection or disease*, and 25% of new cases are found in teenagers[1]. STDs are *easily spread* through sexual contact, including anal and oral, and can lead to serious long-term problems including *infertility, chronic illness, permanent disability, and death*.

The only *sure way* to prevent a STD is *abstinence*, or not being sexually involved at all. The only other way to prevent an infection is to use a *male or female latex condom*, and to get checked by a doctor on a regular basis. This is important for both males and females, especially if one or the other has had more than one partner. Homosexuality or bisexuality is *not a guarantee* against STDs. Several infections can be spread from female to female. Remember that the *only contraceptive* that is effective against infections and disease is a *condom*, and there is still some possibility of error. Abstinence is the only sure means of preventing disease.

Activity: Alyssa's Knowledge Of STDs

As a group take a look at Alyssa's story. What are Alyssa's **opinions** about sexually transmitted diseases and infections? How does she think she can avoid getting them? What does she do to protect herself, and do you agree with what she has to say? Why or why not?

Activity: Is AIDS A Current Epidemic?

Break into groups of three or four and take a look at some recent newspapers or magazine articles. Can you find any articles about AIDS or HIV statistics or infections? Does the occurrence of the disease happen locally, or is it widespread? Who is affected by the disease, and what can be done to prevent the future spreading of the disease?

INFORMATION ABOUT INFECTIONS AND DISEASES

While there are now over twenty infections and diseases that can be spread through sexual activity, there are certain infections that occur more frequently than others. Here are some of the diseases and their symptoms. Remember, if at any time you think you might have an infection, it is important to see your doctor as soon as possible. As a group discuss the causes, symptoms, consequences for the diseases shown in *Causes, Symptoms, and Treatment for STDs* below.

[1]Found at the Department of Health: TeensHealth website

Causes, Symptoms and Treatment for Sexually Transmitted Diseases

Chlamydia

Pronounced *kluh-mid-ee-uh*, this infection is caused by bacteria called *Chlamydia Trachomatis*. One of the most common diseases, this bacteria can move through sexual intercourse, oral-genital contact, and also through the eye. While a person cannot catch this bacteria from a towel, doorknob, or toilet seat, it can be passed from mother to baby while the baby is being delivered.

Symptoms: The difficulty with Chlamydia is that both guys and girls may have a hard time telling whether they have the infection or not. In fact, most girls don't have any symptoms at all, which means they can have the disease and not even know it. When symptoms do occur, between a week and a month after contracting the infection, they can cause unusual vaginal discharge, pain during urination, pain in the lower abdomen and during intercourse, and bleeding between periods for girls. In guys, the bacteria often causes discharge from the tip of the penis or an itching or burning sensation around the penis.

If left untreated, the bacteria can cause inflammation of the urethra (where urine comes out) and can lead to pelvic inflammatory disease (PID) in girls, which can cause infertility. If a diagnosis of Chlamydia has been made, an antibiotic will be prescribed and the infection will clear up in about two weeks. If you are diagnosed, anyone you have had sex with will have to be tested, because remember you can have this disease without any symptoms!

Genital Herpes

Pronounced *her-peez*, this disease is caused by a virus called *herpes simplex* (HSV). There are two different types of the herpes virus, HSV-I and HSV-II. The most common one is HSV-I, which causes cold sores or fever blisters that appear on or around the mouth, lips, or nose of many people. It can be passed by sharing eating utensils, towels, razors, or kissing a person with a cold sore, and can also be spread through sexual activity between females.

HSV-II is a *sexually transmitted infection* that causes sores in the genital area and is spread through intimate sexual contact (vaginal, oral, or anal). A person cannot catch herpes from a toilet seat or doorknob because the virus does not live outside the body for long.

Symptoms: A person who has been exposed to genital herpes may first notice itching or pain around the genitals, followed by sores that appear a few hours to a few days after contraction. The sores, which may appear on the genitals, buttocks, or anus, start as red bumps that turn into red, watery blisters that can make it very painful to urinate. The sores then open up, ooze fluid or bleed, and then scab over and clear up in about 3-4 days. The entire genital area may feel tender or painful, and a fever or swollen lymph nodes may occur. The infection occurs in about 2-20 days after first being exposed, and the sores usually appear a few days later.

Although the symptoms may clear up within days, the virus itself hides in the body until the next breakout. Most people have about five outbreaks a year, although the number will lessen over time. Herpes can still be transmitted, or passed from one person to another, even if there aren't any sores. There is NO cure for herpes, although a doctor can prescribe a medication to help control the recurring virus. The only sure way to prevent Herpes is *abstinence*, and a latex condom must be properly used for people who do choose to have sex.

Genital Warts

Genital warts are caused by a group of viruses called HPV (human papillomavirus), which is similar to the warts found on people's hands and feet, although those warts are not sexually transmitted. The warts are passed from person to person during sexual intimacy (vaginal, oral, or anal sex), and cannot be contracted from a towel, doorknob, or toilet seat, but *can be spread* from female to female.

Symptoms: Genital warts look like regular warts and are small, hard, skin colored, and don't hurt, but may be itchy. As they grow bigger, they may look like tiny cauliflowers. Girls usually get them at the bottom of the vaginal opening, on the vaginal lips, on the cervix, or around the anus. In guys, they often appear near the tip of the penis, on the shaft of the penis, or on the scrotum on guys, and often are so small they can't be seen by the naked eye. Warts may appear anytime from 3 weeks to 3 months after being exposed, and the virus can live in the body for a long time without causing symptoms.

If left untreated, the warts may grow bigger and multiply, and may lead to cervical cancer in females. A doctor will be able to prescribe a special medication to dissolve the warts, and in some cases may "freeze" them off using chemical or laser treatment. They may reappear after treatment.

Gonorrhea

Pronounced gone-uh-ree-uh, this infection is caused by bacteria called Neisseria gonorrhea. The bacteria can be passed through sexual activity (vaginal, oral, or anal) as well as from a mother to her baby during birth. Gonorrhea cannot be contracted from a towel, doorknob, or toilet seat, but it can be spread from female to female, male to male, or male to female.

Symptoms: Similar to chlamydia, a person may have no symptoms at all, or the symptoms are so mild that a person won't notice them until they lead to more severe health problems. A guy is more likely to notice symptoms earlier than a girl, and often the disease causes a *burning sensation* when urinating, and sometimes a green discharge or pus may ooze out of the tip of the penis or from the vagina. A girl may notice the first symptoms from about 1-3 weeks later, while a guy may notice the symptoms from about 2 days to 2 weeks later.

If left untreated, *gonorrhea* can cause scarring and infertility in both males and females, as well as cause a rash, fever, and painful or infected joints, most commonly in the knee. After a doctor has diagnosed gonorrhea, an antibiotic will be prescribed. Gonorrhea, however, can cause *blindness, meningitis, or death* in an infant if the mother has contracted the disease.

Hepatitis

Pronounced *hep-uh-tie-tiss*, this infection causes a disease of the liver. Although a virus usually causes it, alcohol and other toxins can also cause it. There are several different forms of hepatitis, but hepatitis B and C can move from one person to another through blood and other bodily fluids. It can be passed through sexual intercourse and needles shared by intravenous drug users who have the virus. Hepatitis B and C can also be passed from a mother to her baby, although it cannot be contracted from a towel, doorknob, or toilet seat.

Symptoms: A person with hepatitis may feel tired and lose their appetite, similar to the flu, and may be nauseated or have a mild fever. Vomiting, abdominal pain, or pain underneath the right rib cage where the liver is located may also be experienced. After being exposed to the virus, symptoms may occur 1 to 5 months later, with some people having few to no symptoms until the disease has progressed. Some people will be contagious for the rest of their lives, and may not show symptoms until later in life.

Hepatitis can lead to *liver damage* and an increase in liver cancer, and is easily passed through most body fluids. *Immunization against hepatitis B* has become common, especially in newborn babies.

HIV And AIDS

One of the most *serious and deadly* diseases in human history, AIDS has spread incredibly fast since the first cases were identified twenty years ago. AIDS is caused by the HIV virus (human immunodeficiency virus), which destroys a defense cell in the body that fights infectious disease. People with the virus begin to get serious infections that they would normally fight off, causing them to die from common things such as pneumonia.

AIDS and HIV can be spread through blood, genital fluids, and breast milk and most often is *contracted through unsafe sex* (oral, vaginal, or anal) and sharing needles. It *cannot be passed* through hugs, sneezes, coughs, insects, towels, toilet seats, doorknobs, or any other contact that does not involve an exchange of bodily fluids.

Symptoms: The most dangerous thing about HIV infections is that a person can have the virus for a long time before ever getting symptoms. It is only when a person's blood does not have enough cells to fight infection that a diagnosis of AIDS is given, and although most people will develop AIDS within ten years of contracting HIV, they may not have any symptoms for years before that. Once symptoms occur, they usually consist of extreme weakness, rapid weight loss, frequent fevers that last for weeks, sweating very heavily at night, swollen glands, minor infections like rashes, chronic diarrhea, and a cough that won't go away. Girls may also experience yeast infections that won't respond to usual treatment.

There is **no cure** for HIV and AIDS, which makes *prevention extremely important*. Early detection also can play a role, as there are now drugs that can boost the immune system and prevent infections, preventing many people who are HIV+ from developing AIDS and prolonging their lives. But these medications however, are not a cure for being HIV+.

Syphilis

Pronounced *siff-ill-iss*, this infection is caused by bacteria called *Trepenoma Pallidum*. This bacteria is known as a *spirochete*, which is extremely small and can live almost anywhere in the body. This infection can be passed from one person to another through sexual intercourse (vaginal, oral, or anal), as well as from a mother to her baby during pregnancy. It cannot be contracted from a towel, doorknob, or toilet seat, but it can be spread from female to female, male to male, or male to female.

Symptoms: Syphilis occurs in four different stages.

Stage one: Red, wet sores that don't hurt appear on the vagina, rectum, mouth, penis, or under the foreskin. The sore, called a chancre (*shank-er*), appears in the first place that the spirochetes move from one person to another. After a few weeks the chancre will disappear, but this infection is highly contagious during this stage. A chancre may be noticed from 3 days to 3 months after being exposed.

Stage two: If syphilis hasn't been treated, the person will usually break out in a rash, especially on the soles of the feet and palms of the hands. Sores can appear on the lips, mouth, throat, vagina, penis and anus. Flu-like symptoms, such as fever and achiness, can also be present, and this stage lasts from 1 to 2 weeks. This stage may occur anywhere from about 3 to 6 weeks after the original chancre.

Stage three: During this stage, the illness will become what is called *latent syphilis*. The symptoms of the disease go away, but the spirochetes are still moving around the body. Syphilis can remain latent for many years.

Stage four: If the disease has not been treated by this point, it becomes what is known as *tertiary syphilis*. The spirochetes have spread all over the body and can affect the brain, the heart, the spinal cord, and the bones.

It is important to keep in mind that many people never notice any symptoms of syphilis. Depending on the stage, a doctor can make a diagnosis by examining the chancres or by doing a blood test to look for the spirochetes. An *antibiotic* will be prescribed if syphilis is diagnosed.

Trichomoniasis

Pronounced *trick-oh-moh-nye-uh-sis*, this infection is caused by a parasite that can be passed from one person to another during sexual intercourse. Unlike most sexually transmitted infections, *trichomoniasis can live for a few hours on a damp towel*, washcloth, and bathing suits. This is one of the most common infections.

Symptoms: While a guy most often won't notice any symptoms of "trich," a female will usually have thick gray or yellowish green discharge that may have a foul odor. The vagina may feel very itchy, and may be very painful to urinate. The parasite can also cause an achy abdomen and pain during sex. Symptoms usually appear 3 to 28 days after a person has been exposed to *trichomoniasis*.

Although "trich" is not very dangerous, it can be uncomfortable. It does, however, often occur with *gonorrhea* and *chlamydia*, as these infections tend to occur together. If a doctor's diagnosis of "trich" occurs, then a *prescription antibiotic* will be given in order to get rid of the parasite.

Activity: Alyssa's Mistake

Take a look at why Alyssa thinks she can't get a STD, especially if she is involved with only females. Why is Alyssa wrong? What diseases can she get from being with another female? Why wouldn't Alyssa know if a guy she is with has an infection? What can Alyssa do to prevent catching a disease? What diseases are only associated with males and females having sex together? Which can be contracted by same sex partners?

Although these are some of the common sexually transmitted infections and diseases, there are more out there than can be fit in this session. In order to avoid contracting an infection, *prevention methods are absolutely important.* While latex condoms can prevent the spread of certain diseases, **abstinence is the only sure** way to prevent being exposed to a disease or infection. Regular checkups and tests from a doctor are also very important if you decide to become sexually active.

Activity: Speaking About Diseases

We know it can be difficult to talk with an adult or another person about something that is wrong, especially if we think we have something seriously wrong with our health that we might have been able to prevent. On a card write down a problem or question that would be difficult to discuss with an adult, such as thinking you have a specific disease or being pregnant or having confusion over sexual identity and orientation. Then place the card in a bag, which your counselor will mix up, and then select someone else's card. Then break into pairs and try to discuss the difficulty that is on the card with your partner. How might you bring up the problem to an adult? How will the adult act? Try to use the past couple of sessions in order to solve or prevent the problem your partner is trying to communicate. Be sure to use the active listening and sharing skills we have talked about. Then return to the larger group and share the results of your discussion.

If you have any concerns about sexually transmitted disease discuss them with your counselor and she or he will advise you of what steps to take from here.

IT IS IMPORTANT TO GO FORWARD WITH YOUR LIFE, NOT TO BE HELD BACK BY THINGS YOU DID IN THE PAST

Putting It Together

- Alyssa thinks that she can't get an infection from another female. Why is she wrong, and what diseases can she get?

- Is being only with "clean" guys an effective way for Alyssa to avoid getting a disease, and what should she do to keep herself healthy?

- What is the only way to prevent a STD, and what are *some alternatives* to help lower the risk of catching a STD?

- Using the *Table of Diseases*, how can you tell *if you have an infection*, and what can be done in the area of treatment?

- Who would be the best person *with whom to discuss* any of your concerns about sexually transmitted diseases?

- What are your *personal choices* about how to prevent sexually transmitted diseases?

Table 3

TABLE OF DISEASES

Diseases	Symptoms	Cures
Chlamydia (Kluh-mid-ee-uh)	• Vaginal or penile discharge • Pain during urination • Pain in lower abdomen and during sex • Spotting between periods (girls) • Sometime **NO SYMPTOMS**	Doctor-prescribed antibiotics, although pelvic inflammatory disease (PID) or infertility may occur if left untreated.
Genital Herpes (Her-peez)	• Red sores or bumps that develop into watery, red blisters • Painful to urinate • Tender or painful feeling in genitals • Fever or swollen lymph nodes	**No known cure**, although doctor can prescribe antibiotics and antivirals to reduce and control symptoms.
Genital Warts (Human Papillomavirus)	• Small skin-colored bumps that are not painful, yet may be itchy • Look similar to cauliflower as they get larger • May occur on vaginal opening, cervical opening and anus as well as penis tip, shaft, and scrotum	A doctor will medicate, or "freeze" off the warts, although they may come back.
Gonorrhea (Gone-uh-ree-uh)	• Burning sensation when urinating • Green discharge or pus from the penis or vagina • Similar to Chlamydia, symptoms may not appear	Doctor-prescribed antibiotic, although infertility and scarring may occur if left untreated.
Hepatitis (Hep-a-tie-tis)	• Fatigue, tiredness • Loss of appetite • Nausea or vomiting • Pain in abdomen or right under rib cage where liver is located	**No known cure**. Most people recover in six months but will remain contagious for the rest of their lives.
HIV and AIDS	• Extreme weakness • Rapid weight loss • Frequent fevers • Swollen glands • Chronic diarrhea and cough • Some people can have the virus for up to 10 years with **NO SYMPTOMS**	**No known cures.** Doctor can prescribe antivirals and antibiotics to help a person stay healthy longer, but there is no cure for AIDS yet.
Syphilis (Siff-ill-iss)	• Stage 1: Chancre's (Shank-er) found on genitalia • Stage 2: Rash on soles of feet, hands and mouth • Stage 3: No symptoms • Stage 4: Damage to brain, heart, spinal cord and bones	Doctor-prescribed antibiotic, although once the disease has hit the fourth stage, very little can be done about the damage.
Trichomoniasis (Trick-oh-moh-nye-uh-siss)	• Gray or yellowish discharge from vagina • Vagina very itchy and painful to urinate • Achy abdomen and pain during sex • Most males **DO NOT** experience symptoms of "trich"	Doctor-prescribed antibiotic, and testing for Chlamydia and Gonorrhea, as these diseases tend to occur together.

So I kissed a girl. And even though it was a bet, and I feel a bit weird about it, I kind of liked it. But I also like boys still. So does that make me bisexual? Or gay?

Last night I went to a party with my best friend. I didn't really know many of the people there, and most of them were a lot older than us, like seniors and graduated people. I don't usually even drink because it gets in the way of soccer, but she really wanted to go see this guy who would be at the party, and I figured it never hurts to try something different. At first I felt all immature and young, but then as people got drunk they started being stupid and acting like fools and I felt better about how young I was compared to almost everyone else. These people were totally not in our clique, but some of the guys were really cool.

Especially these two guys. They were older, I think like freshmen in college and had graduated from our school. They bet my friend and I a beer that we wouldn't kiss each other. We figured "what the hell, after all we are best friends." She's like the only person who knows all my secrets, and when my parents got divorced, I didn't want to tell anyone, but I told her almost as soon as I found out.

So we kissed, and the guys made a lot of noise, and we got some more beer. It was kind of weird this morning when we woke up, but then we talked about it. We both felt guilty and we're not going to worry about being in a relationship or anything. It was just a kiss, and she's like my best friend. So now that we talked it out, I'm not weird about it. I'm just a little confused. I'm like the most guy crazy of all my friends, but I sort of enjoyed the kiss with her, I'm not so sure why, maybe because everyone was cheering us on. So now I don't know if I'm gay, or straight, or both.

And I guess there are some benefits to sleeping with girls. I mean, I don't have to worry about getting pregnant. That is pretty much impossible between two girls. And in health class we are always learning about STDs and AIDS, which would also be impossible to get if I was only with girls.

But the thing is, I really like guys. Everything about them, even their sloppiness. I mean, girls are softer, and cleaner, and a lot more classier, and if I got involved with a girl I could share clothes with her, which would like increase my wardrobe by like two times. But there is something about a guy picking you up, and dancing with you, and looking at you with those eyes that guys get, especially when they want sex.

And sex is the biggest thing. I'm like only fifteen, and I can't imagine never having sex with a guy. And I want to get married and have kids and a normal life, and how do you do that with another girl? I could not imagine being in a relationship with just a girl, no matter how good a kisser she is.

Things would really be weird if I had kissed a guy last night; they aren't weird right now between my friend and I. It's not like I'm wondering if she still likes me or if she's gonna ask me out again or if I shouldn't have done it. And we don't have to do it again.

At least I'm not a guy right now. I mean, when a guy kisses another guy, he's gay right? There is no bisexuality for guys. They are either gay or not. How can a guy be with another guy and not be gay, ya know? So at least I don't have to worry about that. I can be bisexual if I want to be bisexual.

But I'm not even sure what it means to be bisexual. Am I supposed to have a girlfriend and a boyfriend? Am I supposed to love girls and fool around with boys? Am I supposed to share them with each other? This sex stuff is getting way too confusing. I mean, maybe I should just choose one or the other. One the one hand I really like boys. I've always liked boys. But on the other hand, I kissed a girl and I really like my friend.

So the question is, am I gay or not? Or bisexual? It's so confusing. The truth is I don't think I would like to have sex with a girl, despite no pregnancy or STDs. But if I got bet again that I wouldn't kiss a girl, I would do it in a heartbeat. **You can bet on that.**

Chapter Thirteen:
Problem Solving and Decision Making

JORDAN'S STORY

I can't believe I did this....again. I should have learned from my last time, but I didn't. Last night my friend and I were hanging out at his house, playing games and listening to music. Suddenly the door slammed open and his older brother was there with his friends. The next thing I knew I was playing by myself. I turned around to find powder on the table and all three of them with rolled up bills about to take a hit. My friend looked at me and offered me a hit. At first I said no, but then his brother was like, come on man, we'll have a great time tonight. So I figured what the hell. My friend's brother decided he wanted a Slurpee.

He invited us along with them. So we were walking down this alley and got to the corner, and there was this fence up. So we just stood there and stared at the fence. Then my friend's brother started pulling at the fence. He's like, I'm gonna tear this thing down. So we all started pulling and pushing and swearing while trying to take down this fence that was in our way.

NO TRESPASSING

Because I was last, I didn't notice the cops until I was on the other side staring at the guys spread out on the fence. So here I sit in the police office, waiting for my mom. My friend got picked up just a few minutes ago, and as he was walking by he whispered at least it was fun while it lasted. But I wonder, was it?

SESSION 27: PROBLEM SOLVING

Objectives

- Review *Chapter 12: Exploring Individual Intimacy*
- Discuss steps to problem solving
- Understand how to consider different solutions to problems
- Learn how to cooperate and look for solutions for the good of everyone

Jordan's Story

So after we all got high and we had played video games forever, my friend's older brother said he wanted to get a Slurpee from the convenience store and he invited us to go with them. We decided to walk, and that's good because I wasn't going to get in a car with them. Maybe I would have, I dunno. So we were going down this alley and we were at the part where we cut across the lot of this bar, when suddenly there was a fence in our way.

We couldn't believe it. We were like no way, no way there is a fence here. We took the alley because it cut off like five blocks, and to go all the way down the alley meant we would have to go back to hit the store, and that added like six blocks. My friend's brother started pulling on the boards, saying he was gonna pull the fence down. I felt uncomfortable and my stomach got upset, but I thought it was just the drug. Next thing I know the cops are there. Destruction of property and public intoxication.

Review of exploring individuality and intimacy

In the last chapter we began discussing emotional intimacy, sexual intimacy, contraceptives, sexually transmitted diseases and infections. We indicated that *emotional intimacy*—built on mutual respect, communication and trust—is vital and necessary before *true sexual intimacy* can occur. And in order to achieve intimacy, it is first necessary to develop our own *sense of identity* and to become clear about our *personal values and morals*. While the decision to have sexual intimacy is a personal choice, it is very important to have knowledge about contraceptives and STDs before thinking about becoming sexually active with another person. While pregnancy is definitely a negative when it is unexpected, and especially so for teenagers, sexually transmitted infections and diseases can have lifelong effects such as death and often aren't noticed before they become serious.

Some people think that sexually transmitted diseases only occur in "dirty" people or only between homosexual male partners. This is far from the truth. It is estimated that 1 in 5 people in this country have a sexually transmitted infection, and 25% of the new infections occur in teenagers. That means there is a serious risk of becoming infected if one does not take precautions to prevent any of the diseases. It is not true that females cannot pass diseases to each other, since some diseases like gonorrhea, genital warts, and herpes are carried on the outside as well as inside the genitalia. It is also important to keep in mind that a lot of the diseases, although they do have symptoms, may not appear symptomatic in most people. Diseases like chlamydia do not have symptoms for most of the people who have them, which is why they have become so common.

SESSION 27: PROBLEM SOLVING

Activity: The Factor Of Disease

Your counselor will use a flip chart, and as a group think of the different diseases covered in the last session. List them down the left side of the paper, and then **next to each disease list the symptoms**. With a colored pen, mark each disease that **does not have any symptoms** for some people. With a different colored pen, mark the diseases that can have **lifetime effects** such as infertility or scarring. With a black pen circle the ones that have **serious damaging effects** such as heart and liver damage or death. Then mark on the right side **which ones can be cured**. Are there any of the diseases that cause serious damage or death that can be cured? How can the diseases be avoided? Can you only have one STD at a time, or can some occur together?

The only *sure means* to prevent the occurrence of STDs is *abstinence*, or not becoming sexually involved with anyone. The only other means of protection—for both yourself and your partner—is a latex condom, male or female, although they may not prevent something like warts, herpes, or syphilis if the condom does not cover the affected area. Condoms made of animal tissue, such as sheepskin, are not effective as the virus or bacteria can move through the condom skin into the other person. If a person is to become sexually active, *they must be checked by a doctor on a regular basis* in order to remain healthy, especially if a person has more than one partner. While most of the diseases can be treated with antibiotics, some such as HIV, AIDS, herpes, and hepatitis B and C have *no known cure* and genital warts can reappear after treatment.

Becoming Good At Solving Problems

In the last chapter we dealt with *problems that may occur* as the result of unsafe sexual actions. Although problems are a part of life and happen almost daily, most problems do not carry the *enormous weight* of those associated with unsafe sexual activity. However, most of us are here because we have not been very good at coming up with successful solutions to many different types of problems. These may include the need to get money, coping with disrespect, being upset about how you are being treated, or an invitation to get high.

In fact, most of us try solving our problems in the *spur of the moment*. Sometimes we focus on *blaming the people* involved and not dealing with the problem itself. Unfortunately, that often leads us to *using drugs* in order to forget the problem or *committing crimes* in a search for a quick way to get out of a tight situation. But if we get the facts and use good problem-solving skills, then we can take pride in how effectively we can manage our lives and help others as well. People who develop good problem-solving skills don't have to turn to substances or crime in order to find a way around a difficult situation.

But in order to become good problem solvers, we first have to become *aware that a problem is occurring* and then think about the problem before we act. Sometimes that is difficult, though, because it's easier act impulsively on feelings instead of taking time to focus on the thoughts that are happening in our minds.

How Can We Tell If A Problem Exists?

One of the big things in being able to solve problems is to *know that there is a problem*. There are a couple of things we can pay attention to that will let us know when something is wrong. Most important is to pay attention to our bodies and behavior, and to keep a lookout for these signs:

· Feeling signs of stomach problems, nervousness, or depression
· Not doing our work as well
· Not acting like we want to with the people close to us
· Not getting along with people or having people avoid us
· Feeling uncomfortable with a situation.

If any of the above is happening to you, it is likely that you have a problem that is not being taken care of or is being ignored.

Activity: Jordan's Problem

Take a moment to look at Jordan's story. What symptoms of a problem does Jordan exhibit? Why is he having the symptoms? What do you think the problem is?

STEPS FOR EFFECTIVE PROBLEM SOLVING

Like we said before, everyone has problems sometimes. In fact, problems are a daily thing that happens all the time, whether it is a social situation or our thoughts, attitudes or beliefs that are causing the problems. So then the question is how do we begin to solve our problems. The first step, as in almost everything we've talked about in this program, is *knowing what our thoughts* are. Everything else is as easy as 1-2-3.

1) Define the problem and your goal
Identify *what is wrong*. What is it you *want* from the situation? What is your *goal*, and what is keeping you from attaining that goal? What do you need to change?

2) What are all the facts?
What is the *information* that is important to have? What other facts or information might you need before solving the problem? Get more facts if possible. Have you *dealt with* this problem before, and if so what did you do that time? Although the solution may have changed, if it was successful in the past, it may be a good place to start looking for a solution this time.

3) Consider alternatives—Brainstorm
Can you think of some *different solutions*? What might other people see about the problem? Remember our discussion about empathy, how might another person feel in this situation? How does the problem look to the other person involved? Come up with *as many ways as possible* to solve the problem. They don't even have to be good solutions, just ideas on how to resolve the situation.

4) Choose the best solution

After taking a look at the positives and negatives, choose the solution that *best solves the problem* with the most positive outcomes or least amount of negative outcomes. Be sure to make an effort to get the solution to work, and if it doesn't, start over. Choose several of the best alternative solutions and begin to consider the positive or negative outcomes from using that solution. Be sure to look at the *long- and short-term results* from solving the problem in that means.

5) Study the results

After choosing a solution and giving it a try to solve the problem, it is important to then study the results of the solution. Ask whether the solution did what was expected of it, and what the outcomes were. If the solution was successful, continue to use it and even begin applying it to other problems. Even if it wasn't successful, how can it be revised to better meet the needs of the situation.

Activity: A Moment Of Problem Solving

Take a moment to fill out *Worksheet 35, Problem Solving*. Use a problem that is currently bothering you, and be as honest as possible. Use the steps above to help you answer the questions as thoroughly as possible. After everyone has filled out their worksheet, break into small groups of three or four and **discuss your problem** with the group. Allow the other group members to offer different solutions to your problem. What are some of the group's suggestions? Have they had this problem before, and will their solution work better or worse than the one you chose? Are you able to help them with their problem, and maybe offer some suggestions? What part does experience play in solving problems?

The reason that we learn and practice the *Steps for Effective Problem Solving* is so that it can become habit, allowing us to solve similar problems with ease. The more successful solutions we have in our *set of tools for change*, similar to the *arsenal of thoughts* we discussed in **Chapter 9, Zeroing In On Negative Thoughts**, the easier solving problems will become. The more tools we have at our disposal, the easier it will be to move through life avoiding conflict and difficulties. And the more problems we successfully solve, the easier it will be to stay away from substances and crime.

> ### SOLVING PROBLEMS HELPS US TO AVOID DRUGS AND CRIME

Activity: A Solution To Some Problem

In looking at Jordan's story, do you think he and his friends solved the problem well? How do you think they could have **better solved the problem**? What obstacles did Jordan have to overcome, and how could they have found several different solutions?

Worksheet 35

PROBLEM SOLVING

Pick a problem that you are now having. Go through the steps below. Use the simple steps for studying and coming up with solutions to this problem.

1. Identify or describe the problem.

_____

_____

2. What is your goal?

_____

_____

3. Give the key facts.

_____

_____

4. What are your alternatives? Brainstorm all of the possible solutions.

_____

_____

_____

5. What are the possible outcomes or consequences of all these different solutions?

_____

_____

6. Choose the solution.

_____

_____

7. What do you think the outcome will be?

_____

_____

CREATING "WIN - WIN" SOLUTIONS

When confronted with conflicts and problems there is usually more than one person involved. This means that the skills we learned earlier about *empathy and communication* are vital to effective problem solving. Discuss the following steps to include other people's point of view in your problem solving skills.

1) **Keep your attention on the problem being solved and not on the person involved.** Although it is really difficult for us to keep the other person out of it, it is the problem that we are having difficulties with and it is the problem that needs to be solved.

2) **Keep your attention on the needs and interests of the people involved and not on the positions they take.** Everyone has opinions, and quite often everybody has a different opinion when interacting with other people. The point of problem solving is not to get people to change their opinions; rather, it is for all people involved to benefit and find comfort in a problem being solved.

3) **Don't argue about the positions people take.** Opinions differ, and it's likely that most people do not agree with everyone else. The situation is not a debate about opinions, but rather a problem that needs to be solved. Getting distracted in opinions merely slows down the solution process.

4) **Pick solutions that help everyone, and not just one person.** If a solution only benefits one person involved, then it is likely that the problem will occur again and possibly with more negative influence and outcomes.

Activity: The Problem Of The Acid River

The room will be divided into three parts, with the entire group standing on one side of the room. The middle part of the room is going to be the acid river, and there are carpet squares (or pieces of paper) in the river, about half as many as there are group members. The far side is the other bank that the entire group is trying to reach by crossing the river on the squares. There are certain rules that may be changed by your counselor that must be followed:
· You cannot touch the floor of the room
· No sliding or inch worming on the squares
· No unattended squares. Some part of someone's body must be touching the squares at all times
· All group members must arrive on the bank at the same time
· Any violation and the entire group must go back to the beginning.

What did you learn about problem solving from the acid river game? Did the solution to the problem follow the *Steps for Problem Solving and Creating Win-Win Solutions* that we covered in this lesson?

Putting It Together

· Jordan and his friends ran into a problem while trying to go to the store. What was the problem, and how did they solve it?

· How could have the *Steps to Problem Solving* been used in the example shown in Jordan's story?

· What are some other *solutions* they could have used?

· Think of some problems you have had lately. How did you solve the problems, if you solved them at all?

· How would the steps of problem solving help you to resolve some difficulties?

· Review your *Thinking Patterns* ratings on your *Self-Portrait*. Do these get in the way of good problem solving?

SESSION 28: DECISION MAKING

Objectives

- Review *Session 27: Problem Solving*
- Discuss the difference between fact and opinion
- Understand the importance of propaganda
- Learn the skills of decision making

Jordan's Story

I didn't really want to take a hit. When I turned around it was all laid out on the table, and they were all taking a hit. At first I said no, that I didn't like how it made me feel last time I had tried it, but my friend said this stuff was much better, and that it wouldn't make me feel like the other stuff I had tried. I still felt awkward, but his brother was like come on we'll have a great time and I didn't want to be the only sober one.

And I figured what the hell. I might as well have fun on a weekend night. And I'm only young once, or so everyone always tells me. So I took a hit.

Review of problem solving

In our last session, we began discussing the *steps to solving a problem*. We tend to jump at the *first or easiest* way to get over, without looking at the *possible outcomes* or long-term consequences. If we don't learn how to problem solve effectively, the problems will continue to come back, usually bringing other problems with them. This is similar to the *Cycle of Anger* that we talked about in *Chapter 10, Handling Anger, Guilt and Depression*. Similar to anger, *when a problem doesn't get recognized,* resolved, or resolved well, then it will *continue to erupt* within our lives, causing us even more difficulties to overcome. After awhile we become weak or are unable to control the problem, and that is when we may turn to drugs or crime for an easy way to forget or temporarily escape the problem. Review *Figure 8* on Forming a *Habit and the Addiction Cycle* that we covered in *Session 4*. This shows an important example of poor problem solving.

Unfortunately, drugs and crime merely shove the problem out of view, and in the long run will cause more problems than before. That is where the skills for problem solving become an important factor in us controlling and having freedom within our lives.

> ### PROBLEM SOLVING INCREASES PERSONAL CONTROL AND FREEDOM

Activity: A Group Of Problems

Take a moment to look back at the last session and go over the **steps to problem solving**. Then, individually, write a **problem situation** on a piece of paper and put it into the bag your counselor will hand around. An example of a problem may be that you want to be nice to your mom, but every time you are around her you get angry and start a fight. After everyone has finished a problem, the first person will **choose a problem** out of the bag, and read the problem to the group. **As a group, use the steps for problem solving** to solve the problem written on the piece of paper. Go around the group as often as time allows or as long as there are problems in the bag. How do the problem-solving skills help in solving real life problems? How will you use the skills to solve your own problems?

Of course, learning how to anticipate and avoid problems in the first place is a great start in how we can gain control and have freedom in our lives. One way to prevent problems is in *good decision making*, since most problems can occur from the decisions we choose.

CRITICAL THINKING AND DECISION MAKING

Just as with problem solving, often our decisions are made impulsively and are based on our *thoughts or feelings at the moment* of decision. An example might be smoking marijuana or drinking a beer. If you feel stressed or tired, and you think you deserve to *really cut loose* once in awhile, then it is more likely you will impulsively use the substance without even thinking about the consequences of your decision.

CRITICAL THINKING, also known as logical or rational thinking, is when we make sense out of something and get all the facts before making a decision. Often when it comes to *substance use or criminal actions*, we don't always get all the facts and we become swayed by emotions or *shortsighted thinking*. In order to be able to make decisions logically, we first have to make sure we take the following elements of critical thinking into account.

· **Get all the facts.** We can't make good decisions when we don't have all the correct information, so it's important we *get all the information* first.

· **Do not let our emotions make the decision.** A lot of times we make our decisions because of our feelings— *such as we are angry*—and so we punch or slam the door, or we don't like a person so we aren't going to hang out there anymore. The problem is those kinds of decisions tend to cause us more problems than before. Now we have to fix a hole in the door, or now we can't hang out with our friends because that person is going to be there. This kind of decision can do more damage to us than the thing or person we are trying to offend or injure.

· **Make sense of the facts.** Part of good decision making is being able to *piece together the facts* in order to *make a picture that seems correct*. The idea is not what we think or feel about the situation, but what the facts tell us.

· **Are you being misled?** When we come to a conclusion because we have been swayed to the wishes or desires of another person, we have been conned or misled. When we *allow someone to convince us* of making a certain decision before we get all the facts, we are allowing that person to *con us* (notice the similarity between con and **con**trol). When a person tries to **con**vince us to take their side, sometimes telling us the truth but *more often lying* to us to tell us what we want to hear, this is called *propaganda*. Propaganda gets in the way of good decision making because we don't get all the facts or the correct facts.

SESSION 28: DECISION MAKING

Activity: A Bag Of Decisions

Individually **write out a decision** that needs to be made. It can be something simple, like deciding what to eat at a specific restaurant, or it could be something complicated, like deciding to have sex for the first time. Then put the decisions in a bag and mix them up. Each person will **take a decision**, and then use the above elements to help in making the decision. The decision should be made **based on facts** the group decides apply to the situation, and it should be to the agreement of everyone in the group.

THE PROPAGANDA CON

Decision making, unlike problem solving, tends to take on a group atmosphere. Often there are other people around when we have to make a decision, and it is easy to be swayed by other people's desires and needs when we are trying to make a decision. But what another person wants is not always what is good for us. As we said, propaganda is when a person tries to talk us into doing something, usually by telling us something we want to hear. Here are some methods to propaganda:

- **One-sided arguments**
  The one-sided argument is when the other person *plays up the aspects* that are *likely to influence* the other person to make a decision that agrees with the first person's desires. An example of this would be a friend trying to convince us to smoke a joint: "This weed is so fine and mellow, you will feel good for hours without any paranoia. And there is no way you're gonna get caught. Besides, one joint is not gonna hurt you."

- **The bandwagon approach**
  This approach is *designed to make us feel left out* or *not part of the "in" group* if we do not try or do what they are selling to us. An example of this might be being offered the joint from a friend and the friend telling us when we refuse: "hey man, everyone is doing it. You'll be the only one not high, and everyone knows that it can't hurt you."

- **Repetition**
  We often see this approach on television, radio, or even on billboards. The idea is to *repeat the product* so often in an amount of time that the slogans become ingrained and the specific product is the one we think of when it is time to buy something. Television ads, which might be shown four times in one hourlong program, is an example of this. Sometimes drugs are made to seem more attractive simply by the amount of times you hear about them through friends and people you hang out with.

- **Transfer**
  Advertisers, especially for alcohol and tobacco, use this approach in which they *associate the product with an attractive person* we would like to be or a fun situation that we would like to be in. One example is a beer commercial that shows everyone having fun and the guys getting really attractive twin females to like them.

- **Testimonial**

  A testimonial advertisement is when a *famous or important person* does a commercial to promotes a product. The idea behind this propaganda is the hope that the loyalty or desire to be like the person in the commercial will transfer to the product being sold. An example of this would be sports clothing commercials with a famous hall of fame athlete.

- **Emergency**

  This is when the buyer is told that *there is a limited time* in which they can get the product at the special price, or there are a *limited number of products* to be sold. An example of this would be "come on down today because the sale ends tonight at 5."

- **Bargain**

  This is often used with the emergency propaganda in that they encourage a person to buy because something is *offered for free or reduced price*. An example would be "Buy a subscription to this magazine and you get a poster for free!"

Activity: Jordan's Decision

As a group, look at Jordan's story. How does he make his decision? What sort of **propaganda** does Jordan's friend and his brother use to convince him to use? Who do you think the decision and the propaganda benefits?

Activity: Application Of Propaganda

Take a moment to fill out *Worksheet 36, Propaganda Advertisements*, with advertisements you have seen on television, read in a magazine, or heard on the radio. How has propaganda played **a part in your life**? Then as a group go around and discuss how advertisements use each propaganda technique. Which ones seem more effective than others? How **can you tell** if someone is using propaganda on you? What can you do to avoid being conned to make a decision that is not in your favor? **What has been the relationship between propaganda, drug use and criminal activity in your life?**

Propaganda And Decision Making

As we said before, group opinion tends to be involved when we try to make a decision. When the group is our friends or family, it can become really difficult to tell when they have our interests in mind or their own. Because of thoughts and feelings that can become involved in making a decision, we have to make sure we have all the facts before attempting to make a decision for ourselves.

Another thing we have to keep in mind is how propaganda and decision making play a part in our use of substances or our criminal activities. Often we are influenced to do these things by the group we are around, and they often use the propaganda techniques above. "Everyone is doing it" is something we hear when it comes to trying to resist substances, and the facts are that not everybody is doing it. In fact, there are a large number of people in the country, and people you know, who are not doing drugs. Similar to this is when we get involved in crime. Sometimes we may think that we can have the lifestyle of a celebrity or have people desire to be around us if we only dress a certain way. When we don't have money to dress that way, some people might begin stealing in order to dress in a way they think is going to attract attention and respect. The

Worksheet 36

PROPAGANDA ADVERTISEMENTS

Describe five different advertisements that you have seen either in newspapers or on TV. What technique did they use? Use the information in the Workbook above.

Ad 1)

_____

_____

_____

Ad 2)

_____

_____

_____

Ad 3)

_____

_____

_____

Ad 4)

_____

_____

_____

Ad 5)

_____

_____

_____

truth, though, is that respect comes from who we are and how we respect other people. Stealing will only get us the attention from the cops and a negative identity (like what we talked about in *Session 23*).

Activity: Relative Propaganda

Individually, fill out **Worksheet 37, Relating Propaganda to Your Drug Use and Criminal Conduct**. For each method of propaganda, write a statement as to how that method has played a part in your using substances or getting involved in crime. An example for transfer would be seeing someone who dresses how you want to dress and they say they steal their clothes. That in turn leads you to decide to steal your clothes in order to look good as well. After everyone has filled out their worksheet, discuss as a group how propaganda affects your lives. Who has control over some of your decisions? Who do you want to have control? In what ways can you make your decision making better, and how can you avoid propaganda?

In learning how to see through the propaganda, we are able to make *decisions that are best for us*, and don't fit the needs of other people using us. We all prefer to have freedom and control over our lives, and by listening and believing in propaganda without gathering all the facts, we give up our freedom and control to another person and that person's desires.

Putting It Together

· Jordan's decision is greatly influenced by his friend. What propaganda does his friend use in trying to convince him? How might have Jordan *resisted the propaganda*?

· What sort of propaganda has *influenced* your decision making? Which techniques are more influential than others?

· How would you use the *problem-solving and critical-thinking skills* in helping to make a decision?

· Look at your *Drug Use Patterns* on your *Self-Portrait*. Did your use of drugs get in the way of critical thinking and good decision making?

· Look at your *Thinking Patterns* on your *Self-Portrait*. Do some of these errors in thinking cause you to make poor decisions?

· Update your *Plan for Change*.

RELATING PROPAGANDA TO YOUR DRUG USE & CRIMINAL CONDUCT

Describe how the five ads from the previous Worksheet have played a part in your life.

Ad 1)

_____

_____

_____

Ad 2)

_____

_____

_____

Ad 3)

_____

_____

_____

Ad 4)

_____

_____

_____

Ad 5)

_____

_____

_____

I can't believe I did this… again. I should have learned from my last time, but I didn't. I listened to my friend, and here I sit again, waiting for my mom again, only this time I think it's more serious.

Last night my friend and I were hanging out at his house, playing games and listening to music. Suddenly the door slammed open and his older brother was there with his friends. They told us to move over because they needed the coffee table, and so we ended up sitting on the floor trying to finish our game while they were talking and laughing behind us. As we were playing, his brother asked my friend if he wanted any. The next thing I knew I was playing by myself.

After I had died, I turned around to find powder out on the table and all three of them with rolled up bills about to take a hit. My friend snorted, coughed, and then laughed with tears streaming down his cheeks. He looked at me and offered me a hit. At first I said no, I had done it before and didn't really like how I felt afterwards. My friend just said that this stuff was better, and that I would enjoy it more, and that it really wouldn't affect me like that other stuff. I felt kind of awkward, and I kept saying no, but then his brother was like, come on man, we'll have a great time tonight.

So I figured what the hell. Might as well have a good time on a weekend night. Besides, I'm only young once, or so they kept telling me. A tingle began to spread over my body and a rush went through my head just after I took a hit. And I sat back. Everyone was staring at me with dumb ass grins, but I didn't care because I felt so good.
I don't know how much longer we stayed there playing video games. Time became irrelevant, and life felt like it was moving too slow and too fast all at once. My friend's brother decided that he wanted a Slurpee, and he invited us to go along with them. I couldn't seem to keep myself from moving, so I didn't think sugar was the thing for me, but I also needed to get out of the house to stop from rocking back and forth while I twitched my feet and smacked my gum.

We decided it was better to walk since the store wasn't too far away, and I knew I wasn't gonna get in a car with those guys. Maybe I would have, I dunno. So we were walking down this alley and got to the corner where we usually cut through this bar's lot, and there was a fence up. At first we were like no way, there's no way there's actually a fence here. I started walking back and forth, partly because I couldn't stand still and partly because I was looking for a way around it. We had gone down the alley because it cut five blocks off our walk, but to go all the way down the alley would mean we would have to walk back to the store and that meant adding like six blocks. So we just stood there and stared at the fence.

Then my friend's brother started pulling at the fence. He's like, I'm gonna tear this thing down. I started feeling really uncomfortable, and my stomach was getting upset, but I thought it was from the drug. I thought about walking to the end of the alley and back down to the store, but then I noticed that he had one of the boards off already. So we all started pulling and pushing and swearing while trying to take down this fence that was in our way.
Finally it was big enough for the older guys to squeeze through, and then it was my turn. Because I was last, I didn't notice the cops until I was on the other side staring at the guys spread out on the fence with their hands on their heads.

Destruction of private property and public intoxication. I guess my friend's brother had tried resisting them and running, so he's gonna get resisting arrest and assault on an officer. I just went along quietly, partly because my teeth were so clenched that I could barely speak, and partly because there was nothing I could do.

So here I sit in the police office, waiting for my mom. I guess they could have shipped me straight to a juvie hall because I had a prior, but they took it easy on me because I didn't give them any hassle and I'm so young. My friend got picked up just a few minutes ago, and as he was walking by he whispered something like at least it was fun while it lasted. **But I wonder, was it?**

NOTES

Chapter Fourteen:
Lifestyle Balance

GOALS OF THIS CHAPTER
· Review Relapse and Recidivism
· Understand how imbalances in our lives can lead to RR
· Develop a RR prevention plan
· Continue discussing critical thinking and decision making
· Learn when to walk away

ZACH'S STORY

I can't take it anymore. About a year ago I was caught for grand theft auto. I had stolen a car from a house down the block while I was stoned. Before I knew it, though, there were cops behind me pulling me over. I kind of panicked because I knew I would get in trouble for not only taking the car, but for being stoned, too. So I kept driving. And driving and driving, all the while trying to go faster than the cops, until I bumped off the curb and ran into a tree. Grand theft auto, minor under the influence, destruction of public property, and on and on and on. My parents bailed me out. The judge looked over my profile, looked at my past record, and then ordered me into a treatment facility for six months, community service when I got out, and reparation for damages.

So here I am, going to school so I can graduate within the next couple of years, and working after school to pay back all the damages. And not doing a single thing that's fun. 'Cause when I get home from work, I'm not to leave the house. Yesterday my friend showed up at work. He asked me to take off early 'cause there was something he wanted to give me. I told him I couldn't, I had to work my full shift. But I said he could give me a ride after work if he wanted.

I told him he should take me home. He just started driving in the other direction and said I would thank him for this. At the stoplight I got out of his car. I have a year of being sober, and they say that if I'm good they'll reduce my community service time. I told my friend all that. And then I started walking away. So last night, my girlfriend called and asked why I had dissed my friend like that. I told her I couldn't be around him if he was gonna risk my chances of being good. It's just so hard sometimes, though. I feel left out and like I don't have a life anymore. To tell you the truth, if this is what responsibility is, I'm not sure I want to be responsible.

SESSION 29: STAYING STRONG WITHOUT DRUGS & CRIME

Objectives

- Review *Chapter 13: Problem Solving and Decision Making*
- Discuss high-risk thinking and situations
- Review triggers and stages of relapse and recidivism
- Learn how imbalances in our lives can lead to relapse and recidivism
- Learn how to stay on the road to self-discovery and change

Zach's Story

I really am trying to do things right, and get my life back on track. But it's not fair. I work and go to school all the time, and I don't even get to keep the money I make. And I don't have a life because my parents have put me on house arrest. I'm young, and I should be having the time of my life right now. But it doesn't seem that way to me at all.

Yesterday my friend asked me to ditch work, and I said no, so he picked me up after work. I thought he was going to take me home, but instead he drove in the other direction. He told me that I would thank him later. At the stoplight I got out of the car. I mean, I really wanted to go with him because lately I feel so old and like life is pointless, but I also have a drawing at home I've been working on and that I'm really into. Besides, I need to do right and he doesn't understand that.

Review of decision making

In the last session we began discussing how to make decisions that are best for our situations. Unlike problem solving, *decision making* usually involves a group of people, such as family or friends. Having many people involved can make it even more difficult to act in our own best interest. The important part of any decision is to keep a *realistic view* of the situation. That means keeping *emotions out of the way*, and knowing the *difference between opinion and fact*.

When it comes time to make a decision, there often are other people who are trying to get what they want or need. The pressure from the other people to decide in their favor can sometimes become overwhelming. But the best way to be able to decide in our best interest, as well as the best interest of others, is to be able to tell *what is fact and what is not*. This is where *propaganda* can emerge. *Opinions and fact selection* are used to try to sway a person to one side or the other. In order to think straight and make decisions that are truly in our best interest, we have to be able to see *through the propaganda* and stick to the facts.

Activity: Examples Of Sway

Take a moment to look over the **different propaganda methods** listed in *Session 28, Decision Making*. Then write down a **situation or experience** you have had this past week that can fall into one of the propaganda methods. Were you the one experiencing propaganda or were you the one using it? What was the result of the situation? Break into small groups and discuss your situations together. Is there one propaganda technique that is used more frequently than the others?

Which one do you think is most effective, and why? Help each other brainstorm about **ways to avoid propaganda.**

The purpose of *discussing propaganda* and *decision making* is that they both play a part in using substances and committing crimes. By practicing decision-making skills we can recognize when someone is trying to sway us in a manner that is not in our best interest. This also means that we can spot the times when we attempt to use propaganda, or excuses, against ourselves.

Review Of RR Definitions

As discussed in *Chapter 4, Backsliding to Drugs and Crime*, there are two very powerful forces that may put us in danger of returning to drugs or crime: 1) *High-Risk Situations;* 2) *High-Risk Thinking.*

HIGH-RISK SITUATIONS—Put us at risk for re-offending or reusing.

HIGH-RISK THINKING—Thought habits that cause and allow us to return to substance use and crime.

Certain things from our past can become a *trigger* when we are trying to avoid relapse and recidivism. Hanging out with *friends* we used to commit crimes with or use substances with can be a trigger that will be hard to overcome. *Emotions and thoughts* also can cause us to begin the erosion of relapse/recidivism. Feelings of anger, frustration, or even happiness can bring about the craving for a substance or lead to an urge to commit a crime. Here are some HR situations that you will need to keep an active lookout for:

HIGH-RISK SITUATIONS

· Conflict with another person
· Social or peer pressure
· An unpleasant feeling of anger, depression, or guilt
· A change in self-image

Activity: A Misstep Or Not?

As a group take a look at Zach's story. What do you think about **Zach's situation**? Do you think he is **close to relapse or not**? Why or why not? What HR situations do you think Zach is finding himself in? What can Zach do to avoid those situations, but still feel comfortable and happy?

Remember that *relapse* (returning to substance use) and *recidivism* (returning to crime) are erosions that begin in our minds. Although using drugs or committing a crime is the finale or *end point* of RR, it really begins with *allowing ourselves* to think the *high-risk thoughts* or putting ourselves in *high-risk situations*. Just as with change, there are recognizable stages in relapse and recidivism.

RR STAGES OF RELAPSE AND RECIDIVISM

· *High-risk situation* and *high-risk thinking*
· Lack of mastery skills and *loss of self-confidence*

- *Expecting* substance use or criminal activities to *improve your feelings or situation* in life
- *Tendency to give up* after beginning substance use or criminal thinking (*Rule Violation Effect*)
- *Belief that you were weak* and couldn't handle the thinking or situation
- *Backsliding* to where you were with drugs and crime before you began treatment

For a better idea of how these work, review *Figures 11 and 12*, in *Session 9, Learning How to Avoid Trouble*. Keep in mind that *negative or distorted thinking* is the first stage of RR.

Activity: Evaluation Of Personal Risk

As a group, make a list of all the **thinking skills** you have learned throughout the course of this program, such as the "thought stopping" or "positive thought arming." Then make a list of all the **action/refusal skills** you have learned throughout the program.

When the group has completed the list of thinking and action skills, individually fill out the three parts of *Worksheet 38, Evaluation of Personal Risk*.

FIRST, fill out the section on *Thinking And Action Skills* you have used in the past three months in order to avoid RR.
SECOND, fill out the section on *High-Risk Thinking Patterns* by listing high-risk AOD use patterns of thinking and criminal conduct thinking patterns you were involved in the past three months. Which **thinking skills or behaviors** did you use to deal with these thoughts?
THIRD, fill out the section on *High-Risk Situations* to list high-risk AOD use situations and high-risk criminal conduct situations you placed yourself in the past three months. Take note of the thinking or action skills you used to deal with these situations.
FINALLY, evaluate how successful you were in avoiding the RR thinking and situations. In comparing with others in the group, did you find some situations or thoughts that most people ran into? Did you all deal with the situations alike or did you have different ways of dealing?

MEETING OUR NEEDS THROUGH LIFESTYLE BALANCE

High-risk situations and thinking play a large role in whether we fall back into our previous use and choices, but there is also *another element* that has a large role in RR. Living drug and crime free requires a *balanced lifestyle*, and life can quickly get out of balance. Too often we feel the pressure of *should* and *ought*, and we end up feeling deprived or even cheated. With the demands of work, school, and family, we often leave no time for ourselves and can become overwhelmed.

When life gets out of balance, we often begin to feel a strong desire to meet our needs right away, whether it is the need for relaxation, happiness, or material things. This can lead to *cravings and urges for substances* (both drugs and alcohol) and to get what we want right away through *committing a crime*. Often when this happens, especially after we made a commitment to living drug and crime free, we make excuses for what we want to do.

EVALUATION OF PERSONAL RISK

List up to 5 examples for each category to evaluate your Personal Risk.

Thinking Skills You Used in the Past 3 Months to Manage or Avoid RR	Action Skills You Used in the Past 3 Months to Manage or Avoid RR

High-Risk Thinking Patterns You Engaged in the Past 3 Months	Thinking or Action Skills You Used to Deal with Each of These Thinking Patterns

High-Risk Situations You Placed Yourself in the Past 3 Months	Thinking or Action Skills You Used to Deal with Each of These High-Risk Situations

Relapse And Recidivism Excuses

- "I deserve more than this"
- "I work hard and don't get anywhere"
- "They have more than I do—I deserve as much as they do"
- "I deserve to have fun"
- "I have something coming, they owe me"

These thoughts *can and do* lead to relapse and recidivism. With relapse or recidivism, we get what we want quickly. Both give us immediate *gratification* and *reward*. But the choice we have made to indulge may be hidden. We make choices that don't seem important. This is called *Seemingly Irrelevant Decisions* (SIDs). This becomes the doorway to high-risk thinking and situations, such as letting a friend come over when you know he's going to smoke marijuana and offer to share the experience with you. Or letting yourself hang out with friends that participate in criminal activity because you feel you deserve to go out and have fun.

Activity: It's Not Fair

Discuss Zach's story, and make sure to cover these questions. Has Zach made a *Seemingly Irrelevant Decision?* What was the decision, and why did he think it was irrelevant? How could it have affected him negatively? What thoughts or excuses is Zach beginning to think? How might Zach combat those thoughts, and is he doing that already?

It's All in Being Prepared

We can *prevent* this slide into relapse and recidivism. By developing a *balanced lifestyle* and arming ourselves with a *relapse and recidivism prevention* (RP) plan, we can help stop ourselves before we go very far down the RR road. Below are some recommendations for how to maintain a balanced lifestyle and to stay on the right track when faced with high-risk thoughts and situations.

PREPARING FOR THE ROAD TO SELF-DISCOVERY AND CHANGE

1. *Arm ourselves with a self-control plan.* When we relapse or re-offend, we have made a choice to do so, and when our *lifestyles are out of balance*, we are likely to make those choices. Through this program we have learned skills to prevent relapse and recidivism, which we reviewed in *Worksheet 38 above, Evaluation of Personal Risks*, but we are always faced with high-risk thinking and situations that can lead to RR. That is why it is important for us to come up with a plan for self-control: so that we are not caught off guard every time we run into a situation. This plan is similar to our arsenal of solutions that we discussed in *Chapter 13, Problem Solving and Decision Making*. The figure shown on *Worksheet 39, My Personal Strategies for Relapse and Recidivism Prevention* will help us develop a plan for any risky situation.

2. *Maintain a balanced lifestyle.* To begin, we can achieve a *balanced lifestyle* by building in *daily activities* that can give us *positive feelings* and gratifications. That way, when we feel the need to use substances, we can immediately make ourselves feel good with a *positive activity* and thus replace the desire for the substance. An example of this may be drawing, or playing

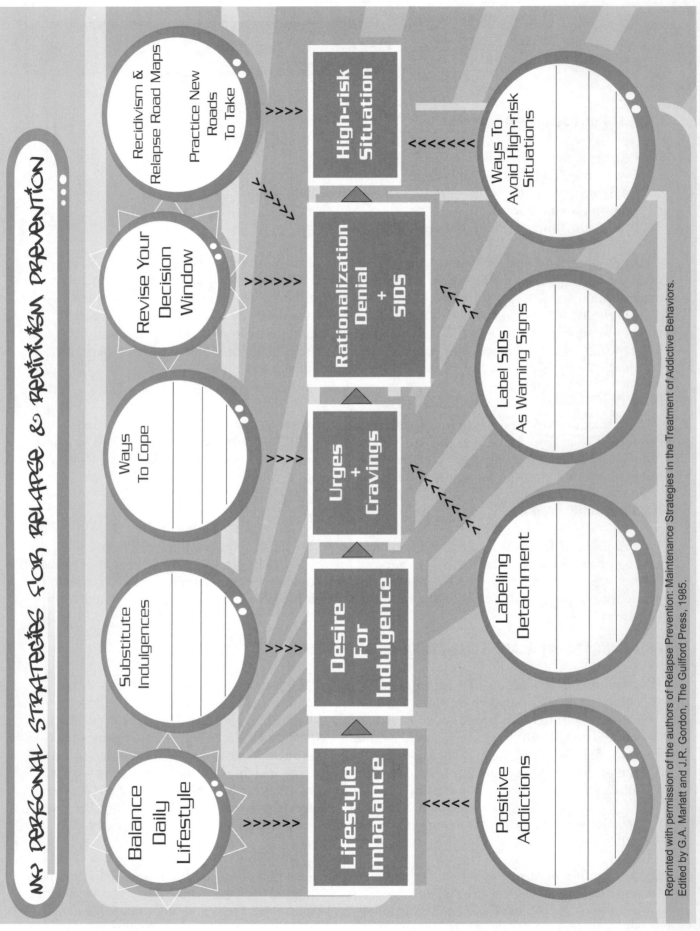

MY PERSONAL STRATEGIES FOR RELAPSE & RECIDIVISM PREVENTION

Recidivism & Relapse Road Maps

Practice New Roads To Take

Revise Your Decision Window

Ways To Cope

Substitute Indulgences

Balance Daily Lifestyle

High-risk Situation

Rationalization Denial + SIDs

Urges + Cravings

Desire For Indulgence

Lifestyle Imbalance

Ways To Avoid High-risk Situations

Label SIDs As Warning Signs

Labeling Detachment

Positive Addictions

Reprinted with permission of the authors of Relapse Prevention: Maintenance Strategies in the Treatment of Addictive Behaviors. Edited by G.A. Marlatt and J.R. Gordon, The Guilford Press, 1985.

Worksheet 19

music. If we set aside time every day to draw, we can turn towards our drawing and replace a desire to do drugs with interest in our art.

3. ***Detaching and labeling.*** This means that every time you have a *craving or an urge* to use a substance or commit a crime, you remove yourself from the situation. You can also label the urge so you are aware it's happening, then ride it out and wait for it to go away. Recognize cravings and urges as thoughts and feelings that you can *detach yourself from*; in other words, they are not all consuming, and you don't have to follow them.

4. ***Carefully watch the decisions that seem like they aren't important.*** Remember these *SIDs (Seemingly Irrelevant Decisions)* are the doorway into the slide to relapse and recidivism. The best thing to do is to be aware of what you are thinking, and do not make excuses. If you catch yourself thinking "I deserve it," stop the thought and call it a "poor excuse." It is also helpful to look at the *short-term and long-term* good and bad parts of any decision to use substances or participate in crime. This is called a *decision window*, and it will help you to become aware of your thoughts that will lead towards RR. For a reminder of how to make a good decision, review *Session 28, Decision Making in Chapter 13*. Of course, the most effective means of preventing RR is to avoid the situations that are likely to lead to it.

Activity: Decision Window

Take a look at *Worksheet 40, The Decision Window*. Complete the windows for both substances and **criminal behavior**. What do you get **right now** and **later** by not using substances? What do you miss out on by not using substances, both in the short and long run? Be sure to do the same for criminal behavior. What do you get in the short and long run by living a crime-free life?

One suggestion that may help you in preventing RR erosion is to think of RR as a highway map. This is the same map that we covered in *Chapter 4, Backsliding to Drugs and Crime (Figure 13, Road to Relapse and Recidivism)*. During this program, you may have found yourself on this highway several times as you faced urges and cravings. You have resisted and stayed straight or abstinent, and although you may have lapsed or did and thought things that brought you close to relapse and recidivism, you have been set on staying on *Road 101* to *Recovery City*. It may be helpful to keep this map in your mind, not only to remind yourself where you want to be but also to remember that one slip does not mean all is lost. Whichever direction you take, though, remember that it is your choice as to your destination.

Activity: My Strategies For Relapse And Recidivism Prevention

Develop your **relapse and recidivism prevention plan** by filling out the blank spaces on *Worksheet 39, My Strategies for Relapse and Recidivism Prevention*. Try to figure out things that are realistic and that will actually help you in the case of a RR situation. Think of the things that have confronted you while in this program, and think of the things that have led to you be in this program. How might you avoid them by substituting **positive activities** and having an arsenal of **ways to cope** with negative thoughts or urges? Break into small groups and discuss your strategies. Then have a member of your small group present the different strategies to the entire group.

DECISION WINDOW
Adapted from Marlatt (1985)

Decision Window: Example of Decision Window for AOD Use & Abuse

	IMMEDIATE OUTCOME		DELAYED OUTCOME	
	POSITIVE	NEGATIVE	POSITIVE	NEGATIVE
LIVE AN ALCOHOL & DRUG FREE LIFE				
CONTINUE TO USE ALCOHOL & DRUGS				

Decision Window for Criminal Conduct

	IMMEDIATE OUTCOME		DELAYED OUTCOME	
	POSITIVE	NEGATIVE	POSITIVE	NEGATIVE
LIVE A CRIME FREE LIFE				
CONTINUE TO COMMIT CRIMES & OFFEND				

Putting It Together

- Zach really wants to *start over again*, but he's having some problems. What are some of the things that are causing Zach to become frustrated? What are some of his *thoughts* that could lead to relapse/recidivism?

- Peer pressure tends to be a difficult HR situation to deal with. How is Zach dealing with the *peer pressure*?

- What are some of the thoughts *you catch yourself thinking* when it comes to your life?

- What are ways you can help yourself to *avoid relapse and recidivism*?

Objectives

- Review *Session 29: Staying Strong Without Drugs or Crime*
- Continue discussing critical reasoning
- Review negotiation
- Understand complaint making
- Learn to decide the best for everyone involved

Zach's Story

My friend came to my work yesterday, and was trying to convince me to get off early. I told him I couldn't do that. He said no one would care if I played hooky for a day, but I still said no. I did tell him he could give me a ride after work if it was that important to him. So after work he picked me up. I thought he was going to take me home, but he turned in the other direction. I asked where he was going and he said that I would thank him later. I wanted to go, but I knew where we were going and what we would end up doing. So at the stoplight I got out of the car. He told me to get back in but I've had a year of being sober, and if I stay clean they'll reduce my community service. I told him that and started walking.

My girlfriend called to ask me why I dissed my friend like that. I told her I couldn't be around him if he was gonna risk my chances of being good. I like him and all, but there's a line that has to be drawn if he doesn't respect what I've got to do. He's my best friend, but I've got to keep an eye out for me first. It's just so hard sometimes.

Review of lifestyle balance

We have discussed *relapse and recidivism prevention* in several chapters up to this point. The reason for this is because once we are out of this program, most of us *return* to our old lives with the *same situations* that can make us think and feel how we used to. But in order to be *strong in our choices* and keep our freedom, we have to be prepared to *resist the cravings and urges* to go back to the way we were.

In order to do that, we should have a *plan* that will be there in case a situation arises unexpectedly. Last session we discussed some *more signs of relapse and recidivism*, and we also discussed a few *more traps* that can lead us into the RR erosion pattern. Often we feel the pressure of what *we have to do* or what we *ought to do*, and we tend to think that the *oughts are ruling our lives*. This type of interpretation can lead to excuses for an action that we know will only cause us harm and negative consequences. Some common excuses are:

- "I deserve more than this"
- "I work hard and don't get nowhere"
- "They have more than I do—I deserve as much as they do"
- "I deserve a good time—I've earned it"

When these excuses occur, our *choice and responsibility* for relapsing or re-offending becomes masked by *seemingly irrelevant decisions* (SIDs), which begin the process of RR erosion. In order to avoid the RR erosion, and to recognize all the possible situations and thinking habits/excuses that can lead us to RR, we have completed *"My Personal Strategies for Relapse and Recidivism Prevention,"* (review *Worksheet 39* from the previous session on *Staying Strong Without Drugs or Crime*).

Activity: The Art Of Reflection

On a piece of paper, draw situations in your life when you become **frustrated**, unhappy, or lead to **craving or urges** to participate in **substances or crime**. Make sure to draw **facial expressions** (frowny or smiley faces) to show how you feel in the situations. Then draw some **alternative activities** that you can do to help you with those negative feelings and urges. Make sure the drawings represent you and your situation. Then go around the group and explain **what the drawings mean**, and how you think you can **help yourself** get over the cravings and urges.

Of course, a major part of *avoiding relapse and recidivism* depends upon our ability to make responsible decisions. SIDs can sneak up on us. We have learned and practiced skills to catch *ourselves* when we start to make *excuses for bad behavior and then drift into SIDs*. These important strategies and tools give us *much more strength* to avoid backsliding into old patterns of destructive behavior. An important part in *responsible decision making* is the ability to *think critically or logically* about our situation.

CRITICAL REASONING AND RESOLVING CONFLICT

In *Chapter 13, Problem Solving and Decision Making,* we began discussing how to solve problems and make good decisions. We learned the importance of *getting all the facts, recognizing propaganda* and to *keeping our emotions from interfering* with a sensible decision. Because we are here in this program, all of us, to some extent, have failed to do either effectively. It is likely that we have used one or more of the following styles to inappropriately deal with conflict or stress.

- **FIGHT:** becoming aggressive and forceful in order to get our way, which only increases friction and conflict

- **FLIGHT:** withdrawing or removing ourselves from the conflict or friction so that nothing is resolved

- **FAKE:** going along with the other person while aggressively attacking them, leaving things up in the air.

These styles are *unhealthy*, and they usually lead us to not getting what we want or causing conflict with people around us. As we discussed, **FAIR** (being *assertive* about what we want without attacking the other person) is the positive way to deal with any conflict. In order to be fair, though, we must use our critical reasoning.

Critical reasoning, which we started discussing in *Session 28*, is also considered *logical or rational* thinking. This means we look at the facts, *separate from our feelings* about the situation, and come up with a *resolution that benefits everyone* involved. Critical reasoning is an important part in both *problem solving* and *decision-making*.

Resolving Conflict Through WIN-WIN Solutions

In order to solve a problem or make a decision to the benefit of everyone involved, there are certain skills that ensure an agreement can be reached and no one loses completely. This means that the result is a *win-win situation*.

· You tell the other person(s) your ideas about the problem or conflict

· You ask the other person(s) what they think about the situation

· You tell them why you think your idea is better, or how you think the two ideas can be combined

· You give them a chance to consider what you have said before expecting them to make up their mind.

Activity: A Debate Among Friends

Write your name on a piece of paper and place it in a bag. If there are an odd number of people, the counselor will place their name in the bag as well. Randomly draw out your partner for this activity. The **two of you will sit in front of the group**, and the group will **think of a situation** for you to debate. The person who chooses the name out of the bag will be *"pro,"* or **for the situation**, and the person who had their name picked will be *"con,"* or **against the situation**. For example, the situation is **lowering the minimum drinking age from 21**.

Using the **win-win guidelines** try to convince the other person that your side is correct. See if the debate team can arrive at a solution that includes **both people's point of view** (win-win). Remember to keep your emotions from interfering with the discussion and be able to point out the difference between facts and opinions. Have the **group decide** whether the two people reached a solution where both sides were given fair consideration.

In order to become really effective at using the *guidelines for win-win solutions*, it is necessary to use *critical thinking* (getting the facts, recognizing propaganda and keeping our emotions out of the picture). Here are a few more important elements to critical thinking that will benefit you in a situation.

IMPORTANT ELEMENTS OF CRITICAL THINKING

· *Words are important.* Our lives are filled with language and words. That is how we communicate with each other. But there can be a *breakdown in communication* if the *words* we are using *mean something different* to the other person.

- ***People often don't say what they really mean.*** Learn to recognize what people imply by what they are saying. Don't always *assume* you understand what is being said, and *ask questions* if you are not sure. There aren't any dumb questions, only dumb answers, so ask if they mean *what you think* they mean. This goes along with words are important, sometimes we don't always know what the other one is saying but we can if we ask questions.

- ***Listen to what people are assuming.*** Everyone makes the mistake of *assuming something that is not true* at least once in awhile. Remember to listen carefully to the feelings portrayed when a word is used, and pay attention to body language and facial expressions. Use your good communication skills (*Chapter 3*).

- ***Fact versus opinion.*** In *Session 28, Decision Making*, we discussed propaganda and how to recognize when it is being used. Often propaganda is used to sway us to another person's opinion. Here is how to *recognize opinion*:
  - Phrases that use words such as "in my opinion," "I think," or "it seems to me."
  - *Emotional statements* such as "I hate that person."
  - *Extreme statements* or generalizations: "He always does that."

Activity: The Act Of Persuasion

Take a moment to look at Zach's story. What is his friend **trying to convince him** to do? What signs are there that Zach's friend is basing his argument on **opinion** and not fact? Does Zach use good **critical thinking** skills, and why or why not? Use as much detail as possible.

The Role of Negotiation in Critical Thinking

While the above skills help us to think *logically and rationally* in order to solve problems and make decisions, they will *not always* help us to resolve a situation to our liking. In fact, we will not be capable of resolving all conflicts easily or in our own manner. Negotiation, which we discussed in *Chapter 7, Avoiding Trouble and Playing Fair*, helps us to reach a *win-win* situation easier and with less friction. Here are some guidelines for how to negotiate to achieve a win-win solution.

NEGOTIATION GUIDELINES

1. ***Decide:*** Decide what it is *you want and need* from the situation. Are you having a difference of opinion? Tell the other person your opinion, and then describe how you see the other person's position. Be careful to not attack or be aggressive.

2. ***Listen:*** Did you *understand* where *the other person* was coming from? Keep an open mind, and try to not let your beliefs build a wall against the other person.

3. ***Think:*** Think about the *other person's opinion* or position. What are the *options* or possible solutions that can benefit both? Your arsenal of solutions can be beneficial here.

4. ***Suggest a compromise:*** Can you suggest a *middle meeting ground* where both people will be happy?

5. *Discuss:* Discuss the *solutions and options* you have come up with and decide which works *best for both people* involved.

Activity: The Role Of Negotiation

Each person writes about a situation that **requires negotiation** in order to resolve it. Then break into groups of two or three, and randomly pick out one of the situations. Then as a group **create a skit** in which the **negotiation is reached effectively**. The rest of the group will then discuss and evaluate how the negotiations were reached and how realistic the situation would be in the real world.

WHEN CRITICAL THINKING AND NEGOTIATION FAIL

Sometimes *our conflicts* with other people *cannot be solved* with them seeing things from our point of view or *even through negotiation*, especially at a workplace or at school. In order to *avoid negative consequences*, sometimes it can be necessary to *involve a third person*. This is not always easy, however, and can be a risk if not done correctly. Here are several steps in how to make a formal complaint successfully.

1. Find a way to *express your complaint clearly*. This means with logical thinking without an excess of emotion. Emotion will likely harm your case.
2. Find out who the *best person* to complain to is.
3. Decide on the *best time and place* to make the complaint.
4. Understand *how you would like to have the complaint resolved*. Tell the third person *what you want* from the situation, and what you are not getting from the other person.
5. Listen to the *third person's response*. They have a more removed and objective view of the situation.
6. Try to offer *suggestions to resolve the problem* so you are taking an active part in the solution.

Activity: A Complaint Made

In Zach's story, who is the person that made the complaint? Why was the complaint made? Does Zach have a reason to make a complaint? What is the suggestion, if any, that Zach is making in order for his friend and him to hang out? Do you think his friend will respect his wishes, why or why not?

In the event of conflict it is most important to remain capable of critical reasoning. It is true that *not all conflicts, problems, or decisions can be resolved*. Certain situations will remain at conflict, and it becomes a *test of personal strength* to be patient and do what you can to avoid or reduce harm from the situation. We will not always get along with everyone, and not everyone is willing to negotiate and meet in the middle with us. It becomes a sign of our personal growth and change to *let some things be and walk away*.

Activity: Situations In Life

Your counselor will use a flip chart to record your answers. As a group, think of situations in your life that require **decision making, critical reasoning, negotiation, and problem solving**. Then, as a group, using the skills that you have practiced, think of solutions or **positive approaches** for the different situations. Are some situations easier to resolve than others? Why or why not? What solutions do you think will really work, and which ones don't seem like they would work all that well? How can you use the skills that we have been practicing to deal with some of the more difficult situations in your life?

Putting It Together

- Zach is trying to become a person that is *substance and crime free*, but his friend wants to take him somewhere that Zach knows isn't good. How did he try to tell his friend how he felt about the situation? How did Zach's friend react?

- After his friend didn't listen to him, what did Zach do? Did he have any other options, and if so what were they?

- What situations are difficult for you? How might the skills of *decision making, problem solving, negotiation and critical reasoning* help you to better deal with those situations?

I can't take it anymore. I am going to go crazy if I don't do something soon, and I'm afraid that what I'll do isn't going to be a good thing.

About a year ago I was caught for grand theft auto. I had stolen a car from a house down the block while I was stoned, and ended up getting into a wreck. At first I was just taking the car for a joy ride. I would have it back before the owner, my parents' friend, ever knew that it was missing. Before I knew it, though, there were cops behind me pulling me over. I guess I wasn't driving straight or something. I don't know. I kind of panicked because I knew I would get in trouble for not only taking the car but for being stoned too.

So I kept driving. And driving and driving, all the while trying to go faster than the cops, until I bumped off the curb messing up the tires, alignment, and rims, and ran into a tree. While I sat on the curb, I couldn't believe the charges that were piling up against me. Grand theft auto, minor under influence, destruction of public property, destruction of private property, resisting arrest, and on and on and on.

My parents bailed me out, and I had to meet with a probation officer before I came before the judge. She said according to my profile that I was an incipient drug addict and criminal, whatever incipient means. The judge looked over my profile, looked at my past record (which was just a bunch of kids stuff), and then ordered me into a treatment facility for six months, community service when I got out, and reparation for damages to the owner of the car and the tree.

So here I am, going to school so I can graduate within the next couple of years, and working after school at a chicken joint to pay back all the damages. And not doing a single thing that's fun. I'm young, and I have all these things I want to do, and no time to do them with. Cause when I get home from work, I'm not to leave the house. My parents said I could consider it house arrest. I don't deserve this. I deserve to be having fun and being young while I still can. I don't even get to keep the money I earn; it all goes to other people. It's not fair.

But just because I'm not happy doesn't mean I don't want to do right. I don't want to be a common criminal my whole life. I don't want to be in the big house with all those murderers and rapists. I'm just a kid. I'm really trying to do right.

Yesterday my friend showed up at work. He asked me to take off early cause there was something he wanted to give me. I told him I couldn't, that I had to work my full shift. He told me I was young and that I should be living life, and no one would care if I played hooky for a day. But I said no, I couldn't do that. But I said he could give me a ride after work if he wanted.

So when he picked me up he told me he was going to take me somewhere. I told him that he should take me home. I had a drawing that I was working on. He just started driving in the other direction and said I would thank him for this. At the stoplight I got out of his car. I really did want to go, but I knew where we were going and what we would end up doing. He told me to get back in the car, and I told him I couldn't unless he was going to take me home. I have a year of being sober, and they say that if I'm good they'll reduce my community service time. Besides, I would really like to get into an art school when I graduate. I told my friend all that. And then I started walking away.

So last night my girlfriend called and asked why I dissed my friend like that. I told her I couldn't be around him if he was gonna risk my chances of being good. I like him and all, but there's a line that has to be drawn if he doesn't respect what I've got to do. He's my best friend, but I've got to keep an eye out for me first.

It's just so hard sometimes, though. I know what I've got to do. I know I did wrong, and that I have to make it right somehow. But when my friends are talking about going to a football game or getting drunk at a party, I feel left out and like I don't have a life anymore. To tell you the truth, if this is what responsibility is I'm not sure I want to be responsible. **But if I get less community service and into a good art school, it will be worth it.**

Chapter Fifteen:
Stability and Growth

LUKE'S STORY

Every day is a struggle. I was in a detention treatment center for about nine months after getting into some serious problems with the law. In the center, I spent a lot of time working with group therapy to change my thoughts, feelings, and actions. After my completion of the program, my probation officer, counselor, and I decided it was best that I didn't go back to my family, and now I'm out on my own. At first there was a sense of freedom, of control. I'm in a place of my own, I'm back in school, and I have a job. I don't really talk with my old friends all that much. I find myself becoming bored and depressed. When I'm not at school or work, I sit in this apartment staring at the television. What I really want to do is write.

The other day I was at my job, when a guy from my group therapy came in. He asked me to go have coffee with him. He began talking about how hard it is right now staying sober and on the right side of the law. A door opened for me. Suddenly I wasn't alone. Saturday we went into the mountains and took a small hike. He took out his guitar, and I just sat there taking deep breaths and relaxing. For the first time in weeks, I felt the urge to write. So now we make a point of spending at least one day a week together. He's convinced me to join a book club. I don't watch television much anymore. I spend that time writing. It's still really hard though. Every day is still a struggle. I just keep writing and thinking about how much better I feel now then I did then.

Objectives

- Review *Chapter 14: Lifestyle Balance*
- See how family can support your *Ownership of Change*
- Understand how friends can support your plans for success
- Discover how healthy ways to have fun can keep your lifestyle balance

Luke's Story

My probation officer, counselor, and I decided it was better that I didn't go home to my family, and since I'm sixteen, I was able to emancipate myself. So now I'm on my own in my own apartment with a job that pays the bills and less than a year of school left to go. But it's really hard. There is a, I dunno, an empty space inside me. Like something that was essential to me is gone now.

I started talking with a guy from my group therapy, and we realized that we are dealing with some of the same problems. We decided to go on a hike together one day, and it was really enjoyable being out in the mountains while he played his guitar and I wrote. He convinced me to join a book club, and they convinced me to submit some of my writings. So now my life isn't just a job and school. Now I have things I enjoy and people I can share things with, even when I'm in the midst of an urge to do something I shouldn't. Even my counselor has become an important person in my life.

A reminder of critical reasoning and its importance

In *Session 30* we continued our discussion about critical reasoning. Critical reasoning, also called logical or rational thinking, is what we use when we try to make a decision or solve a problem. Without critical reasoning, our thoughts, attitudes, and beliefs can begin to get in the way of finding a solution that works.

The first goal of critical thinking is to find a win-win situation. That means that everyone in the situation has gained something from the solution, and everyone is happy with the results. In order to do that, we must first:
- Share our ideas with the other person
- Ask the other person what they think about the situation, and be sure to actively listen to their response
- Offer them a reason why your idea is better or a way to combine the two situations
- Give them time to absorb and think about the information before making a decision.

It is important in this event that we pay attention to the words that are being used, especially a difference of meanings, the assumptions that both people are making about the situation, and that we know the difference between the facts and the opinions of the situation.

Of course, not every situation can be a win-win. That is when the negotiation skills we learned in *Chapter 7* and we reviewed last session will become useful. Finding a compromise, or a settlement that both parties are willing to accept, becomes the main goal of the problem solving.

As life has taught most of us, though, not all problems can be solved to the satisfaction of both parties. It is sometimes helpful to get a third party involved. In making a complaint, be sure to use critical, unemotional thinking with the facts and not very many opinions. It is important that the other person does not think that you are using propaganda to sway them to your side.

A Change In Lifestyle

We have worked hard on learning about ourselves and on how to change our lives to become a healthier and a more responsible person in the community. Making these changes means that we are committing ourselves to staying away from drug use and criminal behavior.

In the past, drug use and criminal activities have been a large part of our life. They have taken up a lot of space in our life. They have been part of our identity—but it has been a *negative identity*. Committing to change means that we commit ourselves to replacing drug use and crime and *finding positive resources* to support our change. These resources may be in our family, in positive friends and in fun and pleasurable, healthy activities. This session will explore how these can become resources to support your *Ownership of Change*.

Family As A Support For Change

Some of you may think "my family is so messed up, that it can't support me in my ownership of change." Others will think, "Yes, my family can become a support for my change and growth." This session will not solve your family problems. We will do a quick study of your family to see if it can become a source of support for you, and if so, to see how you can build on the strengths of that support. If you conclude that it cannot be a source of support, then we will look at ways you can find support in adult caring relationships that can take the place of your primary family.

First, look at how you rated yourself on the Family Disruption, Lack of Closeness and Lack of Family Support scales on your Self-Portrait. If you scored in the high or even moderate range, then you may want to ask for further help and counseling in the area of family and parent relationships. Some of you are or have been in a multifamily group or individual family therapy.

Now, let's take a look at your family. First, we will do a *family sculpture study* to see how and whether your family can give you positive and healthy support for your change goals. At the end of this exercise, you will be asked to come to the conclusion as to whether you *can* or *cannot* depend on your family to support your ownership of change.

Activity: A Sculpture Study Of Your Family

Break into two groups. Then you are asked to have members of the group **represent the members of your family**. Identify who those family members are. Then, **place them in a position** to show whether you **can count** on these members to give you support in your effort to change. If a member represents your father, and you cannot count on him supporting you, then put him at a distance away from you. If you have a sister that will be a positive source of support, put her close to you. Then, place the family members to show whether they support each other. If you think that neither your father nor mother can be counted on to support you, but they support each other, then place them close to each other, but at a distance from you. When you have finished, **come to the conclusion** as to whether you will try to seek support from any of your family members or from your family as a whole. Get some feedback from group members as to what they think you should do

If you decide that you will seek support from certain family members or from the family as a whole, then here are some ways to do this.

· *Make amends*—Take an honest look at how your involvement in drugs and criminal conduct caused problems with your family and share with them your intent to change and that you understand the stress and grief your behavior might have caused them.

· *Use the thought-changing skills from this program*—so that you have better outcomes in your
   relationships with your family.

· *Use the communication skills from this program*—use *active listening* and *active sharing* in your desire to seek your family's support and build more positive relationships with your family.

· *Ask your counselor for at least two family counseling sessions*—if you have not already done this, for the purpose of "clearing the air," making amends, defining your needs for support and then develop a family plan to achieve this.

Ways To Find Support Outside Of Your Family Unit

There are some families that are *not supportive* and would do us more harm than good in our road to a healthy life. If you conclude that, at this time, you will *not be able to count on* family members or from the family as a whole to support your ownership for change, then here are some ways to find support in adult caring relationships that can take the place of your primary family.

First, you may want to *further explore* whether your family can be a source of support by requesting at least one counseling session with family members to look at this issue and to *share with them* that you think you will be *unable to count on them* to support your *ownership of change*. If you think such a session will do more harm than good, don't do it. If you still think that your family will not be a source of support for you, you can do these things.

· Seek out and build other adult sources of support and trust, which could be *other relatives in your life* such as an uncle, aunt, and grandparent.

· Build positive relationships with *other adults* who are *good role models* and who support your goals for change. These could include your counselor or your probation worker.

· Become part of a *strong support group* such as *Alcoholics Anonymous* (AA), a church group or another community group that is positive and that will support your goals for change.

Positive Friends Are A Source Of Support

Friends can also be a source of support for you. Yet, some of your past or current friends **will not understand and cannot support your goals for change**—*your goals to live a crime-free and drug-free life*. Finding new friends who support these goals may be a very difficult part of your lifestyle change. The first important step will be to take an honest look at your friends and friendship patterns. This will give you an idea of how much change you will need to make in your friends and how difficult this will be.

Activity: A Sculpture Study Of Your Friends

Break into two groups. Then ask members of the group to represent the **friends** you have in your life. Sort these friends into four groups: 1) Those who are **involved in** using (or selling) **drugs**; 2) Those who are **involved in** doing **crimes**; 3) Those who **do both**; and 4) Those **who are positive** and who are not and will not be involved in doing drugs or crime.

Now, take groups 1, 2 and 3 and **put them at a distance from you**, as far away as you can. As you do this say out loud the **assertiveness and refusal skills** you have learned in this program to distance yourself from these friends. Have the group help you with how to do this and what skills to use. Then, select some other group members to represent **positive friends**—and put them in group four. What skills will you use to develop and build up group four?

Trust is an important part of finding support from your family or from other family-like adults or groups. We hope that you have been able to develop trust with the people in this group as well as learned the *importance of trust* in relating to your community and society at large. Trust is a big part of developing closeness and intimacy, and trusting people who are around us will help us to live a substance- and crime-free life.

Activity: A Circle Of Support

As a group, take a look at Luke's story. What is the situation with Luke and his family? How has Luke been able to **build a support system** without a family? Do you think his support system is healthy for Luke? Why or why not? Where does trust fit in for Luke?

As we said above, drug use and criminal activities have been a large part of your life. Without these activities, we might find ourselves being *lonely, depressed or even bored*. Being lonely or bored may also cause us to have urges and cravings to participate in crime and drug use. Support from *family, family-like adults, community or school groups, and from good friends* will help us stay committed to change, to help us replace drug use and crime, and help us deal with being lonely, depressed or bored.

Another way to fill that space of drug use and criminal activities is to *replace them with healthy fun and pleasurable activities*. These activities will support our goals for change and will help us deal with the boredom or loneliness. Yet, we might be so bent on reaching our goals for change that we get caught up in only doing the things we "should" or "ought" to do, that we fail to take time to have fun and to take part in healthy play. Healthy or fun play is an *alternative* to the "grindstone" of doing what "we must" to prevent relapse or recidivism. Those "shoulds" and "oughts" can lead to relapse or recidivism. Making *healthy choices for fun living* will help us meet our *goals for change* and lead a crime-free and drug-free life.

Activity: My Personal Interests

Take a moment to look at *Worksheet 41*. Then fill in the interest and desire you have to participate in the activities listed with a number of 0-4. What are some of those things that you did while on substances? Do any of these things on the worksheet have to do with crime? Can you see yourself doing some of these things in your free time?

There are four broad areas of interest that most people fall into. Although some people will be strong in more than one area of interest, most of us are strong in one area specifically. These areas are:

· Physical expression

· Focus on self

· Artistic or aesthetic activities

· Group harmony or working with others.

Activity: Scoring Our Interests

Take all your scores from *Worksheet 41*, and then fill out *Worksheet 42*. This worksheet is intended to show you your specific interests, as well as how strong your interest is in each of the four broad areas. This allows you to have a guideline to what activities will keep you interested and motivated, as well as keep your boredom down and your happiness up.

The emphasis on the personal pleasure inventory worksheet is that the more we know about what we like and take interest in, the easier it will be to find alternative methods of mental happiness other than substance use and crime. The best thing about these interests, though, is that they give us the choice and freedom within them instead of making us give our freedom away. Instead of believing the drug will make us happier or the crime will give us more, we are deciding what we can do to make ourselves happier and give us more.

Some of these interests, though, can be done with other people. When we share an interest with someone, or if we participate in an activity with someone, we are not only more likely to do that activity but we also grow closer to the other person. The emptiness of not using substances or participating in crime comes in part from missing the friends we used to do those things with. Taking part in an activity will also bring us in contact with more people who share the same interests as we do outside of substances and crime, allowing our circle to grow larger and our support system to become stronger. The more we share with a person, the more we are likely to trust a person. The more people we know who we don't associate with substance use or criminal behavior means the more people we have to turn to when things are bringing us down.

Activity: Leisure Time Together

When looking at Luke's story, which broad area of interest do you think Luke fits in? Keep in mind that you can have more than one area of interest. How has Luke's friend helped Luke develop a schedule that makes him feel more content? Do you think that Luke would have done those things by himself, why or why not?

THE PERSONAL PLEASURE INVENTORY

Using one of the five choices below, rate the following items as to degree of pleasure that you derive from each activity. Place the appropriate number corresponding to your choice in the blank line opposite the item. Then put the total score for each group of items on the line marked Total Score.

0= Never engaged in activity or no pleasure derived from activity
1= Low degree of pleasure derived
2= Moderate degree of pleasure derived
3= High degree of pleasure derived
4= Very high degree of pleasure derived

1. Sports
------ Playing basketball
------ Wrestling or Boxing
------ Playing sports
------ Playing softball
------ Going to football games
------ Playing rough games
------ Playing football or soccer
------ Playing volleyball
Total Score _____

2. Challenging Nature
------ Flock climbing
------ Canoeing
------ White water rafting
------ Camping out
------ Hiking
------ Skiing
Total Score _____

3. Physical Fitness
------ Eating healthy
------ Exercising
------ Biking
------ Working out
------ Running
Total Score _____

4. Romantic
------ Holding hands
------ Being physically close
------ Kissing and hugging
------ Going on a date
Total Score _____

5. Soothing Sensations
------ Listening to soft music
------ Warming self by fire
------ Soaking in hot tub
------ Having back rubbed
------ Massage
------ Eating at a nice restaurant
Total Score _____

6. Material Comforts
------ Making money
------ Buying clothes
------ Spending money
------ Going out for an evening
------ Improving how you look
Total Score _____

7. Seeking Adventure
------ Driving to new places
------ Visiting different cities
------ Experiencing new places
------ Experiencing new things
------ Traveling to foreign cities
------ Visiting different cultures
Total Score _____

8. Experiencing Nature
------ Being in nature
------ Being in the woods
------ Watching wildlife
------ Watching the stars
------ Watching the sun rise
Total Score _____

9. Fun at Home
------ Redecorating a room
------ Helping around the house
------ Doing home projects
------ Having friends over
------ Hanging out in the yard
Total Score _____

10. Reflective Relaxation
------ Meditation
------ Relaxation exercises
------ Daily meditations
------ Self reflection
------ Journal writing
Total Score _____

11. Artistic Stimulation
------ Going to the movies
------ Going to a concert
------ Creating art work
------ Reading books
------ Writing poetry
------ Playing a musical instrument
Total Score _____

12. Mental Games
------ Playing word games
------ Playing cards or board games
------ Solving puzzles
------ Playing fantasy games
------ Playing video games
Total Score _____

13. People Closeness
------ Helping family members
------ Playing with children
------ Being with family
------ Spending time with friends
------ Instant Messaging with friends
------ Being with a SO
Total Score _____

14. Religious Involvement
------ Spiritual thinking
------ Worship
------ Bible study
------ Church work
------ Going to church
------ Praying
Total Score _____

15. Helping Others
------ Counseling others
------ Helping friends
------ Teaching others
------ Volunteering services
------ Writing letters to friends or family
Total Score _____

When you have finished scoring all your responses, place the Total Score for each scale on the next Worksheet in the appropriate box under the Raw Score column. Then find your raw score on the row for each scale in order to find your percentile rank for that scale. The percentile rank shows you the degree of pleasure that you derive from each orientation compared with others. For example, if your Raw Material Comforts is 17, then you enjoy this category 80% more than most people.

Worksheet 42

PERSONAL PLEASURE INVENTORY PROFILE

Name: _____ Date: _____

Gender: ☐M ☐F Age: _____

Category	Scale Name	Raw Score	Low 1	Low 2	Low 3	Low-Medium 4	Low-Medium 5	High-Medium 6	High-Medium 7	High 8	High 9	High 10
PHY EXP	1. Sports		0 2 3 4	5 6 7	8 9 10	11 12	13	14 15	16 17	18 19 20	21 22 23	24 26 32
PHY EXP	2. Challenging Nature		0 2 3 5	6 7	8	9 10	11 12	13	14 15	16 17	18 19	20 21 24
SELF FOCUS	3. Physical Fitness		2 5 6 7	8	10	11		12	13	14	15	16 18 20
SELF FOCUS	4. Romance		1 6 8 9	10 11 12	13	14	15	16	17	18		19 20
SELF FOCUS	5. Soothing Sensations		4 10 11	12 13 14	15	16	17	18	19	20	21 22	23 24
SELF FOCUS	6. Material Comforts		4 7 8 9	10 11	12	13	14	15	16	17	18	19 20
AESTHETIC DISCOVERY	7. Seeking adventure		4 7 8 9	10 11 12	13	14 15	16	17 18	19	20 21	22	23 24
AESTHETIC DISCOVERY	8. Experiencing Nature		1 6 7 8	9 10	11	12	13	14	15	16 17	18	19 20
AESTHETIC DISCOVERY	9. Domestic Involvement		0 1 2	3	4	5 6	7	8	9	10	11 12 13	14 15 19
AESTHETIC DISCOVERY	10. Reflective Relaxation		0 1 2	3	4	5	6	7	8	9 10	11 12	13 15 20
AESTHETIC DISCOVERY	11. Artistic Stimulation		0 2 3	4 5 6	7	8	9	10 11	12	13 14	15 16 17	18 20 24
COLLECT HARMONY	12. Mental Exercise		0 2 3	3 4	5	6	7		8	9	10 11	12 14 20
COLLECT HARMONY	13. People Closeness		4 11 12	13 14	15 16	17	18	19	20	21	22	23 24
COLLECT HARMONY	14. Religious Involvement		0	1 2	3	4 5	6	7 8	9 10	11 12	13 14 15	16 19 24
COLLECT HARMONY	15. Helping Others		1 6 7	8	9	10	11	12	13	14	15	16 17 20
	PERCENTILE	0	10	20	30	40	50	60	70	80	90	100

DECILE RANK

Making Time

One difficult thing is having enough time to do the things that interest us while still taking care of what needs to be done. As we mentioned earlier and in Session 29, often things that we are required to do begin to take over our lives so that we can no longer do what we want to do. This causes us to become frustrated and depressed, which often leads to relapse and recidivism. In order to avoid this imbalance, there are three key ideas to keep in mind:

· **Prioritize.** Always keep in mind what is the most important thing at the moment and for the future. Instead of picking up the extra shift in order to have more money, go out for a picnic with friends. It is true the money can be important, especially in getting some of the material things we want, but our mental happiness and contentment is often more important than material things.

· **Work out a schedule.** Set aside time every day for personal time that can be used towards an interest that is separate from things that have to be done. School and work are important, but so is just one hour a day for things that interest you and make you happy.

· **Don't over-schedule.** While it is important to have a schedule in order to have personal time, make sure that you aren't on the go all the time. People need some down time, otherwise they can become stressed and anxious, which can lead to substance use. Leave time for relaxation and rest.

Activity: Leisure Time Activities

Break into groups of three or four and fill out *Worksheet 43* with all the activities you can think of, outside of school and work. Then decide how many times a month the activity can be participated in, and whether it replaces substance use or criminal activities. Then individually write a list of activities you would be interested in taking part in that would replace your own substance use or criminal participation. While you are writing down the activities, think of how long each activity would take and how you might rearrange your schedule in order to fit it into your life. Don't forget to place it where you think it would go in your priority list.

Putting It Together

· Luke is having problems with depression and loneliness. How is interacting with his friend and other people helping him? What are Luke's interests?

· Who is part of your support system and how close do you feel to them?

· What are your specific interests outside of what you have to do? How can you fit those into your schedule?

· How can you become closer to people you trust and admire?

Worksheet 43

LEISURE TIME ACTIVITIES

List the leisure time activities that you are now taking part in. In the second column, write down how many times a month you do these activities. In the third column, check the activity that has replaced drinking alcohol and drug use time or activities.

LEISURE TIME ACTIVITIES	TIMES A MONTH	REPLACES AOD ACTIVITIES

SESSION 32: PLANNING FOR THE FUTURE

Objectives

- Review *Session 31: Building Community Support—Family, Friends and Fun Time*
- Discuss the difference between work and a job or school
- Understand how to be effective
- Plan for your future

Luke's Story

When I'm not in school, I bus tables for a living. It's a job and it helps pay the bills and put cash in my pockets, but what I really want to do is write. It wasn't until we went hiking, though, that I really had a chance to write. And I really enjoyed it. But I never thought I could pay the bills with it.

But then my friend convinced me to join a book club, and with them he convinced me to submit some of my writings to be published. One even got accepted, with some editing of course. So now I'm working on my application to a school for writing, and if I keep getting my submissions accepted, I can quit my job. Even though my counselor told me that I could get a job doing whatever I wanted, I never really believed him. But now there is a chance that I can do what I want and what I'm good at for the rest of my life. And now the void doesn't seem as big anymore.

A look back at support and leisure activities

In *Session 31* we discussed some of the difficulties that will be facing us once we're out of this program. Up to this point we have been learning and practicing knowledge and skills that will help us maintain the change and growth that began in this program. In *Session 29* we began talking about how, even when we think we are doing the right things by working all the time, we can be setting ourselves up for a relapse or recidivism episode. So in the last session we started discussing how we can avoid the loneliness, depression, and boredom that can come from a lack of balance in our lifestyles.

In order to maintain a balance in our lives, there are certain things that we must make an effort to develop and maintain. These things are:
- A support system that consists of family or friends, as long as they are people we trust and care about
- Activities that we can become interested in mentally and physically that do not involve substance use or crime
- A schedule of priorities so we always know what is most important to us
- Personal time to take us away from the things that have to be done sometimes

As long as we have the above things set into our schedules and lives, then it will be easier to maintain balance and control in the changes we've made to our lives.

Activity: My Balance

Take a moment to fill out *Worksheet 44, Personal Time*. List the interests or activities that you did this past week. Then write down the time on the day that you did the activity, and how you felt after the activity was finished. How did you schedule your time this past week? Do you think you included enough interests, or do you think you did only what you have to do?

Break into groups of three and four and compare the activities and time spent on them. Who spent more time on things they enjoy than others? How can you help each other schedule more interests? What are some of the common interests you have?

Another aspect of maintaining balance is understanding our strengths and weaknesses in order to find a future path that will help us maintain our new control and freedom. In order to do that, we must first know what our interests and abilities are, separate from our jobs, and how to develop our work into something we are happy doing.

A Difference In Terms

Productive and meaningful work, doing something that we enjoy, is a strong alternative to substance use and crime. Although we have worked most of our lives, and school is considered work, it is often not something that we think expresses ourselves and who we are. In fact, most of us work to pay bills or buy things or because we have to, not because we see it as a productive and healthy aspect of our identity. Often work and job/school mean the same thing, but in truth there is a difference between our work and going to school.

Our work, (a combination of our interests and abilities -- Luke's work is writing), is a physical or mental activity and effort that is directed toward accomplishing or gaining something. Work is made up of our talents and desires in order to practice our skills and earn a livelihood. We own and control our work; it is ours and ours only. School is just given to us in order to find and fulfill our work. One example of a person's work may be art. Let's say that you like to draw, or write, or play guitar. That is your work. But if you only go to school to socialize and you are not in any classes that help develop your skills, then school is not giving you a healthy place to fulfill your work. Your work, art, writing, guitar, snowboarding, is a way to define your lifestyle.

Activity: Story Of Work

Break into pairs or groups of three in order to write two short fictional stories: one will be about a person involved with their work, their interests and abilities, and the other will be about a person who is just involved with their job or school. Be sure to include what each person is thinking or feeling in their situation.

Effectively Working

It would be nice if everyone could find a job or classes in which they can do their work in the best manner possible. And the truth is, we can find a school environment that supports our work to the best of its advantages. But it is not something that falls into our laps. In order to find a situation that fits our work, we first must be effective in developing our work. Dr. Steven R. Covey is famous for what he calls the *Seven Habits of Highly Effective People*, and the following list summarizes his findings.

Worksheet 44

PERSONAL TIME

First, write down several pleasant activities that you believe you would enjoy doing in the next week. On the following chart, plan 30 to 60 minutes each day that you reserve as your own personal time. Make the time for this in advance. When the time comes, decide which of the things from the above list you want to do and take time to do it. Write down what you did and how it felt to do something for yourself.

Healthy Activities

	Personal Time	Activity and Recreation
Monday		
Tuesday		
Wednesday		
Thursday		
Friday		
Saturday		
Sunday		

These habits can help us develop our work to the best of our ability, and then open doors to find the classes, school, or job that fits our work.

1) **Take a Positive Approach:** Take responsibility for your life by having a personal vision of what you want to accomplish. Set goals for yourself.

2) **Have Your Long-Term Goals in Mind:** After you have set goals, achieve them. Take personal leadership of yourself, and know that no one will get you there but yourself.

3) **Do What is Most Important First:** Prioritize. You manage your time, energies, and focus in order to achieve your goals. This is considered personal management.

4) **Think Win-Win:** Even work like art and professional sports include working with other people in the job situation. Remember what we talked about in decision making and problem solving, and think of how to solve every situation to the best of everyone involved.

5) **Understand Other People's Point of View:** In *Session 16* we talked about empathy, putting yourself in other people's shoes. To effectively work with other people, we must first understand where they are coming from.

6) **Combine Your Resources:** The whole of something is more than the sum of its parts, meaning going to school as an artist isn't a means of living unless there are mentors, advisors, and professors/teachers. By working together with other people, we can project ourselves further than by ourselves

7) **Lifestyle Balance:** This means keeping yourself in balance, physically, mentally, emotionally and spiritually. Refer back to *Session 31* to remember how to maintain balance.

Activity: Work Versus Job

In Luke's story, he mentions that his job is busing tables, but writing is really what he likes to do. What is Luke doing to further his goals? What goals has Luke set for himself? Of the above seven habits of effective people, how many has Luke achieved for himself? What can he do to make himself more effective?

So How Do We Know What Our Work Is?

Now we know how to work effectively in order to achieve our goals and find a situation that matches our talents and desires. But in order to put the skills to work we have to define and figure out what it is we consider our work. As we've said, work does not have to mean your school or job. Our work can be drawing, playing an instrument, learning, thinking, or even building something or tearing something down. Whatever we desire to do, that will benefit us in healthy ways, and makes us content and excited to do, can be considered our work.

Activity: And My Work Is...

Take a moment to fill out *Worksheet 45* in order to identify what your work is. First **give a name to the work you do**. It can be anything from artist to Zen Buddhist, but first a name must be given to it. Then think of all that is contained within your work. All that is physically, mentally, and emotionally involved in your work should be written down. An example is your work as a student. Being a student means you have to take notes, listen to the teacher, respond to questions with thoughtful answers, think about what you have learned, apply it to the outside world, and try to come up with other ideas based on what you have learned. Break into groups of two or three and discuss with each other your individual work. How can each of you apply the seven skills above to your work? What job or school goals can you think of that your work can be applied to?

It is okay, and actually really important, for us to feel pride in our work. We don't have to like our situations, but we can love our work and what we do with ourselves. Make sure you can feel the power and freedom in having pride in what you do for work and how it makes you feel.

Matching Work with School

So now we have an idea of what our work is, where our talents lie, and what we want to do with ourselves. The difficult thing now is finding classes, a school, or a job that we can align with our work in order to feel mental well being and to achieve of our goals. Not only does finding a situation that matches our work help us achieve our goals, but it also plays a major part in building and maintaining a lifestyle alternative to using substances and criminal activities. When we are fulfilled through what we are doing with our lives, there is a lot less risk or desire to search for that fulfillment through negative means. The following are skills that can help us get into the school or situation we want that matches our work. Keep in mind that school can be considered a job, and some schools require the same application process as a traditional job.

1) **Developing a resume:** A resume describes your work history and your desire for work. In order to be effective, it has to be neat, typed, and accompanied with a cover letter. For school purposes, this can be part of your statement of purpose. Try not to leave large open periods of time. Explain periods of lack with phrases such as "I was searching for a situation that defined me."

2) **The job/school application:** This is where you emphasize your personal strengths and strong skills. In a school application, it can be beneficial to say that you are a good writer, or you like participating in class, or something that will set you apart from other applicants.

3) **Research:** This means researching schools that are specifically designed to reach your goal. Keep after it until you succeed, and make sure to use your support system (family, friends, counselor, etc.) to help you with the disappointment if you don't get accepted.

4) **Developing telephone skills:** The telephone is used to set up interviews, discover information needed, and to present yourself to a future employer or school. Make sure to introduce yourself to the person who answers the phone, ask to speak with the specific person to answer your needs, and then introduce yourself again to the next person. Make sure that the person you are speaking with knows who you are and the purpose of the phone call.

WHAT IS YOUR WORK?

First, give a name to your work. The following are some examples: Artist, Writer, Poet, Scientist, Family Provider, Athlete, Student. Then write down everything you think of that defines your work or the important parts of your work. Use extra paper if you run out of room in this Worksheet.

NAME OF MY WORK:

LIST WHAT DEFINES YOUR WORK OR THE IMPORTANT PARTS OF YOUR WORK

SESSION 32: PLANNING FOR THE FUTURE

5) **Interviewing:** Both companies and most schools interview before hiring or accepting prospective candidates, and it can be important to be prepared. In order to be prepared, rehearse for the interview and keep in mind that you are trying to sell your work and your purpose. Know that just because you are not selected to be in one school, does not mean there isn't just as good if not a better one still out there waiting for you.

6) **Set goals:** Most importantly, in all of what we have been trying to teach, is to set goals for where you are going and where you want to be. Use long-term and short-term goals in order to set a plan that is realistic. Keep in mind that the goals have to be realistic in order to be achieved.

Activity: A Plan for the Future

Individually work on *Worksheet 46* in order to set a **plan for your future**. Be sure to include short-term goals as well as long-term objectives in your plan. Think about how you might go about things in order to achieve your objectives. Then get into a circle with the larger group, and one by one discuss your **individual plans for the next three years**. Are the goals realistic? What is the person going to do tomorrow or the next day to begin achieving the goals? What is the order in which things have to be obtained, or what are the separate objectives that can be attained at the same time? Remember, only you have the control over what you do.

Putting It Together

- Do you think Luke has a realistic goal for his future, why or why not? How has Luke made himself more effective?

- What can you do to help yourself maintain the changes you have made?

- What are your goals for the future?

- How has this program helped you to develop and change into a healthy identity?

CONGRATULATIONS! YOU HAVE DONE A GREAT JOB! GOOD LUCK FOR YOUR FUTURE!

Worksheet 46

SCHOOL & WORK PLAN FOR THE NEXT 3 YEARS

List your specific objectives for education, school and work for the next three years.

LIST SPECIFIC OBJECTIVES IN SCHOOL AND WORK PLAN FOR THE NEXT 3 YEARS

LUKE'S STORY

Every day is a struggle. Some days I just want to give up and get drunk or stoned, but other days everything seems all right, that I can make it at least another day.

I was in a detention treatment center for about nine months after getting into some serious problems with the law. In the center, I spent a lot of time working with group therapy to change my thoughts, feelings, and actions. To some extent, I've learned that I'm the one in control of what I do.

After my completion in the program, my probation officer, counselor, and I decided it was best that I didn't go back to my family, or at least what technically is referred to as my family. Mainly it's just my drunk father, neurotic mother, and a little brother that should be in a foster home. Since I'm sixteen, I was able to emancipate myself away from my family, and now I'm out on my own.

At first there was a sense of freedom, of control. I'm in a place of my own, I'm back in school with only a year before I graduate, and I have a job that gives me enough money to pay my bills and have extra to start building a life. But that freedom was quickly replaced by a, I dunno, an empty space. A sense that I've lost something that is important to me, an important part of me.

I don't really talk with my old friends all that much. Most of them are still stoners, and that is a major part of what they do all the time. They aren't at school much, so that's not much of a risk. I do have a couple of friends that I still talk to, but we only see each other at school because they have parents that don't like them to be out on school nights, and I work most weekends. Besides, most of the people at school don't understand what I've been through and how I've changed.

I find myself becoming bored and depressed. When I'm not at school or work, I sit in this apartment staring at the television. What I really want to do is write. Write about what I've been through, what everyone goes through, write stories that, if they don't solve problems, they at least shed light on a little bit of life. But when I get home from my job, get my homework done, and everything ready for the next day, I'm so tired and frustrated that it's hard for me to pick up a pen and write.

The other day I was at my job, cleaning tables and getting my section ready for the next buser, when a guy from my group therapy came in. At first we were a little uncomfortable with each other because there were a lot of things we shared and talked about in group, but then he asked me to go have coffee with him. My shift was over early, so I agreed to spend some time talking with him.

As we walked through the park drinking coffee, he began talking about how hard it is right now staying sober and on the right side of the law, about how he can't talk to any of his friends anymore, and how he feels so depressed after getting home from his job every night. A door opened up for me. Suddenly I wasn't alone, and I think he knew that as well.

We stood and stared at the geese in the lake for awhile, then he asked me if I liked to hike. I said I haven't really had much experience outside the city, that my parents never went anywhere. He asked me to go hiking with him on my next day off, which happened to be the next Saturday. I struggled, because I knew Saturday would give me a chance to get ahead on my homework or maybe pick up a shift, when he began talking about how sometimes it's nice just to get away from everything for awhile. So I agreed. He told me to bring my writing. I was confused but I figured what the hell.

That Saturday we went into the mountains and took a small hike. It was more like a walk beyond the road since we are both smokers and city boys, but we got away from the traffic and sat down on a rock looking towards the surrounding mountains. He took out his guitar, which he brought with him, and I just sat there taking deep breaths and relaxing. For the first time in weeks, I felt the urge to write. We didn't need to do anything, we didn't even need to talk. And I was content.

So now we make a point of spending at least one day a week together. Sometimes we go see a band, which I thought would be difficult being sober, but it's easier with another straight person. Sometimes we go to a poetry reading, or we go hiking, or sometimes we just sit in the park and meet people. He's convinced me to join a book club, and I've begun to meet more people who like to read and write. They've convinced me to submit some of my writings that I did while in the detention center, and one of my writings even got accepted, with some serious editing of course.

I've started the application process to go to a school for writing, and I don't watch television much anymore. I spend that time writing. It's still really hard though. Every day is still a struggle between what I want to do and what I have to do to get there. The void is still there, and I still miss some of my friends and the times we used to have, but the emptiness is getting smaller. **I just keep writing and thinking about how much better I feel now then I did then.**

Excerpt from Nelson Mandela's Inaugural Speech
(1994)

Our deepest fear is not that we are inadequate.
Our deepest fear is that we are powerful beyond measure.
It is our light, not our darkness, that most frightens us.
We ask ourselves, who am I to be brilliant, gorgeous,
talented and fabulous?
Actually, who are you not to be?
You are a child of god.
Your playing small does not serve the world.
There's nothing enlightened about shrinking so that
people won't feel insecure around you.
We were born to make manifest the glory of God that is
within us.
It's not just in some of us, it's in everyone.
And as we let our own light shine, we unconsciously give
others permission to do the same.
As we are liberated from our own fear,
our presence automatically liberates others.

Virginia